Lord Byron's First Pilgrimage

BY

WILLIAM A. BORST

ARCHON BOOKS
1969

SBN: 208 00773 3
Library of Congress Catalog Card Number: 69-15679
Printed in the United States of America

TO

MY MOTHER AND FATHER

PREFACE

IT is the purpose of this book to present more fully than has hitherto been done an account of those two years (1809–11) which Lord Byron devoted to travel in Portugal and Spain, Malta, Albania, Greece, and the Near East. Whenever it has been possible there has been an attempt to go beyond biographical details to a consideration of the effect of his experiences upon the mind and character of the poet. Biographers and critics have, I believe, given insufficient attention to these very impressionable years of Byron's life *before* he awoke to find himself famous.

The proportions of the present study have been determined to some extent by the fact that the most significant poetic product of this extensive tour, the first two cantos of *Childe Harold's Pilgrimage,* and also the chief account in prose, his companion Hobhouse's methodical *Journey into Albania,* treat only the first of the years of travel. The comparative scarcity of materials necessarily makes the record of the second year, which Byron spent alone in Greece, a story more briefly told. Yet from this less documented period one emerges with a keen sense of Byron's growing devotion to Greece and his awareness of the tribulations of her people, less vividly conveyed than the stanzas of *Childe Harold* express, for example, the powerful effect of the Peninsular War upon the intellectual consciousness and imagination of the poet, but no less real.

I should like to express my deep sense of gratitude to those whose counsel and kindness made this book possible. I am in particular debt to Mr. Frederick A. Pottle, under whose direction the work was originally prepared in candidacy for the degree of Doctor of Philosophy at Yale University, where it was awarded the John Addison Porter Prize in 1945. Mr. Chauncey Brewster Tinker generously put at my disposal the resources of his own rich library and the collections of the Rare Book Room of the Sterling Memorial Library. Mr. Robert D. French, Mr. George L. Hendrickson, Mr. Joseph T. Curtiss, Mr. Richard L. Purdy, and Mr. Philip B. Daghlian were kind enough to read the manuscript and make valuable observations, as was also the earliest of my teachers and friends in the Yale English department, the late C. F. Tucker Brooke. To Mr. Antony E. Raubitschek and Mr. Peter G. Phialas I am indebted for assistance with the Greek and to Mr. Raymond T. Hill for guidance through the Portuguese material. Every student of Byron must inevitably direct inquiries to 50 Albemarle Street and like many before me I must thank Sir John Murray and Mr. John Grey Murray for their courteous and informative answers to my questions. My fellow workers in Byron, Mr. E. Dudley H. Johnson of Princeton University and Mr. Harold S. L. Wiener of Sarah Lawrence College, have been ready with helpful suggestions. I wish also to express my gratitude to Mr. Benjamin C. Nangle, editor of the Yale Studies in English, for his aid in the preparation of the book for the press. Finally, special thanks are due to Mr. James T. Babb, Librarian of Yale University, Miss Belle da Costa Greene, Director of the Pierpont Morgan Library, Miss Fannie Ratchford, Director of the Rare Books Collections at the University of Texas, and Mr. John D. Gordan, Director of the Henry W. and Albert A. Berg Collection in the New York Public Library, for permitting me to use previously unpublished material.

W. A. B.

New Haven, Connecticut
February, 1948

ABBREVIATIONS

Galt	John Galt. *The Life of Lord Byron.* London, 1830.
Journey	John Cam Hobhouse. *A Journey through Albania and Other Provinces of Turkey in Europe and Asia to Constantinople during the Years 1809 and 1810.* London, 1813. 2 vols.
LBC	*Lord Byron's Correspondence.* John Murray, ed. London, 1922. 2 vols.
LJ	*The Works of Lord Byron, Letters and Journals.* Rowland E. Prothero, ed. London, 1898–1901. 6 vols.
Moore	Thomas Moore. *Letters and Journals of Lord Byron: with Notices of His Life.* London, 1830. 2 vols.
P	*The Works of Lord Byron, Poetry.* Ernest Hartley Coleridge, ed. London, 1898–1905. 7 vols.
Recollections	Lord Broughton (John Cam Hobhouse). *Recollections of a Long Life.* Lady Dorchester, ed. London, 1909–11. 6 vols.
Travels	— *Travels in Albania and Other Provinces of Turkey in 1809 and 1810.* London, 1855. 2 vols.

Occasional reference will be found to the following standard biographies of Byron:
John Drinkwater. *The Pilgrim of Eternity: Byron—A Conflict.* London, 1925.
André Maurois. *Byron.* Hamish Miles, tr. London, 1930.
Ethel C. Mayne. *Byron.* Revised ed. London, 1924.
Helene Richter. *Lord Byron: Persönlichkeit und Werk.* Halle, 1929.
   In several instances later cited, texts of Byron's letters more complete than those given by Moore and Prothero appear in *The Works of Lord Byron; in Verse and Prose*, FitzGreene Halleck, ed. (New York, 1833); *The Works of Lord Byron, Letters, 1804–1813*, William Ernest Henley, ed. (New York, 1897); and James T. Hodgson, *Memoir of the Rev. Francis Hodgson* (London, 1878, 2 vols.).

CONTENTS

INTRODUCTION

IT is probably truer to say of Byron than of any other English poet that it was inevitable and necessary that he should travel. No poet felt more cramped within the confines of his own land than he, and none came more fully to pride himself upon living as a "citizen of the world." Nor was any poet more dependent than Byron upon influences beyond his native island for the materials and the development of his genius.

Byron's innate restlessness and alert curiosity combined with the chronic and irremediable insecurity of his life in England to lead him to spend two of the most highly impressionable years of his life in a journey to the Iberian Peninsula and the Near East. And four years after his return from this pilgrimage the greatly increased complexity of his personal affairs prompted him again to leave England, with no great reluctance, and to dwell for the remainder of his years in those warmer, freer lands where he felt more naturally at home. The affection for Greece which Byron conceived during his stay there and his sympathy for the country's sad plight together inspired the heroic final act of his life, his ill-fated participation in the struggle for the liberation of Greece.

The Byron who set forth from Falmouth on the second day of July, 1809, was a handsome young man of twenty-one, who had but recently taken his seat in the House of Lords and had attracted some attention during the spring by the publication of his satire *English Bards and Scotch Reviewers*. The letters and poems Byron wrote before the summer of 1809 and the testimony of those who knew him reveal a youth as talented and engaging as he was passionate and headstrong. He must have been a thoroughly delightful person but he could surely be a difficult one as well. Even in his early years Byron was far from being well balanced; indeed, it might almost be said that he was never afforded a chance to be that. His stormy inheritance and family background, the temperamental antagonism that existed between him and his mother, his acute consciousness of his deformity, the lack of any real family or home through his early years—all these factors intensified rather than resolved the discords of a naturally introverted and restless nature.

But the less attractive features of Byron's personality should never be allowed to obscure the essential warmth and integrity of his character. The affectionateness, the disarming frankness, and the humor and high spirits that never completely deserted him find particularly attractive and spontaneous expression in the early letters. The school-boy Byron was ready to admit that "I have been *idle* and I certainly ought not to talk in church, but I have never done a mean action at this School to . . . *any one*";[1] and he did not hesitate to grant that "I am naturally *extravagant*."[2] A capacity for self-criticism is evident in such remarks as "Although I am *violent* I am not *capricious* in my own *attachments*"[3] and "I have *eased* my *conscience* by the atonement, which is humiliating enough to one of my disposition."[4] From Cambridge Byron wrote to Hanson that "I am still the School-boy and as great a *Rattle* as ever."[5] And his mood could not have been one of unmitigated gloom when he wrote to Augusta, "You must know, Sister of mine, that I am the most unlucky wight in Harrow, perhaps in Christendom, and am no sooner out of one scrape than into another."[6] There is here, I believe, an element of consciously humorous exaggeration that persisted in some of his more somber literary works, especially in the portrait of Burun-Harold in the opening stanzas of *Childe Harold.*

There was also a gratifying tendency not to take himself too seriously, the agreeable habit of using himself and his pretensions as material for humorous observation. Writing to Augusta about the Harrow Speech Day, Byron mentioned "the *Gothic omission* of my *superior talents* . . . These are *disappointments* we *great men* are liable to."[7] Some months later he wrote, "I have only just dismounted from my *Pegasus,* which has prevented me from descending to *plain* prose in an epistle of greater length to your *fair* self."[8] And there is something disarming in the tone of the following reference to a review of his rather conventional and self-conscious first volume *Hours of Idleness:* "I have now a review before me, entitled *Literary Recreations* where my *bardship* is applauded far beyond my deserts. I know nothing of the critic, but think *him* a very discerning gentleman, and *myself* a devilish *clever* fellow. His critique pleases me particularly, because it is of great length, and a proper quantum of censure is administered, just to give an agreeable *relish* to the praise."[9]

The ease and felicity of Byron's prose are worth noticing. He takes an evident pleasure, in such passages as the foregoing, in the very wielding of words. There is something of the same kind in his scarcely enticing picture of Southwell, a village notable for "the pleasures of contemplating *pigs, poultry, pork, pease,* and *potatoes* together, with other Rural Delights."[9a] At sixteen Byron wrote facetiously from Harrow, "I am an absolute Hermit; in a short time my Gravity which is increased by my solitude will qualify me for an Archbishoprick;

---

1. *LJ*, I, 14.   2. *LJ*, I, 95.   3. *LJ*, I, 23.   4. *LJ*, I, 117.   5. *LJ*, I, 90.
6. *LJ*, I, 41–2.   7. *LJ*, I, 74.   8. *LJ*, I, 108–09.   9. *LJ*, I, 140.
9a. *LJ*, I, 58.

I really begin to think that I should become a mitre amazingly well." [2]
Perhaps less attractive are references to his mother, whom, as he
sharpens his satirical sword, he calls "my amiable Alecto, this female
Tisiphone, that worthy and lamblike Dame," and "that upas tree, that
antidote to the arts." [3]

As early as 1804 and 1805 there were evidences, too, of a recurrent
mood of melancholy deeply and painfully felt but already expressed
with some sense of its effect upon others—upon relatives and friends,
at this stage, rather than upon a wider public. Byron's thwarted love
for Mary Chaworth was something from which he never let himself
fully recover. At the end of the year 1805, when he was seventeen,
he wrote in a boyishly melodramatic mood of the possibility that a
pistol or a fever might cut short the thread of his existence.[4] Low
spirits, induced in part by strained relations with his mother, financial
difficulties, and dissatisfaction with the treatment of his early poems,
continued to visit him at intervals during the next three years and
returned with especial violence at the end of 1808, after he had left
the rather aimless life of Cambridge and London to settle down alone
in his vast and crumbling abbey at Newstead. There he could at least
entertain the possibility of an alternate solution to his problems: "I
suppose it will end in my marrying a *Golden Dolly,* or blowing my
brains out; it does not much matter which, the remedies are nearly
alike."[5] On the last day of November Byron wrote as if he were a
tired man beyond the prime of life rather than a vigorous youth of
twenty, "I am a very unlucky fellow, for I think I had naturally not
a bad heart; but it has been so bent, twisted, and trampled on, that
it has now become as hard as a Highlander's heelpiece."[6]

It has been observed that Byron's insecurity and sense of doom
were to a large extent attributable to his early instruction in the Cal-
vinist creed.[7] Indeed, he seems never to have been able either fully
to accept the tenets of this harsh faith or to free himself from the

2. *LJ*, I, 26.   3. *LJ*, I, *passim*.   4. *LJ*, I, 92.   5. *LJ*, I, 205–06.
6. *LJ*, I, 203.

7. E. H. Coleridge remarks, in a note to the first canto of *Childe Harold*, that "Byron's
belief, or, rather, haunting dread that he was predestined to evil is to be traced to
the Calvinistic teaching of his boyhood. Lady Byron regarded this creed of despair
as the secret of her husband's character, and the source of his aberrations." (*P*, II,
74, n.) At the age of fourteen, in the poem "On the Death of a Young Lady," Byron
wrote the lines:

> The King of Terrors seiz'd her as his prey . . .
> Oh! could that King of Terrors pity feel,
>   Or Heaven reverse the dread decree of fate.
>
>   .   .   .   .
>
> And shall presumptuous mortals Heaven arraign!
>   And, madly, Godlike Providence accuse!
> Ah! no, far fly from me attempts so vain;—
>   I'll ne'er submission to my God refuse.

tyranny of its gloomier aspects. Byron could attack sects and dogmas
with vigor but he was totally incapable of a pagan attitude; he could
be flippant but never with any lasting satisfaction. At nineteen he
wrote to a friend:

Of Religion I know nothing, at least in its *favour*. We have *fools* in all sects
and *Imposters* in most; why should I believe mysteries no one understands,
because written by men who chose to mistake madness for Inspiration, and
style themselves *Evangelicals?* . . . This much I will venture to affirm,
that all the virtues and pious *Deeds* performed on Earth can never entitle
a man to Everlasting happiness in a future State; nor on the other hand can
such a Scene as a Seat of eternal punishment exist, it is incompatible with
the benign attributes of a Deity to suppose so. . . . I have lived a *Deist*,
what I shall die I know not; however, come what may, *ridens moriar.*[8]

And on the day before his twentieth birthday he glibly summed up
his beliefs for the sober Dallas:

In morality, I prefer Confucius to the Ten Commandments, and Socrates
to St. Paul (though the two latter agree in their opinion of marriage). In
religion, I favour the Catholic emancipation, but do not acknowledge the
Pope; and I have refused to take the sacrament, because I do not think eating bread and drinking wine from the hand of an earthly vicar will make me
an inheritor of heaven. I hold virtue, in general, or the virtues severally, to
be only in the disposition, each a *feeling*, not a principle. I believe truth
the prime attribute of the Deity, and death an eternal sleep, at least of the
body.[9]

Moore stresses the essential warmth and affectionateness of Byron's
nature. From the beginning those qualities tended to be extreme in
their expression. Byron's friendships at Harrow, his early letters to
Augusta, and particularly his strong attachment to the boy chorister
Edleston at Cambridge amply bear out his statement in the *Detached
Thoughts* that "My School friendships were with *me passions* (for I
was always violent)."[1] His love for Mary Chaworth caused him intense agitation at the time of early infatuation and persisted as something more than mere literary self-indulgence for years afterwards.
In a very significant passage Byron later linked the mood of melancholy and ennui, which was especially strong during the months
before he left England in the summer of 1809, with the premature
indulgence of his passions:

My passions were developed very early—so early, that few would believe
me, if I were to state the period, and the facts which accompanied it. Perhaps this was one of the reasons which caused the anticipated melancholy

---

8. *LJ*, II, 19, n.
9. *LJ*, I, 173. Before the end Byron was to affirm his belief in the immortality of the
soul. *LJ*, v, 456–7.
1. *LJ*, v, 455.

of my thoughts—having anticipated life. My earlier poems are the thoughts of one at least ten years older than the age at which they were written: I don't mean for their solidity, but their Experience. The first two Cantos of C^eH^d were completed at twenty-two, and they are written as if by a man older than I shall probably ever be.[2]

The portrait of Childe Harold, originally Childe Burun, in the opening stanzas of the poem that was soon to make Byron famous is, of course, a reflection of this attitude. The grotesque exaggeration of that picture (Stanzas 2–14) does not make its original impetus the less real. Byron's archaized and melodramatized representation of himself and his circumstances before he set forth upon his travels contains, I believe, a mixture of his melancholy and satirical moods. There was a kind of release and even pleasure in the very exaggeration of the picture. I cannot believe that Byron did not derive amusement—though rather dour amusement, perhaps—from applying to himself such lines as the following:

> Ah me! in sooth he was a shameless wight,
> Sore given to revel and ungodly glee.
>
> .   .   .   .
>
> But spent his days in riot most uncouth.
>
> .   .   .   .
>
> Childe Harold basked him in the Noontide sun,
> Disporting there like any other fly.
>
> .   .   .   .
>
> For he through Sin's long labyrinth had run.[3]

In one mood he truly "felt the fulness of satiety," yet in another very closely allied to it he could not resist the incongruity of the situation. This is the very mixture of moods that was so characteristic of the man. It is a mistake to look upon the opening lines of *Childe Harold* with utter seriousness—*or* complete levity for that matter.

If any proof were needed that as a youth Byron was much more than the idle gadabout that many, including himself, have often pictured, there would be strong evidence in the number and especially in the quality of his friends. Lytton Strachey has made the foolish statement that Byron was probably incapable of friendship.[4] Nothing could be further from the truth. The very fact that his closest friends at Cambridge and afterward were such talented and substantial people as Hobhouse, Hodgson, and Matthews is evidence not only of his

---

2. *LJ*, v, 450.   3. *Childe Harold*, I, 2–5.
4. "Indeed, he was probably incapable of friendship. There was no give and take about his nature; and his vanity was such that he preferred to be flattered by an insignificant mind, like Moore's, to being treated as an equal by a noble one, like Shelley's." *Characters and Commentaries* (London, 1936), p. 59.

companionability but even more of his fine intelligence and essential seriousness.[5]

Byron probably gained more from his own extraordinarily wide reading than he did from the formal education he received at Harrow and Cambridge. His headmaster Dr. Drury wrote that he "soon found that a wild mountain colt had been submitted to my management. But there was mind in his eye."[6] In retrospect Byron observed that "At School I was . . . remarked for the extent and readiness of my *general* information; but in all other respects idle; capable of great sudden exertions . . . but of few continuous drudgeries."[7] The same was doubtless true at Cambridge, where in the early nineteenth century the demands upon a young lord were not very exacting. The list, which Moore preserved, of Byron's early reading makes it clear, however, that even allowing for a good deal of skimming he kept his mind occupied with a vast amount and variety of reading, particularly in history, biography, and poetry. It is significant to our purposes that he showed special interest in Greece and Turkey.[8]

5. Byron's close Cambridge friend and travel companion John Cam Hobhouse (1786–1869) was, as a young man, a poet and scholar. Byron contributed nine poems to Hobhouse's *Imitations and Translations from the Ancient and Modern Classics* (London, 1809). As Lord Broughton he later became an important political figure. Francis Hodgson (1781–1852), poet and scholar also, had already published his *Translation of Juvenal* and *Lady Jane Grey; a Tale; and Other Poems* in 1809. In the latter volume Hodgson included *Gentle Alternative for the Reviewers,* a satirical reply to the *Edinburgh Review's* unfavorable criticism of his *Juvenal;* though it is on a much smaller scale, this poem is an interesting parallel to Byron's *English Bards and Scotch Reviewers.* Hodgson took orders and was eventually Provost of Eton. Byron's own tributes to Charles Skinner Matthews (1786?–1811), Fellow of Downing College, Cambridge, describe a rare and gifted personality. *LJ,* I, 150–60; *P,* II, 95. Mention should also be made of Henry Drury (1778–1841), son of the Harrow headmaster, with whom Byron was intimate and to whom he wrote numerous letters. Byron presented the MS. of the first two cantos of *Childe Harold* to Drury.

6. Moore, I, 38.

7. *LJ,* V, 453.

8. Moore, I, 95–101: "*Greece.*—Mitford's Greece, Leland's Philip, Plutarch, Potter's Antiquities, Xenophon, Thucydides, Herodotus . . . *Turkey.*—I have read Knolles, Sir Paul Rycaut, and Prince Cantemir, besides a more modern history, anonymous. Of the Ottoman History I know every event, from Tangralopi, and afterward Othman I to the peace of Passarowitz, in 1718,—the battle of Cutzka, in 1739, and the treaty between Russia and Turkey in 1790." In Byron's list, dated November 30, 1807, there are also works of law, philosophy, geography, divinity, and eloquence, as well as novels "by the thousand." In a note published in the third edition of Isaac Disraeli's *The Literary Character* (London, 1822), pp. 101–2, Byron added to his list "De Tott—Lady M. W. Montague—Hawkins's translation from Mignot's History of the Turks—the Arabian nights—All travels or histories or books upon the East I could meet with, I had read . . . before I was *ten years old.* I think the Arabian nights first."

A few months before his death in Greece Byron told Count Gamba, "The Turkish history was one of the first books that gave me pleasure when a child; and I believe it had much influence on my subsequent wishes to visit the Levant, and gave, perhaps, the oriental coloring which is observed in my poetry." *Narrative of Lord Byron's Last Journey to Greece* (London, 1825), p. 149. For a thorough study of Byron's Eastern

The idea of foreign travel had been in Byron's mind as early as 1806. On February 24 of that year he wrote his mother from Cambridge declaring his wish "to pass a couple of years abroad, where I am certain of employing my time to far more advantage and at much less expence, than at our English Seminaries." Byron's opinion of Cambridge was not a very high one, judging from his statement that he had already, after four desultory months, gained as much there as if he had pursued his studies for a century; and his remark that "Improvement at an English University to a Man of Rank is, you know, impossible, and the very Idea *ridiculous*"⁹ further demonstrates how little educational value Byron, like many of his contemporaries, derived from residence at Cambridge.

The notion of a Continental tour was clearly much more than a mere whim on Byron's part at this time, for not only did he solicit his mother's approval of the enterprise but he also suggested that she provide him with a tutor to accompany him. Since England was at war with France travel in the latter country was out of the question but Byron still considered Germany and the courts of Berlin, Vienna, and Petersburg safe and worth visiting. In fact, the journey he had in mind was closely along the lines of the conventional grand tour— something very different from the pilgrimage upon which he actually embarked three years later; it is worth noting that Byron visualized this early travel project as a tour "in the regular manner."

But the times were not propitious for a leisurely inspection of the Continent in 1806. The powerful hand of Napoleon dominated the face of Europe as boldly as Britain controlled the surrounding seas. And though Byron had originally intended to embark on his tour even without the consent of his mother (or of his guardian Lord Carlisle and his banker John Hanson) practical considerations, both political and financial, combined to keep him in England.¹

The rather aimless activities of Cambridge, Southwell, and London occupied Byron during the next two years but the impetus to travel lingered on. He was not able to undertake a projected trip to the Hebrides and Iceland in the summer of 1807. In late October of the same year he was looking forward to embarking in January on a four-

reading see Harold S. L. Wiener, "Byron and the East: Literary Sources of the 'Turkish Tales,'" *Nineteenth Century Studies* (Cornell University Press, 1940), pp. 89–129.

Byron's much less extensive information on Portugal and Spain was, however, derived chiefly from noting the swiftly moving events of the contemporary political scene.

9. *LJ*, I, 95–6. Hans Maier, in his *Entstehungsgeschichte von Byrons "Childe Harold's Pilgrimage" Gesang* I *und* II (Berlin, 1911), fails to mention this first indication of Byron's desire to travel. Maier's study, while helpful in details, suffers from a tendency to interpret Byron too literally, as for example when (pp. 13–14) the writer takes seriously Byron's offhand remark about possibly entering the Austrian, Russian, or Turkish military service. *LJ*, I, 225.

1. *LJ*, I, 96.

or five-month voyage with his cousin Captain George Bettesworth "to the Mediterranean, or to the West Indies, or—to the devil."[2] Byron took delight in informing his correspondent Miss Elizabeth Bridget Pigot that Bettesworth, commander of "the *Tartar*, the finest frigate in the navy,"[3] had received more wounds than Lord Nelson himself during his brief but eventful naval career and possessed a letter from the late admiral proving his right to that distinction. But this promising if hazardous enterprise also failed to materialize, and perhaps fortunately so for Byron, since Captain Bettesworth was to receive a twenty-fifth and fatal wound in action off Bergen the following May.[4]

It would be a mistake to overemphasize the significance of this rather vague travel project but, unsuccessful though it proved, the plan could hardly have failed to stimulate in Byron's mind the notion of a journey by sea, of a voyage to distant lands beyond the continent of Europe. By the following winter such a proposal was beginning to take real shape. Byron writes his schoolfellow De Bathe on February 2, 1808, that "In January 1809 I shall be twenty one, & in the Spring of the same year proceed abroad, not on the usual Tour, but a route of a more extensive Description. What say you? Are you disposed for a view of the Peloponnesus and a voyage through the Archipelago?" Byron goes on to state that his intention is "fixed on the *Pilgrimage*, unless some political view or accident induce me to postpone it."[5]

Here, then, is a project that exceeds the conventional grand tour in scope and in magnitude. By November Byron's plans were even more ambitious; he intended to travel as far as Persia and India. Already he had arranged to gain information from the Arabic professor at Cambridge and now he asked his mother to make inquiries of a Major Watson, who was "an old Indian."[6] He felt confident of procuring letters from the Government to the various consuls and governors at Calcutta and Madras; when the Prime Minister, the Duke of Portland, failed to coöperate and grant Byron permission to pass through the East India settlements he earned himself a doubtful literary immortality in *English Bards and Scotch Reviewers* as "old dame Portland." In very convincing manner Byron persuaded his mother that

After all, you must own my project is not a bad one. If I do not travel now, I never shall, and all men should one day or other. I have at present no con-

2. *LJ*, I, 146.   3. *LJ*, I, 146.
4. *Gentleman's Magazine*, LXXVIII, 1 (1808), 560.   5. *LJ*, I, 176.
6. *LJ*, I, 194–5. We may regret that Byron never reached Persia and India but the alteration in plans as the journey progressed and circumstances changed is perfectly understandable. The possibility of going on into Asia was still in his mind when he was in Greece. In a letter to Dallas, written September 7, 1811 (*LJ*, II, 27), Byron wrote that "before Childe Harold left England, it was his full intention to traverse Persia, and return by India."

nections to keep me at home; no wife, or unprovided sisters, brothers, etc. I shall take care of you, and when I return I may possibly become a politician. A few years' knowledge of other countries than our own will not incapacitate me for that part. If we see no nation but our own, we do not give mankind a fair chance; it is from *experience,* not books, we ought to judge of them. There is nothing like inspection, and trusting to our own senses.[7]

To his banker Hanson Byron wrote in much the same vein, taking especial care, however, to point out the financial wisdom of the undertaking:

In the first place, I wish to study India and Asiatic policy and manners. I am young, tolerably vigorous, abstemious in my way of living; I have no pleasure in fashionable dissipation, and I am determined to take a wider field than is customary with travellers. If I return, my judgment will be mature, and I shall still be young enough for politics. With regard to expence, travelling through the East is rather inconvenient than expensive: it is not like the tour of Europe, you undergo hardship, but incur little hazard of spending money.[8]

In late April he vowed to Hanson his intention of quitting the country as soon as possible and begged him to provide sufficient funds to "allow me to depart from this cursed country, and I promise to turn Mussulman, rather than return to it."[9] But whatever happened Newstead must not be sold: "The Abbey and I shall stand or fall together, and, were my head as grey and defenceless as the Arch of the Priory, I would abide by this resolution."

The initial impulse to travel came, I believe, from the natural curiosity and restlessness of Byron's nature. This impulse was intensified, to be sure, by other factors but there is an element of motive-hunting in Byron's presentation of now one, now another of these, in the manner we have just seen, as the prime reason for his departure.[1] Once he resolved to leave England he could look upon the journey as an escape from all that was displeasing to him and could play with the fancy that any or all of these motives and grievances drove him from his home.

In early March of 1809 *English Bards* appeared. Thus Byron had his revenge upon the uncomplimentary *Edinburgh Review.* He also attacked vigorously most of the leading poets of the day while declar-

7. *LJ,* I, 195.
8. *LJ,* I, 199–200. Byron was not entirely dependent upon Hanson for funds, however; before leaving England he borrowed £4,800, repaid in 1814, from his friend Scrope Davies. *LJ,* I, 165, n. Thus amply provided, Byron in turn lent to Hobhouse sufficient funds to cover the latter's traveling expenses. *LJ,* II, 328, n.
9. *LJ,* I, 222.
1. There are two farewell poems to Mary Chaworth, who had long since been Mrs. Musters. One is called "To a Lady, on Being Asked My Reason for Quitting England in the Spring," the other "Stanzas to a Lady on Leaving England." The latter has the refrain "Because I cannot love but one."

ing his allegiance to those neoclassical ideals in poetry that, despite his
practice, he was to believe in to the end of his life. Later in the month,
betraying no strong political convictions beyond a rather mild and
mechanical Whiggism, he took his seat in the House of Lords and by
his behavior on that occasion showed how insecurely and self-con-
sciously he carried his rank as a peer of the realm.[2] Hobhouse agreed
to be his friend's traveling companion. During the spring Byron
gathered miniatures of his other friends to take with him; and in late
May he invited the most intimate of these friends to Newstead for a
farewell frolic. There Matthews, as well as Hobhouse, was urged to
go along on the travels but dismissed the notion as a "wild scheme."[3]
Byron left London on June 11, after adding the following lines to a
new edition of *English Bards:*

> Yet once again adieu! ere this the sail
> That wafts me hence is shivering in the gale;
> And Afric's coast and Calpe's adverse height,
> And Stamboul's minarets must greet my sight:
> Thence shall I stray through Beauty's native clime,
> Where Kaff is clad in rocks, and crowned with snows sublime.
> But should I back return, no lettered rage
> Shall drag my common-place book on the stage:
> Let vain Valentia rival luckless Carr,
> And equal him whose work he sought to mar;
> Let Aberdeen and Elgin still pursue
> The shade of fame through regions of Virtù;
> Waste useless thousands on their Phidian freaks,
> Mis-shapen monuments, and maimed antiques;
> And make their grand saloons a general mart
> For all the mutilated blocks of art:
> Of Dardan tours let Dilettanti tell,
> I leave topography to classic Gell;
> And, quite content, no more shall interpose
> To stun mankind with Poesy, or Prose.[4]

Upon his return to England in 1811 Byron was careful to alter the line

To stun mankind with Poesy, or Prose

to read

To stun the public ear—at least with Prose.[5]

2. Robert C. Dallas describes Byron's haughty manner toward the Lord Chancellor
when he was welcomed to the House in his *Recollections of the Life of Lord Byron*
(London, 1824), pp. 50–4.
    3. *LJ*, I, 155, n.   4. These are the lines as they appeared in the second edition.
    5. *P*, I, 380. Byron always professed scorn for pretentious books of travel and the
minutiae of archaeological and antiquarian researches—even when the author happened to be his friend Hobhouse and the travels his own! Lord Valentia's *Voyages
and Travels to India, Ceylon, the Red Sea, Abyssinia, and Egypt,* called by Byron
his "tremendous travels" (*P*, I, 378, n.), appeared in 1809. At that time Sir John Carr
had already gained considerable profit and some ridicule (see *LJ*, I, 235) from his

This last alteration must surely have been intended to smooth the way for *Childe Harold*.

After waiting over a week for suitable winds Byron and Hobhouse finally sailed from Falmouth Roads on Sunday, July 2, 1809, aboard the *Princess Elizabeth* packet, which was carrying mails for Lisbon.[6] In addition to Byron and Hobhouse and their attendants William Fletcher, Joe Murray, and young Robert Rushton, the passengers included "two officers' wives, three children, two waiting-maids, ditto subalterns for the troops, three Portuguese esquires and domestics, in all nineteen souls."[7] It could hardly have failed to appeal to Byron's imagination that the commander of the *Princess Elizabeth* happened to be a Captain Kidd.[8]

The rollicking verses enclosed in Byron's farewell letter to Hodgson[9] give a vivid picture of preparations for departure and suggest thus early something of the tone and facility of *Beppo* and *Don Juan*. They stand, indeed, in marked contrast to the closing words of the letter itself, where Byron writes "I leave England without regret— I shall return to it without pleasure. I am like Adam, the first convict

accounts of travel in Ireland and on the Continent. Sir William Gell's *Topography of Troy* (London, 1804), *Geography and Antiquities of Ithaca* (London, 1807), and *Itinerary of Greece* (London, 1808) were the fruit of extensive travels in the Near East. These were but a few of the countless books of travel and investigation, particularly in the Near East, which appeared in England in the early part of the nineteenth century. Many were of considerable importance, as Wallace Cable Brown has pointed out in his article, "The Popularity of English Travel Books about the Near East, 1775–1825," *Philological Quarterly*, xv (1936), 70–80.

6. Byron gives (*LJ*, I, 236) July 2 as the date of departure. The *London Chronicle* for July 4–5, 1809, reports that "FALMOUTH, July 2. . . . sailed . . . Princess Elizabeth packet with two mails for Lisbon." *The Times* for September 26, 1809, announces the arrival from Lisbon of "the Princess Elizabeth, KIDD."

7. *LJ*, I, 227. Fletcher, Murray, and the boy Rushton had all been attached to the household at Newstead. In the letter written to his mother from Falmouth on June 22 (*LJ*, I, 224–5) Byron mentions that he is taking with him a German servant Friese, recommended to him by Dr. Butler of Harrow. And in a postscript to the same letter he expresses his regret at leaving behind the aged Murray. Once the journey is under way, however, there is no mention of Friese among the servants and it seems safe to infer that for some reason Friese did not sail on the *Princess Elizabeth* from Falmouth. Since Murray did finally accompany his master, it seems likely that he took the place of Friese at the last moment.

8. I have been unable to identify Captain Kidd beyond Byron's enthusiastic descriptions of him as "our gallant, or rather gallows commander" (*LJ*, I, 226), "a gallant commander as ever smuggled an anker of right Nantz" (*LJ*, I, 227), and "that experienced navigator, Captain Kidd" (*LJ*, I, 230). In the valedictory "Lines to Mr. Hodgson"

 . . . lo! the Captain,
 Gallant Kidd, commands the crew.

9. *LJ*, I, 230–2. The letter is dated June 25 from Falmouth but it was apparently not sent until at least five days later, since the enclosed poem is dated June 30 from Falmouth Roads. On or shortly before the thirtieth, the preliminaries so graphically described in the poem must have taken place: the customs inspection, departure by rowboat from shore, and the installation of the passengers aboard the *Princess Elizabeth* in the Roads. Once aboard the packet they were further delayed until July 2.

sentenced to transportation, but I have no Eve, and have eaten no apple but what was sour as a crab;—and thus ends my first chapter." [1] With very much this same theatrical and morbid self-consciousness Byron was soon to endow his shadowy Childe Burun.

> On, on the vessel flies, the land is gone,
> And winds are rude in Biscay's sleepless bay. [2]

Byron describes the trip to Lisbon as "a very favorable passage of four days and a half." [3] Yet favorable as the trip was from the point of view of speed, Hobhouse found it a "rough passage" [4] and Byron himself admits to having been "sea-sick, and sick of the sea." [5] One suspects, also, that in the real feelings of Rushton and Fletcher there was some basis for the homesickness of the "little page" and the "staunch yeoman" who were to come into being a few months later in *Childe Harold's Good Night.* The misanthropic, cynical mood of the Childe himself as, in that same poem-within-a-poem, he bids farewell to his native shores is again an embodiment of the darker, more theatrical side of Byron's own nature, grotesquely attired in antique dress.

Moore has recorded a strange tale that Byron heard from the lips of Captain Kidd during the crossing to Portugal and repeated to his friends in later years. As Moore retells the story, one night in his cabin the Captain

was awakened by the pressure of something heavy on his limbs, and, there being a faint light in the room, could see, as he thought, distinctly, the figure of his brother, who was, at that time, in the naval service in the East Indies, dressed in his uniform, and stretched across the bed . . . To add to the wonder, on putting his hand forth to touch this form, he found the uniform in which it appeared to be dressed, dripping wet . . . A few months after, he received the startling intelligence that on that night his brother had been drowned in the Indian seas. Of the supernatural character of this appearance, Captain Kidd himself did not appear to have the slightest doubt. [6]

The impression made upon Byron by the story of the incident is an early indication of that fatalism and belief in the supernatural that remained with him to the end of his life. [7]

---

1. *LJ*, I, 230. Miss Mayne, speaking of this contrast between the farewell letter and the poem to Hodgson, observes that "No more striking example of the difference between the real and the self-imagined Byron is to be found." *Byron* (Revised ed., London, Methuen & Co., Ltd., 1924), p. 104. The manuscript of the poem to Hodgson is now in the Wrenn Library at the University of Texas. Mr. William H. McCarthy calls my attention to the fact that in the MS. the third word of Stanza 2, line 15, is "genial" rather than "general," as it appears in the standard text.

2. *Childe Harold*, I, 14.   3. *LJ*, I, 236–7.   4. *Recollections*, I, 6.

5. *LJ*, I, 233.   6. Moore, I, 193, n.

7. Lady Blessington noted this characteristic in 1823. See *A Journal of the Conversations of Lord Byron with the Countess of Blessington* (New York, 1893), pp. 36–7.

THE SCENE OF BYRON'S TRAVELS
1809–1811

THE SCENE
of
BYRON'S TRAVELS
1809 ~ 1811

LORD BYRON'S FIRST PILGRIMAGE

I

Portugal and Spain

I. The Peninsular War to July, 1809

WHEN Byron visited Portugal and Spain in the summer of 1809 English eyes were focused on the Iberian Peninsula.[1] Since May, 1808, England's war with Napoleon had entered on a new phase. Ostensibly to enforce his Continental System, but more particularly as part of a carefully prepared plan to subdue his wavering ally Spain, Napoleon had, immediately after the Treaty of Tilsit in August, 1807, called upon Prince Regent John of Portugal to declare war on England, to join his fleet to those of Napoleon's allies, to confiscate all British goods in his harbors, and to arrest all British subjects in his domain. When the Prince Regent protested that he could not meet these excessive demands, Napoleon prevailed upon the impotent Spanish king Charles IV and his minister Manuel de Godoy to allow a French army to pass through Spain en route to Portugal—this with the twofold purpose of conquering Portugal and of establishing French troops in Spain without arousing suspicion. In return for Spanish support against Portugal Napoleon promised that a division of the conquered country should be made between France and Spain.

Portugal offered no resistance to the invading forces. By November 30, 1807, the royal family and fifteen thousand of their leading subjects had fled to South America and, without firing a shot, the French general Junot had gained complete control of Lisbon. Junot wasted no time in disbanding the Portuguese army, confiscating the property of those who fled, and imposing heavy taxes and imposts, in accordance with orders from Napoleon.

With the subjugation of Portugal thus easily accomplished Napoleon turned attention to his ostensible ally Spain. Now, instead of

1. This introductory account of affairs in the Peninsula during the year and a half before Byron's visit is based primarily upon Charles Oman's *A History of the Peninsular War* (Oxford, 1902–03, 2 vols.) and W. F. P. Napier's *History of the War on the Peninsula and in the South of France, from the Year 1807 to the Year 1814* (London, 1886 [originally published in 1828–40], 2 vols.). The Whig bias of Napier's brilliant work, much of which is based upon firsthand observation, is largely corrected by Oman's more objective if less animated treatment. For a briefer account, written with vividness and discernment, see the latter chapters of Arthur Bryant's *Years of Victory* (London, 1945).

ceasing to pour French troops into Spain after the fall of Portugal, he kept adding to their numbers and the conciliatory attitude of the weak Spanish Government helped to hasten his process of occupation. When the Spanish people, beginning to suspect Napoleon's treacherous designs on their country, forced Charles IV to abdicate the throne in favor of his son Ferdinand, Napoleon was unwilling to recognize the new king. Instead he proclaimed his brother Joseph Bonaparte king of Spain. Thus by the first of May, 1808, Napoleon seemed to have the entire Peninsula at his feet.

It was at this point that the Spanish people rose in fury against their French oppressors. On May 2, 1808, there was a rising at Madrid and soon afterward all the Spanish provinces had thrown off the French yoke. Envoys were dispatched to England to be greeted with great enthusiasm. Two months after the revolt in Spain the English Tory Government sent help in the form of money and arms to the Juntas which had sprung up all over Spain; and in July, 1808, a force of nearly ten thousand men under Sir Arthur Wellesley sailed from Cork for the Peninsula. In January, 1809, England made a formal treaty of alliance with the Supreme Junta at Seville.

Ill-prepared though the Spaniards were to wage war against Napoleon, they held their own against his armies through the spring and summer of 1808. The heroic defense of Zaragoza, preserved by its citizens for three months until finally in mid-August the French raised the siege, stirred the imaginations of Englishmen as well as Spaniards; and Augustina, the heroine whose exploits in defense of her country were among the most thrilling in Spain's history, became immortalized as the "Maid of Zaragoza." The decisive victory of the Spanish general Castaños over the French at Baylen in June had been a factor in relieving the pressure upon Zaragoza; it also checked the plan of Napoleon's lieutenant General Dupont to cross Spain and reduce the important cities of Seville and Cadiz.

Meanwhile in August Wellesley had landed his troops at the mouth of the Mondego River and marched southward toward Lisbon to meet a French army under Junot. At Vimiera, a few miles north of Lisbon, Wellesley decisively defeated Junot on August 21 but was prevented from following up his gains by Sir Henry Burrard who, arriving during the battle to take over the command from Wellesley, refused to sanction a vigorous pursuit. The situation approached the ludicrous the following day when a third general, Sir Hew Dalrymple, arrived and in turn took over the command from Burrard. As Napier, the first great historian of the Peninsular War, pointed out, "Thus in the short space of twenty-four hours, during which a battle was fought, the army fell successively into the hands of three men, coming from the ocean with different views, habits, and information, and without any previous opportunity of communing even by letter, so as to arrange a common plan of operations."[2]

This combination of circumstances led to the notorious "Convention of Cintra," by the terms of which the French evacuated Portugal but on the condition that they be transported back to France in British ships with their artillery and arms. The leniency of this arrangement raised a tremendous outcry in England and in November the three generals, including Wellesley who had signed the agreement only with reluctance, were brought before a court of inquiry in London. They were acquitted but many months passed before Englishmen, especially those who inclined toward the Whig opposition, ceased to condemn the Convention of Cintra.

Upon the recall of Wellesley, Burrard, and Dalrymple, Sir John Moore took over command of the allied army in Portugal and in the early fall of 1808 was ordered by the British Government to march from Lisbon to meet a force under Sir David Baird. Together they were to carry on the battle against the French in concert with the Spanish troops. However Napoleon's own sudden seizure of the offensive in Spain, culminating in his capture of Madrid on December 3, thwarted Moore's plans. By threatening Napoleon's lines of communication and then retreating northward to Corunna Moore was at least able to divert Napoleon from his plan of overrunning southern Spain. Moore, whose difficulties were increased by the impolitic interference of the British Minister to Spain, John Hookham Frere, was killed at Corunna shortly before his troops managed to embark for England. Napoleon, after his forces had pursued Moore to the very ocean, retired into France leaving southern Spain still unconquered. In England, however, the Corunna retreat and evacuation seemed a negative triumph at best. Disappointment was widespread and in the winter and spring of 1809 the British cause on the Peninsula looked to be at its lowest ebb.

But Wellesley, redeemed, returned to Portugal in late April. Since Napoleon was back in Paris, military affairs on the Peninsula were being carried forward by his lieutenants under the Emperor's orders. Advancing north Wellesley seized the opportunity to drive a French army under Soult from Oporto in the middle of May and then turned his attention toward Spain and the approaches to Madrid. During June and the first days of July Wellesley moved to Abrantes in central Portugal and on July 3 he entered Spain for the first time to offer opposition to the French forces near Madrid. On the day of Byron's arrival in Lisbon Wellesley's army was advancing toward the town of Talavera, in the close vicinity of Madrid.

2. *Op. cit.*, I, 141.

II. Byron's Early Political Sympathies

It is impossible to say with any precision how much thought Byron had given to affairs in Portugal and Spain before he set forth upon his travels. His complete silence about the Peninsular War in his early correspondence and poems may be adduced as negative evidence. Almost certainly if so articulate a young man as Byron had felt the passionate zeal for the Spanish cause that animated many of his fellow countrymen, there would have been at least some passing reference to the war in his many letters to his friends or in the poetry he wrote in late 1808 and early 1809.

To be sure, Byron was but twenty when the war broke out. His energetic defense of Fox,[3] his membership in the Cambridge Whig Club,[4] and the scornful remarks in *English Bards* concerning the Tory Government[5] indicate that his early political sympathies inclined toward the Whig opposition. Writing with admirable candor and objectivity to Hanson before taking his seat in the House of Lords, he had insisted that he did not strongly favor either party; yet he betrayed some preference when he remarked that, "though I shall not run headlong into opposition, I will studiously avoid a connection with ministry."[6] It is safe to assume that the Byron who came of age in the year 1809 tended to take rather for granted the Whig point of view but was not very actively concerned either about foreign affairs or the domestic political scene. There is no real reason for doubting his sincerity when he closed the letter to Hanson with the statement, "So much for Politics, of which I at present know little and care less."[7]

Even before England's intervention to assist Portugal and Spain against Napoleon in 1808, almost the entire Whig party had opposed the conduct of the war with France.[8] The extent of this opposition ranged within the party from criticism of the Government's methods to the opinion that it was futile to continue the war at all. There had been almost universal rage among the Whigs against England's "ruthless" seizure of the Danish fleet at Copenhagen in September, 1807, and this was succeeded at the end of the year by scorn for British assistance in transporting the Portuguese royal family and their fifteen thousand attendants to Brazil. When Spain rose in May, 1808, most

3. See the poem, "On the Death of Mr. Fox," written in 1806.
4. *LJ*, v, 424. In a letter to John Murray, which appears in *LJ*, iv, 499–500, Hobhouse lists the ten members of this club.
5. See chiefly ll. 1011–6.   6. *LJ*, i, 209.   7. *LJ*, i, 210.
8. The best single treatment of the Whig attitude during this period is Michael Roberts' "The Whigs and the War," *The Whig Party 1807–1812* (London, The Macmillan Co., 1939), chap. ii, pp. 103–71. See also A. F. Fremantle, *England in the Nineteenth Century* (London, George Allen & Unwin, Ltd., 1930), ii, 196–362. *The Spanish Journal of Elizabeth Lady Holland* (London, 1910) reflects faithfully the views of the strongly pro-Spanish climate of Whig opinion.

of the party at first joined the Tories in rallying behind the Spanish cause. But three months later the Convention of Cintra checked this enthusiasm considerably, seeming, contrary to the facts of the case, to bear out the Whig distrust of the Tory general Wellesley. The Whigs had to content themselves with a parliamentary investigation that availed nothing; and later, after the unhappy campaign of Sir John Moore, with criticism, partially justified, of the Government's treatment of Moore and the behavior toward him of their representative in Spain, Frere.[9] When Austria renewed war upon Napoleon in the spring of 1809 the wisdom of the Government's decision to send a new army to the Peninsula was seriously questioned and the choice of Wellesley as its leader became a party matter. Most Whigs were discouraged by the impotence of Portugal, by the inefficiency of the Spanish Juntas, and by what they considered the apathy and uncooperativeness of the Spaniards. In 1809 among the influential members of the party only a small group, headed by Lord Holland, supported the war on the Peninsula with any genuine conviction.

Many Whigs visited the Peninsula to investigate the situation at first hand. The greater number of these, including Thomas Sheridan, Lord John Russell, and that J. W. Ward whom Byron met in Lisbon, belonged to the Holland faction which was enthusiastic about the war but there were also some who went in a more critical frame of mind.[1] Byron, however, belonged to neither group, for his visit to the Peninsula was purely accidental. Up to the eve of departure his plan had been to sail directly to Gibraltar and on to Malta and Constantinople. Only because expediency suggested sailing first to Lisbon did he do so. Once there, to be sure, Byron took the time and trouble to see something of the Peninsula but he had originally had no intention of visiting either Portugal or the interior of Spain.

It is important to remember this point in estimating the effect of his experience in the Peninsula upon Byron. We shall see that a rather indifferent and inarticulate attitude of opposition to the conduct of the war was inflamed there into vigorous expression and, more important, that some acquaintance with the people and the land which Napoleon was despoiling aroused in Byron a bitter hatred for such wanton oppression and also a deep concern and sympathy for the fate of the people of Spain who waged what he considered an all but hopeless struggle against the might of Napoleon.

9. "But the Whigs were not fertile in positive suggestions; and they were too ready to assume that, as long as Tories managed the war, our victories would be fruitless and our reverses irretrievable." H. W. C. Davis, *The Age of Grey and Peel* (Oxford University Press, 1929), p. 121.

1. Roberts, *op. cit.*, pp. 167–8. These names appear in the pages of Lady Holland's *Spanish Journal*. Sheridan was the son of the dramatist and orator; Russell in later life became the well-known Lord Russell of the Reform Bill.

III. Portugal[2]

On July 7 the *Princess Elizabeth* came within sight of the Portuguese coast and shortly afterward proceeded up the river Tagus,
guided by native pilots through its narrow eight-mile channel.[3] The
lines in *Childe Harold* describe the approach to Lisbon:

> Four days are sped, but with the fifth, anon,
> New shores make every bosom gay;
> And Cintra's mountain greets them on their way,
> And Tagus dashing onward to the Deep,
> His fabled golden tribute bent to pay;
> And soon on board the Lusian pilots leap,
> And steer 'twixt fertile shores where yet few rustics reap.[4]

The richness and beauty of the land on either side of the channel
rendered Byron's first immediate impressions of foreign shores very
favorable. And as the Tagus channel widened into the inner bay of
Lisbon, on the left bank the city itself rose to view:

> Her image floating on that noble tide,
> Which poets vainly pave with sands of gold.[5]

Byron was indeed fortunate in his first sight of a foreign city, for
the harbor view of Lisbon has been universally admitted to be one of
the most beautiful and spectacular in the world.[6] The long approach

2. The indispensable sources of information concerning Byron's stay in Portugal
and Spain are Prothero's edition of the *Letters and Journals,* especially Vol. I, and
Coleridge's edition of the *Poems,* especially Vol. II. The account of the journey in
Hobhouse's *Journey into Albania* does not begin until the departure from Malta but
there is valuable information in his *Recollections of a Long Life.* Alberto Telles, in his
Lord Byron em Portugal (Lisbon, 1869) gives a few facts that are not available elsewhere. Philip H. Churchman's article, "Lord Byron's Experiences in the Spanish Peninsula in 1809," in the *Bulletin Hispanique,* XI (1909), 55–95, 125–71, is a helpful gath-
ering of details but it suffers from overuse of illustrative material from other travelers
and from the fact that it appeared before Hobhouse's *Recollections.* For a discussion of
chronological details see Appendix A.

3. Telles, *op. cit.,* p. 129, quotes from the *Diario Lisbonense* for July 8, 1809: "No
dia 7 entrou o paquete inglez por nome Princeza Isabel." Byron himself, in the first
of the stanzas quoted above, implies also that the travelers reached Lisbon on the fifth
day.

4. *Childe Harold,* I, 14.   5. *Idem,* I, 16.

6. One example among many is the description of Sir Robert Ker Porter, who, less
than a year before Byron, came to Lisbon to join Sir John Moore's army: "You can form
no idea of the magnificence of the view, on entering what is called the mouth of the
Tagus . . . On its bosom heave the proud fleets of Britain, intermixed with numbers of
smaller vessels, whose lateen sails and copper-hued crews bring the shores of the Nile,
or of Barbary, before your awakened fancy, and produce a stretch of scene as splendid
as romantic." *Letters from Portugal and Spain* (London, 1809), pp. 4–5. Byron himself,
writing facetiously to Murray eight years later, said, "I sha'n't go to Naples. It is but
the second best sea-view, and I have seen the first and third, viz. Constantinople and
Lisbon." *LJ,* IV, 101.

by the river channel, which finally expands to reveal the steep city and its reflection in the bay, gives Lisbon a charm peculiarly her own. Moreover, in 1809 the presence of the British fleet amid the many vessels in the bay added to the impressiveness of the scene. There, as the *Princess Elizabeth* glided into the harbor,

> . . . a thousand keels did ride
> Of mighty strength, since Albion was allied,
> And to the Lusians did her aid afford.[7]

But the approach to Lisbon impressed Byron much more favorably than did the city itself. He wrote his mother that, "except the view from the Tagus, which is beautiful, and some fine churches and convents, it contains little but filthy streets and more filthy inhabitants."[8] The lines in *Childe Harold* emphasize the strong contrast between the outer appearance of Lisbon and its true character:

> But whoso entereth within this town,
>   That, sheening far, celestial seems to be,
> Disconsolate will wander up and down,
>   Mid many things unsightly to strange ee;
> For hut and palace show like filthily.[9]

The original manuscript version of lines 4–5 was even more explicit:

> Mid many things that grieve both nose and ee:
> For hut and palace smelleth filthily.[1]

Though the flatness and pseudoarchaic diction of these lines on Lisbon and its people make them inferior as poetry, they must have had a solid basis in fact, for Byron's opinion of Lisbon was shared by almost every traveler who visited the city in the eighteenth or the early nineteenth century. Henry Fielding, who went to Portugal to die in 1754, called Lisbon "the nastiest city in the world."[2] Forty-five years later the German mineralogist Henry F. Link exclaimed at the squalor of the city.[3] And in January, 1809, even so sympathetic an observer as Lady Holland wrote in her journal that Lisbon was "full as dirty as formerly."[4]

The travelers found lodging in the upper part of Lisbon at the Buenos Aires Hotel, where Hobhouse was shocked when a Mr. Bulkeley charged them thirteen per cent for changing their money. They

---

7. *Childe Harold*, I, 16.   8. *LJ*, I, 237.
9. *Childe Harold*, I, 17.   1. *P*, II, 33, n.
2. *Journal of a Voyage to Lisbon*, p. 119, in *Works of Henry Fielding*, Leslie Stephen, ed. (London, 1882), Vol. VII.
3. *Travels in Portugal, and through France and Spain, With a Dissertation on the Literature of Portugal, and the Spanish and Portuguese Languages*, translated from the German by John Hinckley (London, 1801), pp. 201–03.
4. *Op. cit.*, p. 244.

spent the first two or three days seeing the city.[5] Among the "fine churches and convents" Byron visited were the Convent of Jesus, whose library turned out to contain only two English works, and the handsome Hieronymite Convent of Belem, founded in 1499 to commemorate Vasco da Gama's discovery of the sea route to India. Both Byron and his companion seem to have been more impressed by the behavior of the monks than by the buildings themselves. Byron was amused to find how shaky the monks' Latin was, while Hobhouse was as horrified to discover their ignorance when he was told by one of them that a picture, showing a battle in which firearms were being used, represented an ancient Roman fight! [6]

Despite the squalor of Lisbon the novelty and excitement of the new world he discovered proved irresistible to Byron. To Hodgson he wrote in high spirits:

I am very happy here, because I loves oranges, and talks bad Latin to the monks, who understand it, as it is like their own,—and I goes into society (with my pocket-pistols), and I swims in the Tagus all across at once, and I rides on an ass or a mule, and swears Portuguese, and have got a diarrhoea and bites from the mosquitoes. But what of that? Comfort must not be expected by folks that go a pleasuring.[7]

And to make delight complete there had to be a few depreciatory words about England: "But, in sober sadness, any thing is better than England, and I am infinitely amused with my pilgrimage as far as it has gone."

Byron visited the theaters where he was apparently less shocked than his companion to find the audiences addicted to Iberian dances "of a lascivious character."[8] Captain Gronow, in his *Reminiscences,*[9] remarks that Byron frequently visited the opera at Lisbon, "accompanied by his friends, Dan Mackinnon, Hervey Aston, Colin Campbell, and William Burrell."[1] Mackinnon, a colonel in the Coldstream Guards, and Aston later achieved note as two of the outstanding dandies of Regency London. According to Gronow, at Lisbon Byron heard Italian opera, that very type of entertainment which he had derided a few months before in *English Bards.* Gronow further observes that Byron "became the idol of the women, and the lionizing

5. *Recollections,* I, 6.   6. *Recollections,* I, 9. Also *LJ,* I, 233.
7. *LJ,* I, 233.   8. *Recollections,* I, 6.
9. *The Reminiscences and Recollections of Captain Gronow* (London, 1892), II, 195–6.
1. A William Burrell received the M.A. degree from St. John's College, Cambridge, in 1809. Colin (later Sir Colin) Campbell (1776–1847) became a trusted lieutenant of Sir Arthur Wellesley after serving with distinction in India. As Wellesley's chief aide-de-camp he had been in command of the expeditionary force to Portugal in 1808.

he underwent there might have made him exceedingly vain, for he was admired wherever he went."[2]

Byron emphasizes that no mere sense of the dramatic but actual necessity prompted him to carry his "pocket-pistols" when he went into society. Commenting upon the assassinations that took place in Lisbon in 1809, he relates from personal experience that "I was once stopped in the way to the theatre at eight o'clock in the evening, when the streets were not more empty than they generally are at that hour, opposite to an open shop, and in a carriage with a friend: had we not fortunately been armed, I have not the least doubt that we should have 'adorned a tale' instead of telling one."[3]

Portuguese tradition has also perpetuated an incident that presumably took place as Byron *left* the San Carlos Theater in Lisbon one evening. In 1844 the historian Alexandre Herculano referred to such an occasion when Byron was reputedly struck by a Portuguese husband with whose wife he had been flirting.[4] The episode was later commemorated in a poem addressed to Byron by Joao de Lemos,[5] part of which has been haltingly translated into English as follows:

> You found ignorant and rude all of us
> For finding husbands very serious,
> Who, when you wished to stain their wives' honour
> Stained your body with something to remember.

In 1879 the translator Alberto Telles called this a "tradiccional anecdota de S. Carlos." And again forty years later the cudgels were taken up against Byron by a Portuguese writer D. G. Dalgado, who not only identified the episode with the near-assault mentioned by Byron but, in the spirit of Joao de Lemos' poem, went to the extreme of at-

---

2. *Op cit.*, II, 196. Gronow also mentions that during Byron's stay at Lisbon he was "much amused with Dan Mackinnon's various funny stories." He relates one of these, which "was supposed" to have suggested to Byron the similar scene in the fifth canto of *Don Juan*. Gronow tells the highly picturesque anecdote, which reputedly almost brought Mackinnon to a court martial, as follows: "Lord Wellington was curious about visiting a convent near Lisbon, and the lady abbess made no difficulty; Mackinnon, hearing this, contrived to get clandestinely within the sacred walls, and it was generally supposed that it was neither his first nor his second visit. At all events, when Lord Wellington arrived, Dan Mackinnon was to be seen among the nuns, dressed out in their sacred costume, with his head and whiskers shaved; and as he possessed good features, he was declared to be one of the best-looking amongst those chaste dames." *Reminiscences*, I, 62.

3. *P*, II, 86.

4. *Estudos Morais*, II, "O Parocho de Aldeia," in *O Panorama* (Lisboa, 1844), p. 119. Alexandre Herculano de Carvalho e Aranjo (1810–77), the author of a definitive but incomplete *Historia de Portugal*, is referred to in the fourteenth edition of *The Encyclopedia Britannica* (XI, 481) as "the greatest modern historian of Portugal and the Peninsula."

5. *Cancioneiro* (Lisboa, 1859), II, 242. The translation, by Alberto Telles, appears in his *Lord Byron em Portugal*, p. 51.

tributing Byron's entire animus against the Portuguese to the incident! "In Lisbon," says Dalgado, "he has to submit to an unpleasant
experience at the hands of one Portuguese husband, and he falls foul
of the whole Portuguese nation."[6]

On all sides there must have been talk and signs of the war that was
engulfing the Peninsula. Byron, to be sure, makes practically no
reference to the war in his correspondence but, since those few letters
he wrote from Portugal and Spain were hasty and highly impres-
sionistic, it is not surprising that they deal only scantily with the more
serious side of things. *Childe Harold* gives ample evidence that the
war affected him deeply.

On the eleventh of July Byron and Hobhouse had the opportunity
to review the light brigade of General Robert Craufurd which had
taken part in Sir John Moore's Corunna campaign earlier in the year.[7]
Although Wellesley was penetrating farther and farther into Spain
during Byron's stay in Lisbon, this particular detachment of the
British forces remained in the capital. Less than two weeks later the
three battalions were to hurry forward with almost incredible swift-
ness to reinforce Wellesley's troops at Talavera.[8]

Hobhouse records numerous other details that he picked up in
conversation at Lisbon, particularly anecdotes having to do with the
recent French occupation.[9] He remarks upon the good favor in which
the French general Junot was held by the Portuguese but was told
that when, at the time of the battle at Vimiera, Junot had left Lisbon
in the hands of only a thousand men, the Portuguese had turned on
their captors and repaid their rapacity by murdering many of them.
Service in the Portuguese Army seemed unpopular; men were
rounded up from time to time in the public gardens and, if unmarried,
were taken for service against the French.

As Byron wrote to Hodgson, during the days at Lisbon he undertook and accomplished a very difficult swimming feat. Hobhouse
records that his companion swam the Tagus from Old Lisbon, opposite the town, to Belem Castle down the river and, "having to con-
tend with a tide and countercurrent, the wind blowing freshly, was
but little less than two hours in crossing the river."[1] This exploit was,
indeed, a more hazardous one than the celebrated crossing of the
Hellespont the following spring.

Among the Englishmen at Lisbon Byron met John W. Ward, who
was to attain a position of prominence later in life as the first Earl of
Dudley. Ward's account in 1812 of his first meeting with Byron at
Lisbon is worth recording: "I met him by accident three years ago in

6. *Lord Byron's Childe Harold's Pilgrimage to Portugal* (Lisboa, Imprensa Nacional,
1919), pp. 71–2.
7. *Recollections*, I, 6. Hobhouse misspells the name of the general as "Crawford."
8. Oman, *op. cit.*, II, 560.   9. *Recollections*, I, 7–9.   1. *Journey*, II, 220.

Portugal. I had never seen his first poems or his 'Scotch [*sic*] Bards,' &c., so that I had no prejudice about him one way or the other. But I had not been half an hour in his company before I perceived that he was a person of no common mind."[2] Ward goes on to mention with some glee that "This discovery, however, by no means prevented me from cheating him extremely in the sale of some English saddles with which I equipped him at Lisbon to make the tour of Portugal and Andalusia." With reference to *Childe Harold*, which had just appeared in London when he wrote, Ward observed that "The portrait which he has drawn of himself in the eighth stanza is, I am apt to think, a pretty accurate resemblance.[3] He is lame of both feet, but his figure and face are good."

Byron's harsh words about the city of Lisbon go beyond his indictment of the uncleanliness of the city. Uncleanliness, he insists, characterizes the people as well. Not merely Lisbon itself but also

> The dingy denizens are reared in dirt.[4]

And Byron makes clear his belief that something more degrading than pitch has defiled the people of Lisbon, as of all Portugal, when he calls them, even as he praises the beauty of their country,

> A nation swoln with ignorance and pride,
> Who lick yet loathe the hand that waves the sword
> To save them from the wrath of Gaul's unsparing lord.
>
> .   .   .   .
>
> Poor paltry slaves! yet born 'midst noblest scenes—
> Why, Nature, waste thy wonders on such men?[5]

These are strong words and it is necessary to consider just what led Byron to utter them.

In the first place, Byron must have come to Lisbon with predispositions against the Portuguese. Even before the Peninsular War brought calamities upon the people of Portugal, foreigners had been in the habit of speaking slightingly of them as a people cowed by a despotic ruling family and a greedy, overbearing clergy. Neither the catastrophic Lisbon earthquake of 1755 nor the reforms effected through the next quarter-century by the enlightened statesman Pombal had shaken more than temporarily the absolutism of the reigning house of Braganza.[6] Then, after the royal family and leaders of the state

2. S. H. Romilly, *Letters to "Ivy" from the First Earl of Dudley* (London, 1905), p. 163.

3. This is the stanza, added to the MS. in 1811, beginning "Yet ofttimes in his maddest mirthful mood."

4. *Childe Harold*, 1, 17.   5. *Idem*, 1, 16, 18.

6. See George Young, "Pombal and the Peninsular War," *Portugal Old and Young, a Historical Study* (Oxford, 1917), chap. v, pp. 179–234.

had deserted their country in November, 1807, the meek, bloodless submission of Portugal to the French helped to shatter what prestige Portugal possessed in the eyes of her fellow nations.

In 1809 there was in England such a strong current of opinion hostile to the Portuguese that Wordsworth, in his *Tract on the Convention of Cintra*, felt it necessary to defend them: "But the Portugueze *are* a brave people—a people of great courage and worth!"[7] Porter, in the thick of the fighting in the Peninsula, observed, "I have heard of nations submitting quietly to a generous conqueror; but to sheathe the half-drawn sword, to bend the head without a word to the yoke of violence and extortion, is an abjectness of spirit never before paralleled, I believe, in the history of man."[8] Porter spoke for many Englishmen when he declared that "It has been a growing evil with Portugal, the assistance she has always sought in all her wars from foreign powers."[9]

This was the Portugal to which Byron came in July, 1809. The Council of Regency, set up after the expulsion of the French, proved to be an inefficient and corrupt body and only the presence of a British garrison prevented serious trouble in Lisbon during the latter part of 1808 and early 1809.[1] The efforts of the regency to remedy the military situation were fruitless in the extreme, for instead of attempting to complete a regular army they resorted to a mass levy of the population. Oman gives a vivid picture of the behavior of the recruited soldiery during the winter of 1809:

These tumultuary levies had few officers and hardly any arms but pikes. They were under no sort of discipline, and devoted themselves to the self-imposed duty of hunting for spies and "Afrancesados." Led by demagogues of the streets, they paraded up and down Lisbon to beat of drum, arresting persons whom they considered suspicious, especially foreign residents of all nationalities. . . . Isolated British soldiers were assaulted, some were wounded, and parties of "legionaries" actually stopped aides-de-camp and orderlies carrying dispatches, and stripped them of the documents they were bearing. The mob was inclined, indeed, to be ill-disposed towards their allies, from the suspicion that they were intending to evacuate Lisbon and retire from the Peninsula.

This last fear was allayed to a large extent when General William Beresford arrived in March to take over the organization and

7. *Wordsworth's Tract on the Convention of Cintra,* with Introduction by A. V. Dicey (London, 1915), p. 93.

8. *Op. cit.,* p. 14.   9. *Idem,* p. 37.

1. According to Napier, "When sir John Moore marched from Lisbon, the regency established by sir Hew Dalrymple nominally governed that country; but the listless habits engendered by the ancient system of misrule, the intrigues of the Oporto faction, and the turbulence of the people soon produced an alarming state of anarchy. Private persons usurped the functions of government, justice was disregarded, insubordination and murder were hailed as indications of patriotism." *Op. cit.,* II, 1.

training of the Portuguese Army.[2] And Wellesley's victory at Oporto, following shortly upon his return to Portugal with an expeditionary force in April, helped to bolster confidence and restore some semblance of order. But such improvement was only beginning to show itself in July, 1809. Suspicions lingered on; memories of the recent atrocities were vivid. Indeed, as late as February, 1812, the young soldier Frederick Ponsonby wrote that "The Portuguese, I believe, heartily wish us all at the bottom of the sea, and that no other country than Portugal existed."[3]

Under these circumstances it would be surprising if any Englishman came to Lisbon in 1809 with a very high opinion of the Portuguese. Byron's attitude is made the more understandable by the fact that his politics, as we have indicated, aligned him with that party which took the darkest view of the prosecution of the war and the potentialities of England's allies. Moreover, Byron's observations on the spot served to confirm him in his unfavorable opinion. In connection with the episode in the streets of Lisbon he was led to remark: "It is a well-known fact that in the year 1809, the assassinations in the streets of Lisbon and its vicinity were not confined by the Portuguese to their countrymen; but that Englishmen were daily butchered: and so far from redress being obtained, we were requested not to interfere if we perceived any compatriot defending himself against his allies."[4]

Hobhouse was in substantial agreement with Byron in his judgment of the Portuguese and expressed himself at some length on the subject. The ascendancy and misbehavior of the clergy, as well as their ignorance, particularly horrified Hobhouse.[5] He himself saw some monks in church "pulling about" a woman while close by another monk was praying at a shrine. The Inquisition, he found, was not completely abolished; twenty men had lately been arrested and sent to dungeons under the great square of Roccio. These and similar abuses could hardly have failed to shock two Englishmen looking for the first time upon a country that was not their own but with which the accidents of warfare had allied them. Hobhouse sums up with the remark, "Avarice and immorality appear to be the reigning passions of the Portuguese, both amongst men and women. Amongst such people, controlled by such institutions, what chance of ultimate success can we possess against the French?"

On the twelfth Byron and Hobhouse escaped from the heat and squalor of Lisbon and journeyed to Cintra, fifteen miles away.[6] The

---

2. Oman, op. cit., II, 200.
3. Lady Bessborough and Her Family Circle, Earl of Bessborough, ed., in collaboration with A. Aspinall (London, John Murray, 1940), p. 221.
4. P, II, 86.   5. Recollections, I, 7–9.
6. Hobhouse gives the date in Recollections, I, 8.

lofty peaks of Cintra had attracted the notice of the travelers as they approached the shores of Portugal five days earlier[7] and they were quick to seize an opportunity to visit the little village so magnificently situated on the northern slope of the nearby Serra da Cintra. Upon arriving there Byron was in agreement with almost every traveler who has recorded his impressions of Cintra when he called the village "the most beautiful, perhaps, in the world."[8] To be sure, almost a month later when he wrote his mother from Gibraltar, Byron's geographical superlative was modified to "perhaps in every respect, the most delightful [village] in Europe," but he went on to exclaim that "it contains beauties of every description, natural and artificial. Palaces and gardens rising in the midst of rocks, cataracts, and precipices; convents on stupendous heights—a distant view of the sea and the Tagus. . . . It unites in itself all the wildness of the western highlands, with the verdure of the south of France."[9] One may smile at the readiness of the youth of twenty-one, whose travels were at the moment limited to Great Britain and a very small part of the Iberian Peninsula, to imply knowledge of the geographical features of "the south of France," of Europe, and of "the world" but Byron's enthusiasm is refreshing and contagious.

No lines in *Childe Harold* show the natural buoyancy of Byron breaking through the settled misanthropy of his gloomy Harold more effectively than do the first of those that describe Cintra.[1] Indeed the minuteness of detail makes it difficult to believe that Byron did not put his impressions upon paper until four months after he visited Cintra. Once he has described the general scene, the "variegated maze of mount and glen," the poet would have the reader climb with him to the "toppling convent"; this is the Convent of Nossa Señora da Peña which occupies the peak of a steep, rocky hill and commands a superb view of Lisbon, the surrounding province, and the ocean, and to the northeast reveals the façade of the distant palace of Mafra.[2] From the peaks of Cintra were visible, also, the ruins of an ancient Moorish castle nearby and the various palaces and villas of the region, some in decay, some in full splendor. Among the latter the five-century-old royal palace was an especially attractive sight.[3]

7. "And Cintra's mountain greets them on their way," *Childe Harold*, i, 14.
8. *LJ*, i, 232.   9. *LJ*, i, 237.   1. *Childe Harold*, i, 18–21.
2. The last two lines of Stanza 20 refer, however, not to the Peña Convent but to a Capuchin convent a few miles away known, because its walls were lined with panels of cork, as the Convento da Cortica. It was there that the hermit monk Honorius dwelt in the sixteenth century. Byron included a note in the first edition of *Childe Harold*, explaining that "Below, at some distance, is the Cork Convent, where St. Honorius dug his den, over which is his epitaph." *P*, ii, 85–6. The omission of this note since the first edition has misled many readers and even editors; Coleridge fails to make the matter entirely clear and Chew has jumped to the erroneous conclusion that the two convents are one and the same. *Childe Harold's Pilgrimage and Other Romantic Poems* (New York, 1936), p. 18, n.
3. *Childe Harold*, i, 22.

At Cintra Byron's attention was especially attracted to the elaborate Moorish palace formerly occupied by William Beckford, the wealthy and eccentric author of *Vathek*.[4] "The first and sweetest spot in this kingdom is Montserrat, lately the seat of the great Beckford," Byron wrote to Hodgson.[5] Fifteen years before, upon the occasion of his second visit to Portugal, Beckford had leased Montserrat, a villa dramatically situated on the heights of Cintra, and after going to great expense in decorating the palace and beautifying its extensive gardens had lived there for two years. When Byron visited Cintra in 1809 the magnificent showplace was, however, completely deserted— the mansion bare and unfurnished, the grounds neglected and overgrown.[6] This striking sight, melancholy as it was beautiful, was the inspiration for three stanzas of *Childe Harold*. Two of these appeared in the published version of the poem but Byron omitted the third because he would "be sorry to make any improper allusion, as I merely wish to adduce an example of wasted wealth, and the reflection which arose in surveying the most desolate mansion in the most beautiful spot I ever beheld."[7] The published lines are not, however, altogether free from the suggestiveness that Byron disclaimed.

The theme of the transiency of earthly pleasures is, of course, one of the oldest and most familiar in literature and one which, throughout Byron's life, continued to inspire some of his most powerful and characteristic passages. But in Stanzas 22 and 23, generalized though the last lines are, the personal allusion to the circumstances of Beckford's own life is unmistakable. It would be difficult, in fact, to find a subject more congenial to the melodramatic and fatalistic side of Byron's nature than the career of the highly gifted and enormously wealthy Beckford who, suspected of unnatural relations with William (afterward Viscount) Courtenay, had been driven to the Continent

---

4. Byron had probably read *Vathek* at this time but the first expression of his great enthusiasm for the work did not come until he had returned from the East and was at work on the Oriental Tales. The notes to those poems show that Byron was indebted to *Vathek* for material as well as inspiration. In a note to *The Giaour* he says, ". . . for correctness of costume, beauty of description, and power of imagination, it far surpasses all European imitations, and bears such marks of originality that those who have visited the East will find some difficulty in believing it to be more than a translation." *P*, III, 145, n. In 1818 Byron expressed his desire to meet Beckford and asked his friend Samuel Rogers if he could "beg of *him* for *me* a copy of the remaining *Tales*." *LJ*, IV, 209. *Vathek* was one of the books Byron set aside to take to Greece with him in 1823. *LJ*, VI, 284. Byron's use of material from *Vathek* in composing his own Eastern romances is fully discussed in Harold S. L. Wiener's article, "Byron and the East: Literary Sources of the 'Turkish Tales,'" pp. 89–129.

5. James T. Hodgson, *Memoir of the Rev. Francis Hodgson* (London, 1878), I, 163. Prothero's version of the letter, taken directly from Moore, omits this passage. *LJ*, I, 231–3.

6. Hobhouse's details (*Recollections*, I, 8) amplify the description in *Childe Harold*.

7. *LJ*, II, 47–8.

by the voice of scandal in 1785.[8] Moreover Beckford had been recently in Byron's mind, for previous to sailing from Falmouth Byron mentioned changing horses at an inn "where the great apostle of Pederasty, Beckford, sojourned for the night. We tried to see the martyr of prejudice, but could not."[9] In writing to Hodgson Byron could not resist the temptation to add the provocative detail that "What we thought singular, though you perhaps will not, was that Ld. Courtenay travelled the same night on the same road, only one stage *behind* him."[1]

The omitted stanza, which did not appear until Moore included it as a detached fragment in the 1833 *Works*,[2] was much more explicit than the lines published in *Childe Harold:*

> Unhappy Dives! in an evil hour
> 'Gainst Nature's voice seduced to deeds accurst!
> Once Fortune's minion now thou feel'st her power;
> Wrath's vial on thy lofty head hath burst.
> In Wit, in Genius, as in Wealth the first,
> How wondrous bright thy blooming morn arose!
> But thou wert smitten with th'unhallowed thirst
> Of Crime unnamed, and thy sad noon must close
> In Scorn and solitude unsought the worst of woes.[3]

It is ironic to note with what minor alterations these lines might refer to the Byron of 1816!

Also among the more impressive of the villas of Cintra was the residence of the Marquez de Marialva. There was no reason for Byron to doubt the popular misconception that the infamous Convention of Cintra had taken place at "Marialva's Dome."[4] The sight of the palace

8. Beckford's latest biographer, Mr. Guy Chapman, believes the charges were false. *Beckford* (London, 1937), pp. 186–9. Whether rightly accused or wrongly, Beckford found himself ostracized after the Powderham scandal and spent most of the next twelve years abroad. In 1796 he returned to England to live the life of a recluse at his singular Fonthill Abbey.

9. This passage is quoted from the original letter now in the Sterling Memorial Library at Yale University. There are several omissions in Prothero's version of the letter; a complete text has never been published.

1. This line from the same letter appears also in *LJ*, i, 229–30.

2. The stanzas that originally appeared in *Childe Harold* could hardly have pleased Beckford. And, since he lived until 1844, Beckford probably saw the more offensive third stanza. Beckford's own copy of Moore's *Life of Byron*, now in the possession of Mr. James T. Babb, Librarian of Yale University, has several annotations, in Beckford's own hand, that betray strong animosity toward both Byron and Moore.

3. *P*, VII, 7.

4. Although the arrangements were first drafted at Torres Vedras and were later ratified at Lisbon, the conference became mistakenly known as the "Convention of Cintra." So persistent was this misconception that Henry Matthews, elder brother of Byron's Cambridge friend, recorded on visiting the Marialva palace in 1807 that "The ink which was spilt on this memorable occasion is still visible on the floor, scattered, as it is said, by Junot, in an ebullition of spleen, when he put his name to the instrument." *The Diary of an Invalid* . . . (London, 1820), 17–18.

was sufficient to kindle into full flame his impatience with the easy terms granted Junot after Vimiera the year before. And here was an opportunity not merely for the expression of convictions but also for some of that frequently unattractive and unfair personal abuse that he had unleashed with such success in *English Bards* and was always to relish. Byron originally devoted six stanzas to decrying the follies of Cintra but these he wisely reduced to three before the poem was published.[5] The extra stanzas were well omitted and it is unfair to hold Byron to account for them as bad poetry and bad taste since he never published them. They cannot, however, be completely ignored, for they were an expression of Byron's feelings in 1809.

The central feature of the stanzas on the Convention is the elaborate personification of the event, in what Byron apparently considered the Spenserian manner, as a fiendish dwarf, wearing a foolscap and clad in parchment and pointing with ridicule to names on a scroll hanging beside him. This rather forced personification Byron retained, in slightly modified form, is the published version of *Childe Harold*. But in the stanzas as they originally appeared Wellesley was specially singled out as the first at whose name

> . . . the Urchin points and laughs with all his soul.[6]

In the second of the stanzas, after he had drawn attention to the French general Junot's name at the head of the list, the dwarf directed his scorn at the

> Dull victors! baffled by a vanquished foe,
> Wheedled by conynge tongues of laurels due.

The generals so easily cheated of their victory

> Stand, worthy of each other in a row—
> Sirs Arthur, Harry, and the dizzard Hew
> Dalrymple, seely wight, sore dupe of t'other tew.

There followed a prosaic account of the English reaction to the Convention and the subsequent inquiry in Parliament; the satirical touches here were heavy and the poem was the better for the omission of these lines. On the whole, the rejected stanzas on the Convention of Cintra show Byron trying to do, very clumsily with the Spenserian stanzas, what he was nine years later to succeed so signally in doing with the *ottava rima*. And the Convention stanzas as they finally appeared are more significant as an example of early poetic experiment and as a symptom of Byron's state of mind than they are as poetical achievement.

Even in their softened final form, with proper names omitted,

5. *Childe Harold*, I, 24–6. The six original stanzas are to be found in *P*, II, 38–41, n.
6. *P*, II, 38.

Byron's stanzas are in the mood of the more violent brand of Whig opposition to the conduct of the war. Byron's chief error in judgment was his stubborn insistence upon placing Sir Arthur Wellesley on the same level with the two other generals. Actually Wellesley had opposed the "Cintra" arrangements but as a junior officer was forced to yield. In November, 1808, he had succeeded in exonerating himself before the Council of Inquiry in a very positive manner, much in contrast to the negative acquittal granted Dalrymple and Burrard.[7] But as a Tory and the Tory-appointed leader of the British Peninsular Army Wellesley continued to draw the fire of the opposition long after he had demonstrated his abilities in conducting the campaign. In 1811 Byron had to admit that "The late exploits of Lord Wellington have effaced the follies of Cintra"[8] but, outmoded though the sentiments in his poem were by that time, he was unwilling to drop the matter altogether. Three modified stanzas remained.

While Hobhouse stayed at Cintra Byron traveled on ten miles farther north along the coast to visit the Monumento da Mafra, a "prodigious" pile which was plainly and dramatically visible from the heights of Cintra.[9] This massive structure, built less than a century earlier in imitation of the Escurial at Madrid and consisting of a palace, a monastery, and a church, made a vivid impression upon Byron, who described it as "the boast of Portugal, as it might be of any other country, in point of magnificence without elegance."[1] In the monastery Byron enjoyed speaking Latin with those few monks who still remained after the invasion by the French.[2] It was while he was admiring their large library that one of them surprised him by asking if the English had any books in *their* country.[3] Until the French invasion the tremendous palace which occupies the greater part of the Monumento had been the residence of Queen Maria I,[4]

7. Oman, *op. cit.*, I, 291–300.   8. *P*, II, 86.

9. *P*, II, 87. There exists at Cintra a tradition that Byron spent at least one night there. The Reverend Walter Cotton, after describing an eventful day at Cintra some years later, adds that "we retired at a late hour to rest, Captain Reed, as the Agamemnon of the party, to that chamber which Byron occupied, on his visit to this place." *Ship and Shore: or Leaves from the Journal of a Cruise to the Levant* (New York, 1835), p. 129. Dalgado remarked in 1919 that "Not long ago a room was shown in what was known as Laurence's Hotel, as having been occupied by him." *Op cit.*, p. 32. Laurence's Hotel still stands and modern guide books accept the Byron connection, even going to the extreme of suggesting that Byron wrote part of *Childe Harold* there!

1. *LJ*, I, 237. Beckford spoke of the "vast fronts of the convent, appearing like a street of palaces." *Italy; With Sketches of Spain and Portugal* (London, 1834), II, 129.

2. Hobhouse records the fact that only 30 monks of the original 150 remained. *Recollections*, I, 8. He doubtless gained the information from Byron.

3. *LJ*, I, 237. Hobhouse also mentions this detail, which seems to have startled both men. Dalgado, however, hastens to the defense of his countrymen on this point by suggesting that Byron's Latinity failed him and that what he was really asked was whether there were any *libraries* in England (p. 92, n).

4. For the last twenty-five years of her life Maria was queen in name only, however, for her mind was deranged throughout her latter years. Byron, in the original MS. of

who reigned as sole monarch of Portugal from 1786 to 1816. Less than a year before Byron visited the palace six thousand French soldiers had slept there on the eve of the battle of Vimiera.[5]

Of his reflections on Portugal in *Childe Harold* Byron wrote, "As I found the Portuguese, so I have characterized them."[6] We have already intimated that his scornful words did not pass unnoticed among the natives of the country; the "tradiccional anecdota de S. Carlos" is but a convenient rallying point for the whole cause of Portuguese national honor against Byron. Telles, in his *Lord Byron em Portugal,* brings out the fact that through the early and middle years of the nineteenth century most Portuguese preferred to ignore Byron rather than admit any possible truth in what they considered his outrageous attack upon their country. Telles makes a conscious and rather praiseworthy effort to set aside national prejudice and present the evidence pro and con as objectively as possible. His obvious admiration for Byron's genius makes it less difficult for him to admit that, in large part, Byron's accusations were just in 1809.[7]

A more recent and a more embattled champion is Dalgado, whose treatise is a vigorous and sometimes ridiculous attack upon Byron. Dalgado is correct enough in pointing out that, since Byron did not know the language or the people at first hand, his opinions are necessarily superficial. But Dalgado's case suffers seriously from his eager readiness always to believe the worst of Byron and especially from his grotesque lack of perspective in attributing the whole of Byron's rancor to the legendary San Carlos incident.

In the spring of 1811, after the victory over the French at Barossa, Byron still had sarcastic words for the Portuguese:

> Yet Lusitania, kind and dear ally,
> Can spare a few to fight, and sometimes fly.[8]

By the time he was preparing *Childe Harold* for publication, however, he had to admit that they were "improved, at least in courage." Portuguese troops had gained in ability and confidence during 1810

Childe Harold, referred to Maria as Portugal's "crazy" queen but he softened the adjective to "luckless" before the poem was published.

5. Francis Darwin, *Travels in Spain and the East, 1808–1810* (London, 1927), p. 15.
6. *P,* ii, 87.
7. Telles translated into Portuguese Byron's juvenile "Stanzas to a Lady, with the Poems of Camoens" and his later, not very Portuguese, stanzas "From the Portuguese." Byron's knowledge of the language and literature of Portugal was extremely meager. Like many Englishmen, he had read with interest Lord Percy Strangford's erotic *Poems from the Portuguese by Luis de Camoens* but there is no reason to believe he ever acquired more than a few scattered words of the language from which those poems were very free translations. For the benefit of his own countrymen Telles also translated into Portuguese the first canto of *Childe Harold, Peregrinações de Childe Harold,* Canto Primero, traducção do inglez por Alberto Telles (Portugal e Hespanha, 1881).
8. *The Curse of Minerva,* ll. 233–4.

and 1811 and the fiber of the people began to stiffen with military success. Yet in *Childe Harold* Byron let his early judgments stand. Only with reluctance did he withhold from publication a scorching note in which he insisted "They must fight a great many hours, by 'Shrewsbury clock,' before the number of their slain equals that of our countrymen butchered by these kind creatures . . . if the cowards are become brave (like the rest of their kind, in a corner) pray let them display it."[9]

Since southern Spain had not yet fallen into the hands of the French Byron and Hobhouse determined to take the difficult and hazardous, but more interesting, course of traveling overland to Gibraltar by way of Seville and Cadiz while the servants were dispatched with the baggage by sea.[1] On July 21 they set forth from Lisbon, first crossing to the small town of Aldea Gallega on the opposite shore of the Tagus.[2] They then traveled on horseback in a southeasterly direction across the Portuguese province of Estramadura and the northern part of Alentejo into Spain. As the travelers commenced their long journey they were not without a grim reminder of the disordered country through which their journey was taking them, for the road was "bordered by a vast number of crosses—signs of the murders which from time immemorial had taken place along its track."[3] But Byron (and probably Hobhouse, too) had taken the precaution of wearing an English staff uniform and that, together with the orders which Byron carried from the home government, guaranteed them as safe a trip as possible; in fact, Byron wrote his mother that he had "every possible accommodation on the road, as an English nobleman, in an English uniform, is a very respectable personage in Spain at present."[4]

Byron found the horses excellent and the roads so superior that he and his companion were able to ride seventy miles a day, completing the journey to Seville "without fatigue or annoyance" in four days.[5] Conditions along the way were rudimentary but adequate: "Eggs and wine, and hard beds, are all the accommodation we found, and in such torrid weather, quite enough."[6] The country through which they first passed is a land of valleys and hills:

> O'er vales that teem with fruits, romantic hills
> (Oh, that such hills upheld a freedom race!)
> Whereon to gaze the eye with joyaunce fills,
> Childe Harold wends through many a pleasant place.

. . . .

9. *P*, II, 87–8.

1. Seville was to fall to the French on January 31, 1810. Cadiz was besieged from February, 1810, until August, 1812, when Wellington finally raised the siege.

2. *Recollections*, I, 10. Coleridge dates the departure four days earlier but only on the basis of Byron's remark (*LJ*, I, 233) that "tomorrow we start to ride post near 400 miles as far as Gibraltar, where we embark for Melita and Byzantium."

3. *Ibid.*   4. *LJ*, I, 238.   5. *LJ*, I, 238.   6. *LJ*, I, 234.

Oh, there is sweetness in the mountain air
And Life, that bloated Ease can never hope to share.[7]

This "sweetness in the mountain air" is more than a rhetorical flourish on Byron's part, for a particular shrub native to the highlands of Alentejo gives a real and distinctive sweetness to the air; this is the *cistus ladaniferus,* whose buds and leaves are covered with a gum which gives forth in summer, especially in the evenings, a very pleasant fragrance.[8] Here is but one of many examples of Byron's minute accuracy in the details of his description.

On the first day they probably traveled as far as Montemor, a picturesque little hill town, on the summit and sides of which were ruined Moorish towers and walls; the travelers noticed especially one Moorish castle "with extensive ruins, commanding a beautiful prospect."[9] Prominent in this view must have been the groves of olives which surround the hill on which Montemor stands. From Montemor they traveled on through Arroyolos and Estremoz to the Spanish border. The last town in Portugal was the frontier fortress of Élvas, perched high on an eminence overlooking the border regions of Spain. Here they experienced difficulty when the governor insisted on their presenting themselves with great ceremony to him.[1] A striking feature in approaching Elvas was its immense aqueduct, which Byron was to recall a dozen years later when he answered Bowles's contention that works of nature are more poetical than works of art.[2] As one penetrates farther into Alentejo and nears Spain the hills become fewer and there are immense plains. In summer, as the influence of the sea diminishes, the vegetation is less and less luxuriant and the eastern edge of the province looks arid and barren. So, in *Childe Harold,*

> More bleak to view the hills at length recede,
> And, less luxuriant, smoother vales extend:
> Immense, horizon-bounded plains succeed![3]

Riding down the hill from Elvas to the plain below, but a few miles beyond Elvas, Byron and Hobhouse came to the tiny stream which

7. *Childe Harold,* i, 30.
8. This phenomenon is mentioned by numerous travelers. Beckford, on the same route in 1787, "hastened out to breathe the fresh morning air, impregnated with the perfume of a thousand aromatic shrubs and opening flowers." *Op. cit.,* ii, 265.
9. *Recollections,* i, 10. Hobhouse's special mention of Montemor, and the fact that it is about seventy-five miles from Lisbon, makes it reasonable to believe that this was the first stopping place. Other details in respect to Montemor have been taken from Beckford and George Borrow's *The Bible in Spain* (London, 1843).
1. *Ibid.*
2. *LJ,* v, 552. "Will Mr. Bowles tell us that the poetry of an aqueduct consists in the *water* which it conveys? Let him look on that of Justinian, on those of Rome, Constantinople, Lisbon, and Elvas, or even at the remains of that in Attica."
3. *Childe Harold,* i, 31.

separates Portugal from Spain. Here, at two o'clock in the afternoon, they took care to bathe in accordance with tradition.[4] When Byron wrote *Childe Harold* he expressed wonder that no more formidable barrier divided the "rival realms"—that no Tagus, no "dark Sierras," no "vasty wall" like China's formed the boundary:

> But these between a silver streamlet glides,
> And scarce a name distinguisheth the brook,
> Though rival kingdoms press the verdant sides.[5]

This rivulet with "scarce a name" is, of course, the Caia, a little stream significant only by geographical accident, which farther south flows into the Guadiana. Here, then, Byron bade farewell to Portugal. In *Childe Harold* the farewell is far from affectionate, for Byron could not resist the temptation to take a last fling at Portugal as, catching his first glimpse of a Spanish peasant, he extolled him at the expense of "the Lusian slave, the lowest of the low."

IV. Spain

Thus far in amplifying the account of Byron's actual experiences and impressions with relevant stanzas from *Childe Harold* it has been possible to assume that the chronology of the poem corresponds to that of the journey. Such is not the case, however, with the stanzas on Spain, which show the aroused imagination of the poet playing a large part in determining the structure and ordering of his material. Byron's emotions and sympathies were stirred in Spain as they never were in Portugal. Therefore something beyond the mere delight and excitement of new scenes animates the remainder of the first canto.

Byron begins with an apostrophe to Spain to rise against her oppressors. Then, instead of pursuing step by step the route he himself followed in Spain—through Albuera to the Sierra Morena region, and on to Seville and Cadiz—in the poem Byron gives first, after the exhortation to Spain, an imaginative conception of the battle of Talavera, which he did not witness and which he heard news of only when he reached Cadiz; and then, after some bitter reflections upon military glory, he violates strict chronology by picturing Seville as a city whose gaiety will soon be replaced by the gloom of conquest at the hands of Napoleon. Next come some stanzas inspired by the journey en route *to* Seville over the Sierra Morena and then finally there are the stanzas on Cadiz. This disregard for the actual chronology of the journey has misled Coleridge, in the Itinerary he has prefixed to the *Childe Harold* volume, into placing the Sierra Morena range be-

4. *Recollections,* I, 10.   5. *Childe Harold,* I, 33.

tween Seville and Cadiz rather than in its proper location north of Seville.[6]

Childe Harold becomes a better poem as the dependence upon fairly precise detail is subordinated to a more emotional shaping of the material. It is still of interest, however, to attempt to determine what those materials were and how they were developed; thus we shall continue to reconstruct, as far as possible, the journey as Byron himself made it, presenting passages from *Childe Harold* as they seem to grow out of Byron's experience rather than necessarily in the order in which he presents them in the poem.

About an hour after the travelers had crossed the Caia, above the Guadiana loomed the sturdy Spanish fortified city of Badajoz which, because of its highly strategic situation as the gate to southeastern Spain, had undergone sieges through the centuries. Already since the outbreak of the war on the Peninsula the French had twice failed in their attacks upon this frontier fortress. Through Badajoz the travelers passed and on fifteen miles to a little hamlet called Albuera, where the authorities of the Junta tried in vain to seize their horses.[7] Albuera did not impress Byron particularly until he looked upon it in retrospect over two years later; by that time it had become the scene of one of the bloodiest battles of the war.[8] It is likely that they halted for the second night at Albuera or not far beyond.

Ahead lay the most difficult portion of the journey to Seville, for it was necessary to pass over the broad expanse of the Sierra Morena, the vast mountain range that serves as a formidable natural barrier to travelers and armies alike who approach the province of Andalusia. Progress was much slower once they began to cross the Sierra Morena and the fourth day found them no farther along their way than the mountain village of Monastereo. Here they had their first sight of Spanish troops, which seemed "fairly organized and disciplined."[9]

A curious prose fragment in Byron's handwriting, apparently intended as a preface to Cantos I and II of *Don Juan*, gives what is surely in some degree a reminiscence of this stage of the journey into Spain.[1] The main intent of the passage is clearly that of satirizing Wordsworth's "prosaic raving" and striking a telling blow at Southey but in it we also find, if not a literal episode from Byron's experience in July, 1809, at least a pleasant tableau whose vividness is largely dependent on the author's observations in the Sierra Morena country. As Wordsworth desired the reader to suppose that his poem, "The

6. *P*, ii, xxi.   7. *Recollections*, i, 10.
8. On May 16, 1811, the English forces under Beresford won a costly victory over the French at Albuera. Byron links the stanza on Albuera that he added to *Childe Harold* with his original passage on Talavera. In the standard text these are now Stanzas 38–44 of the first canto.
9. *Recollections*, i, 10.   1. *LJ*, vi, 381–2.

Thorn," was recited by "The Captain of a Merchantman or small trading vessel, retired on a small annuity to a country town, etc., etc.," so in Byron's mock explanation of the origins of his own *Don Juan* we are asked

to suppose, by a like exertion of Imagination, that the following epic Narrative is told by a Spanish gentleman in a village in the Sierra Morena in the road between Monasterio and Seville, sitting at the door of a Posada, with the Curate of the hamlet on his right hand, a Segar in his mouth, a Jug of Malaga, or perhaps "right Sherris" before him on a small table containing the relics of an Olla Podrida: the time, Sunset: at some distance, a groupe of black-eyed peasantry are dancing to the sound of the flute of a Portuguese servant belonging to two foreign travellers, who have, an hour ago, dismounted from their horses to spend the night on their way to the Capital of Andalusia. Of these, one is attending to the story; and the other, having sauntered further, is watching the beautiful movements of a tall peasant Girl, whose whole Soul is in her eyes and her heart in the dance, of which she is the Magnet to ten thousand feelings that vibrate with her own. Not far off a knot of French prisoners are contending with each other, at the grated lattice of their temporary confinement, for a view of the twilight festival. The two foremost are a couple of hussars, one of whom has a bandage on his forehead yet stained with the blood of a Sabre cut, received in the recent skirmish which deprived him of his lawless freedom: his eyes sparkle in unison, and his fingers beat time against the bars of his prison to the sound of the Fandango which is fleeting before him.

Such is Byron's tongue-in-the-cheek description, in what he considers the manner of Wordsworth, of the source of his own *Don Juan*. And, absurd though Byron would have the picture be, it remains highly attractive in its blending of romantic coloring and amusing detail. Moreover there can be little doubt that the two foreign travelers spending the night in the village were Byron and Hobhouse, or at least figures evoked by memories of July, 1809. It is even tempting and rather amusing to go a step further and speculate which of the two travelers more closely suggests Byron himself. From the purely practical point of view, since the jeu d'esprit rests on the acceptance for a moment of the notion that in *Don Juan* the poet tells a story he overheard earlier in a Spanish village, Byron should be the traveler who was "attending to the story." On the other hand, one experiences difficulty in imagining Byron listening intently to a story while the much more sober-minded Hobhouse was "watching the beautiful movements of a tall peasant Girl"!

It is obviously mistaken to insist on the relevancy of each of the details of this description, written with satirical intent, to one particular occasion during the travels; but it is worth noting that Byron and Hobhouse must, on July 24, 1809, have dismounted to spend the night on their way to Seville. Moreover it is highly probable, since servants and baggage had been sent from Lisbon by sea to Gibraltar, that a Portuguese servant familiar with the surrounding country had been hired at Lisbon for the journey into Spain. And Hobhouse, in his *Recollections,* supplies the graphic detail that "At Monastereo, passing over ground every inch of what had recently been fought over by French and Spaniards, we overtook two French prisoners and a Spanish spy on their way to Seville to be hanged."[2] Very much as in the poem *Don Juan* itself the general setting and atmosphere, if not all the precise details of this description, grow out of Byron's recollection ten years later of his experiences in Spain in the summer of 1809.

By an incident he observed in a small town farther on in the mountains Byron was led to observe that "The Spaniards are as revengeful as ever. At Santa Otalla, I heard a young peasant threaten to stab a woman (an old one, to be sure, which mitigates the offence), and was told, on expressing some small surprise, that this ethic was by no means uncommon."[3]

As the travelers crossed the Sierra Morena there were many reminders of the war which was going on about them. In the distance, across the plains far to the south, the mountains of the Sierra Nevada range were visible; here and there among them one could descry scenes of the bitter campaign of the previous summer—the "dragon's nest" of Jena and, farther south, the lofty heights of Granada and Ronda. Byron's observations as he crossed the Sierra Morena enabled him to imagine what must be the even grimmer appearance of those distant regions which had felt the brunt of battle more heavily:

> On yon long level plain, at distance crowned
>   With crags, whereon those Moorish turrets rest,
>   Wide-scattered hoof-marks dint the wounded ground;
>   And, scathed by fire, the greensward's darkened vest
>   Tells that the foe was Andalusia's guest:
>   Here was the camp, the watch-flame, and the host,
>   Here the bold peasant stormed the Dragon's nest;
>   Still does he mark it with triumphant boast,
> And points to yonder cliffs, which oft were won and lost.[4]

Nearer at hand the patriotic red cockades worn by people they passed on the road, and even more the threatening appearance of their surroundings, brought increased awareness of the struggle that was

---

2. *Recollections,* I, 10.
3. *P,* II, 72. Churchman points out (*op. cit.,* p. 128, n.) that "Otalla" is either a misprint or a misreading for "Olalla." In Byron's MS., Churchman discovered, the town is correctly called "Santa Olalla."
4. *Childe Harold,* I, 49.

convulsing Spain.[5] Byron remarks that "The Sierra Morena was fortified in every defile through which I passed in my way to Seville."[6] These sights were vivid in his memory when he wrote:

> At every turn Morena's dusky height
> Sustains aloft the battery's iron load;
> And, far as mortal eye can compass sight,
> The mountain-howitzer, the broken road,
> The bristling palisade, the fosse o'erflowed,
> The stationed bands, the never-vacant watch,
> The magazine in rocky durance stowed,
> The holstered steed beneath the shed of thatch,
> The ball-fired pyramid, the ever-blazing match,
> Portend the deeds to come.[7]

On Tuesday, July 25, the travelers reached Seville where they spent three days.[8] Since the Supreme Junta now had its headquarters at Seville and the population of the city had consequently grown to three times its normal size, Byron and Hobhouse encountered difficulty in finding lodgings. Unable to gain accommodations at the usual resorts of Englishmen—Mrs. Latchford's and the posada—they appealed to Mr. Wiseman, the British Consul, for assistance. It was at his suggestion that they took lodgings at the home of "two Spanish unmarried ladies," Donna Josepha Beltram and her younger sister. So crowded were conditions at this particular house, one of six possessed by the Beltrams,[9] that Byron and Hobhouse and their attendants were all forced to sleep in one small room; and Hobhouse relates ruefully that "we went supperless and dinnerless to bed."[1] Byron's companion also mentions the rather surprising detail that as a temporary substitute for Fletcher, who was still in Lisbon awaiting passage to Gibraltar, they were able to secure a lieutenant in the Spanish army to serve as their valet.

Seville impressed Byron as a town of beauty although he preferred Cadiz when he visited there a few days later.[2] But even when he had reached the easternmost bounds of his pilgrimage at Constantinople he was still to "prefer the Gothic cathedral of Seville to St Paul's, St. Sophia's, or any religious building I have ever seen."[3] The famous paintings of Murillo and Velasquez, however, left him cold.[4]

5. *Idem*, I, 1.   6. *P*, II, 91.   7. *Childe Harold*, I, 51–2.

8. Hobhouse gives the date. *Recollections*, I, 10. Byron writes his mother (*LJ*, I, 238), "I was there but three days."

9. *LJ*, I, 238.   1. *Recollections*, I, 11.

2. "Seville is a beautiful town; though the streets are narrow, they are clean." *LJ*, I, 238.

3. *LJ*, I, 282.

4. *LJ*, IV, 107. At the same time (April, 1817) Byron added, "You must recollect, however, that I know nothing of painting; and that I detest it, unless it reminds me of something I have seen, or think it possible to see, for which [reason] I spit upon and

Something he was never to forget was the sight of Augustina, the famous Maid of Zaragoza, who by command of the Supreme Junta walked each day in the Prado in battle dress, wearing the medals and orders that her brave exploits had won her.[5] In England before he departed on his travels Byron had doubtless heard of Augustina's heroic performance during the siege of her native city[6] and he was struck now with the gently feminine appearance of this heroine[7] who, when an entire artillery unit had been wiped out, stepped over the dead and wounded to fire a cannon and arouse her fellow citizens to renew battle against the French. This was but the first of many acts of heroism that won for Augustina the pay and uniform first of an artilleryman and later of a commissioned lieutenant in the Spanish Army. Augustina not only inspired three stanzas in the first canto of *Childe Harold* but she was also in Byron's mind fourteen years later when, in *The Age of Bronze,* he wrote of a new Spanish fight for freedom.[8]

As the lines in *Childe Harold* show, it was not alone the remarkable military prowess of the Maid of Zaragoza that attracted Byron's attention. She was notable also for her softer, more feminine charms.

abhor all the Saints and subjects of one half the impostures I see in the churches and palaces." The bracketed insert is Prothero's.

5. *P*, II, 91. Byron does not mention her dress but other writers refer to it. Two works in particular give interesting supplementary details with reference to the Maid of Zaragoza, as well as to the social and political situation in Seville and Cadiz in 1809. William Jacob, the author of *Travels in the South of Spain, in Letters Written A.D. 1809 and 1810* (London, 1811), visited Seville from September to November; he emphasized in his book the incapacity of the Supreme Junta, the hatred of the Spaniards for Napoleon, and the free manners of the Spanish people. Sir John Carr was in both Seville and Cadiz at the same time as Byron. Carr was already a prolific writer of travel books and though Byron found him "a pleasant man" (*LJ*, I, 241) he could not resist the temptation to satirize Carr in *Childe Harold* as the potential author of just the sort of travel book on Spain he himself scorned to write. Byron's three stanzas, which with another on Lord Holland were suppressed from the published version of the poem in 1812 (see *P*, II, 78–80), give a fairly accurate prophecy of the contents of Carr's book, *Descriptive Travels in the Southern and Eastern Parts of Spain and the Balearic Isles, in the Year 1809* (London, 1811). Byron wrote to Hodgson from Gibraltar, "I have seen Sir John Carr at Seville and Cadiz, and, like Swift's barber, have been down on my knees to beg he would not put me into black and white." *LJ*, I, 235. Whether consciously or not, Carr granted this favor, for there is no mention of Byron in the *Descriptive Travels.*

6. Charles R. Vaughan's *The Narrative of the Siege of Zaragoza* (London, 1809) was widely reviewed and discussed. *The Quarterly* reviewed it in February and the *Edinburgh* in April used the book as a springboard for a long attack upon the conduct of the war.

7. Both Jacob and Carr emphasize her mild, pleasing countenance and manner. Jacob found her face "altogether the last I should have supposed to belong to a woman, who had led troops through blood and slaughter." *Op. cit.*, p. 123.

8. A French army invaded Spain in 1823 and restored the cruel, reactionary Ferdinand VII to the throne. In *The Age of Bronze,* ll. 366–9, Byron refers to

> . . . the desperate wall
> Of Saragossa, mightiest in her fall;
> The man nerved to a spirit, and the Maid
> Waving her more than Amazonian blade.

And such, Byron insisted, were possessed by most of the young women of Spain:

> Yet are Spain's maids no race of Amazons,
> > But formed for all the witching arts of love:
> Though thus in arms they emulate her sons,
> And in the horrid phalanx dare to move,
> 'Tis but the tender fierceness of the dove,
> Pecking the hand that hovers o'er her mate.[9]

The Beltram sisters at whose house the travelers lodged in Seville gave Byron his most signal experience of the free behavior he was so surprised to find among the young ladies of Spain. Indeed, their example convinced him that "reserve is not the characteristic of the Spanish belles." [1] Of these two sisters Byron told his mother:

They are women of character, and the eldest a fine woman, the youngest pretty, but not so good a figure as Donna Josepha . . . The eldest honoured your *unworthy* son with very particular attention, embracing him with great tenderness at parting . . . after cutting off a lock of his hair, and presenting him with one of her own, about three feet in length, which I send, and beg you will retain till my return. . . . She offered me a share of her apartment, which my *virtue* induced me to decline; she laughed, and said I had some English *amante* (lover), and added that she was going to be married to an officer in the Spanish army.[2]

Byron wrote very little, either poetry or prose, during the weeks he spent in Spain. However, eight lines of doggerel survive that were reputedly written during the stay in Seville. The verses, supposedly composed as a poetical recommendation for his guide in Seville, are as follows:

> All those that travel ever must decide
> 'Tis time ill spent without a skilful guide,
> One who the manners and the customs knows,
> And gives the history of all he shows,
> And all the locks worth picking can undo
> With silver keys, with skill applied thereto.
> If such you want, and one who will not fail ye,
> I strongly recommend Antonio Bailly.[3]

These lines are, indeed, negligible as poetry and if Byron did write them he must have dashed them off very swiftly on the spur of the

9. *Childe Harold*, I, 57.   1. *LJ*, I, 238.   2. *LJ*, I, 238–9.

3. Churchman quotes the lines and describes the circumstances relating to them. *Op. cit.*, XI, 142, n. An article in *Putnam's Monthly* for November, 1907, which mentioned an autographed poem of Byron's in the possession of Dr. Horace H. Furness, led Churchman to inquire directly of Dr. Furness. In his reply Dr. Furness said that he had never possessed or even seen the original MS. but he went on to quote these lines and explain that they were recited to him in Seville in 1855 by his guide.

moment. He was in the habit of composing *jeux d'esprit* in just this manner but the results were usually more diverting.

Byron's guide at Seville was also the source for an anecdote that is of some biographical interest. At the same time Bailly recited the above lines to a later traveler, he described also an incident that allegedly occurred when he took Byron up the tower of the cathedral for the sake of the superb view of Seville and its environs. Bailly's story has been recorded by Dr. Horace H. Furness, to whom it was originally told:

"Lord Byron was so much impressed by the landscape, that he took out a gold pencil-case, and prepared to write on the side of one of the outlooks, whether his name or verses, Bailly did not know. It appears that a little dog had followed them up the tower, and just at the moment that Byron began to write, his lordship looked down and noticed that the little dog was sniffing at his club foot. This put Byron in a towering rage, so Bailly said, and imprecating curses on the little dog, which he kicked away in his rage, he threw the gold pencil far away on the roof of the cathedral below. Bailly showed me the very spot where Byron stood, and I strained my eyes for a gleam of the glittering pencil-case; but Bailly told me that my scrutiny was useless; he had searched for hours and hours on that roof in vain, and the pencil must have bounded off in some extraordinary way into the street."[4]

There is always the possibility that this is but another of those fables that grow up around every famous name and especially thrive when they can be put to the purposes of financial gain but the incident is at least plausible and not uncharacteristic of Byron. Dr. Furness was inclined to believe Bailly's story was genuine and it is tempting to concur.[5]

Seville is also memorable as the birthplace and home of Don Juan. Byron's description of the town in the first canto of *Don Juan* shows how vividly the first journey lingered in his memory when he began his comic epic ten years later:

> In Seville was he born, a pleasant city,
>   Famous for oranges and women,—he
> Who has not seen it will be much to pity,
>   So says the proverb—and I quite agree;
> Of all the Spanish towns is none more pretty,
>   Cadiz perhaps—but that you soon may see;—
> Don Juan's parents lived beside the river,
> A noble stream, and called the Guadalquivir.[6]

4. Quoted in Churchman, *ibid.*
5. The following May Byron asked Henry Drury to "Tell Dr. Butler I am now writing with the gold pen he gave me before I left England, which is the reason my scrawl is more unintelligible than usual." *LJ*, I, 267.
6. *Don Juan*, I, 8.

Donna Julia, also, as with vigor and eloquence she upbraids her justly suspicious husband, gives us some suggestion of the pleasurable routine of life doubtless pursued by such attractive young ladies of Seville as Byron's Donna Josepha Beltram:

> Was it for this that no Cortejo e'er
> I yet have chosen from out the youth of Seville?
> Is it for this I scarce went anywhere,
> Except to bull-fights, mass, play, rout, and revel?[7]

It is scarcely reasonable, however, to believe Byron when he says:

> But that which more completely faith exacts
> Is, that myself, and several now in Seville,
> *Saw* Juan's last elopement with the Devil.[8]

It is unlikely that Byron actually saw a performance of some version of the Don Juan legend while he was at Seville, for Sir John Carr, who was in Seville at the same time as Byron, observes that the theaters were closed.[9] Moreover, the mood of the preceding lines is less one of reminiscence than of facetiousness.

Looking back upon Seville several months later Byron saw it as a doomed city.[1] His emphasis in *Childe Harold,* as in the later, more dramatic passage on the eve of Waterloo in the third canto, rests upon the contrast between the careless, festive spirit of the city and the grim fate that awaits it:

> Yet is she free? the Spoiler's wished-for prey!
> Soon, soon shall Conquest's fiery foot intrude,
> Blackening her lovely domes with traces rude.
> Inevitable hour! 'Gainst fate to strive
> Where Desolation plants her famished brood
> Is vain, or Ilion, Tyre might yet survive,
> And Virtue vanquish all, and Murder cease to thrive.
>
> But all unconscious of the coming doom,
> The feast, the song, the revel here abounds;
> Strange modes of merriment the hours consume,
> Nor bleed these patriots with their country's wounds.[2]

Probably on the twenty-eighth the travelers left Seville for Cadiz.[3] In striking contrast to the unconcern of the pleasure-loving citizens of

7. *Idem*, 1, 148.   8. *Idem*, 1, 203.   9. *Op. cit.,* p. 99.
1. Byron probably wrote the stanzas on Seville in mid-December, 1809, although there is the possibility that he wrote them later and inserted them in *Childe Harold.* As the military situation stood in the late summer and fall of 1809, a French advance into Andalusia in late 1809 or early 1810 was inevitable. And Byron felt that against such an invasion, gallant though some of her defenders were, Seville was powerless to protect herself. Seville surrendered to the French on January 31, 1810.
2. *Childe Harold,* 1, 45–6.
3. Hobhouse does not give a precise date but on July 29 the travelers reached Xeres, which is more than a day's journey from Seville. *Recollections,* 1, 11.

Seville was the acute awareness of the threat of war Byron noticed among the peasants encountered along the route. Their sad plight aroused his compassion and reawakened his contempt for the ruthless intervention of Napoleon.

> Not so the rustic—with his trembling mate
> He lurks, nor casts his heavy eye afar,
> Lest he should view his vineyard desolate,
> Blasted below the dun hot breath of War.
> No more beneath soft Eve's consenting star
> Fandango twirls his jocund castanet:
> Ah, Monarchs! could ye taste the mirth ye mar,
> Not in the toils of Glory would ye fret;
> The hoarse dull drum would sleep, and Man be happy yet![4]

Patriotic songs, combining veneration for King Ferdinand with hatred for Napoleon, were to be heard in city, in village, and along the way.[5] Most of them contained scorn also for the abdicated King Charles and his queen, and the court favorite Godoy; to the last named, Byron said, Spaniards imputed the ruin of their country. Byron found the airs of some of these songs beautiful.[6]

The ride to Cadiz was "through a beautiful country."[7] A pleasant oasis along the route was the prosperous town of Xeres de la Frontera, favorably known to Englishmen through the centuries from the fact that its vineyards produce most of the world's sherry wine.[8] Here the comfortable home of Mr. James Gordon—"a Mr. Gordon of Scotland," Byron calls him—was a regular and welcome point of call for Englishmen in southern Spain. Like most travelers who stopped to enjoy the hospitality of Mr. Gordon, Byron inspected the vast wine vaults and cellars of Xeres and "quaffed at the fountain head."[9] Byron and Hobhouse spent the night with the Gordons at Xeres before proceeding on their way to Cadiz.[1]

It is likely that at Xeres the travelers heard talk of the bullfight taking place on the following day at Puerta Santa Maria, the town from which they would need to sail across the bay to reach Cadiz. The distance from Xeres to Puerta was about ten English miles.[2] In the amphitheater at Puerta Santa Maria, on Sunday afternoon, July 30, Byron viewed the bullfight which he was later to describe so graphically in *Childe Harold*. This was one of the most thrilling, if also one of the most painful, of his experiences in Spain. The bullfight at Puerta Santa Maria was the only such event allowed in Spain at the

---

4. *Childe Harold*, I, 47.
5. *Idem*, I, 48. Carr (*op. cit.*, p. 100) heard in Seville many national airs vowing "Death to Napoleon!"
6. *P*, II, 90.   7. *LJ*, I, 239.
8. The vaults of Mr. Gordon, with whom Byron and Hobhouse stayed, were alone capable of holding between five and six thousand butts of wine. Carr, *op. cit.*, p. 70.
9. *LJ*, I, 239.   1. *Recollections*, I, 11.   2. Carr, *op. cit.*, p. 69.

time and even this spectacle was, strictly speaking, unlawful, since Charles IV had outlawed the national pastime in 1805. In that interdict a fact more weighty than the brutality of the bullfight had been the effect of heavy mortality in horses and oxen upon both the army and agriculture. On Sundays, however, bullfights at Puerta were now countenanced by the Supreme Junta as "a convenient boon to the people."[3]

Byron and Hobhouse were privileged to watch the proceedings, in the company of the principal civil and military officers and several other Englishmen, from the handsome governor's box in the center of the large wooden amphitheater. Hobhouse shared Byron's revulsion at the brutality of the affair and he indicated they did not stay for the complete performance when he said that "The death of one or two horses completely satisfied their curiosity."[4] Yet the spectacle was so intensely dramatic and so illustrative of one side of the Spanish character that Byron devoted to it eleven stanzas of *Childe Harold*. Nor could its sharply drawn contrasts and melodramatic violence have failed of some appeal to such a nature as Byron's. In his highly realistic lines he emphasized the picturesqueness and pageantry, the feverish excitement, the animation and quick action, as well as the callous brutality of the bullfight.

> Hark! heard you not the forest-monarch's roar?
> Crashing the lance, he snuffs the spouting gore
> Of man and steed, o'erthrown beneath his horn;
> The thronged arena shakes with shouts for more;
> Yells the mad crowd o'er entrails freshly torn,
> Nor shrinks the female eye, nor ev'n affects to mourn.[5]

Stanza 68 provides an anticipatory glimpse of the fight which, after the digression on the English Sunday, Byron describes at length in Stanzas 71–80. He refers to it sardonically as the most solemn religious rite of the Spanish Sabbath.

Sir John Carr was also in attendance on that Sunday afternoon and his prose account bears many resemblances in the details of the event to Byron's stanzas. Carr begins:

After dinner, the whole place was alive, and the people in crowds hastened to the theatre of the bull-fight . . . Upon entering the theatre, I was much impressed by the magnitude of the structure, and the immense assemblage of the people. The number of men and women appeared to be nearly equal. Amongst the latter were several females of distinction, and many of great respectability . . . A short time after he [the Governor] took his seat, one of the gates of the arena or circus opened, and a fine corps of volunteers entered, and cleared it of a great number of people who climbed over the sides, and took the seats to which they were entitled.[6]

3. *Ibid.*   4. *P*, II, 522.   5. *Childe Harold*, I, 68.   6. *Op. cit.*, pp. 52–4.

It is interesting to compare Byron's poetic treatment of the same material:

> Then to the crowded circus forth they fare:
> Young, old, high, low, at once the same diversion share.
>
> The lists are oped, the spacious area cleared,
>   Thousands on thousands piled are seated round;
>   Long ere the first loud trumpet's note is heard,
>   Ne vacant space for lated wight is found:
>   Here Dons, Grandees, but chiefly Dames abound,
>   Skilled in the ogle of a roguish eye,
>   Yet ever well inclined to heal the wound;
>   None through their cold disdain are doomed to die,
> As moon-struck bards complain, by Love's sad archery.[7]

Here Byron does little more than render in matter-of-fact poetic form the details of the preliminaries to the event.

Another English traveler, William Jacob, visited the arena several months later when a special bullfight was arranged in honor of the Duke of Wellington. A comparison of his prose version with Byron's corresponding stanzas reveals Byron now embellishing his lines with descriptive details and beginning to introduce an emotional element:

. . . Three men were posted behind each other, about ten yards asunder, mounted on small, but active horses, and armed with a spear about fifteen feet long.[8]

> Hushed is the din of tongues—on gallant steeds,
>   With milk-white crest, gold spur, and light-poised lance,
>   Four cavaliers prepare for venturous deeds,
>   And lowly-bending to the lists advance;
>   Rich are their scarfs, their chargers featly prance:
>   If in the dangerous game they shine today,
>   The crowd's loud shout and ladies' lovely glance,
>   Best prize of better acts! they bear away,
> And all that kings or chiefs e'er gain their toils repay.[9]

According to Jacob's simple statement, "The gates were thrown open, and the bull rushed in. He made towards the first horseman, who received him on the point of the spear, and wounded him between the shoulders." Byron's description becomes much more animated and emotional:

> Thrice sounds the Clarion: lo! the signal falls,
>   The den expands, and Expectation mute

---

7. *Childe Harold*, i, 71–2.
8. This passage and the two from Jacob that follow are to be found in *op. cit.*, p. 173.
9. *Childe Harold*, i, 73.

Gapes round the silent circle's peopled walls.
Bounds with one lashing spring the mighty brute,
And, wildly staring, spurns, with sounding foot,
The sand, nor blindly rushes on his foe:
Here, there, he points his threatening front, to suit
His first attack, wide-waving to and fro
His angry tail; red rolls his eye's dilated glow.

Sudden he stops—his eye is fixed—away—
Away, thou heedless boy! prepare the spear:
Now is thy time, to perish, or display
The skill that yet may check his mad career!
With well-timed croupe the nimble coursers veer:
On foams the Bull, but not unscathed he goes;
Streams from his flank the crimson torrent clear:
He flies, he wheels, distracted with his throes;
Dart follows dart—lance, lance—loud bellowings speak his woes.

Again he comes; nor dart nor lance avail,
Nor the wild plunging of the tortured horse;
Though Man and Man's avenging arms assail,
Vain are his weapons, vainer is his force.
One gallant steed is stretched a mangled corse.[1]

As the climax of the struggle approaches, Jacob's account becomes fuller:

He now becomes furious, and galloped round the circle; but either from the loss of blood, or the pain he endured, he was fearful of facing the horseman; the men on foot then began to irritate him, by sticking small darts in his body, and whenever he made a push at them, threw the cloak over his eyes, and with great dexterity avoided his thrust.

Byron's lines at this point combine vigor and excitement with compassion for the harassed bull:

Foiled, bleeding, breathless, furious to the last,
Full in the centre stands the Bull at bay,
Mid wounds, and clinging darts, and lances brast,
And foes disabled in the brutal fray:
And now the Matadores around him play,
Shake the red cloak, and poise the ready brand:
Once more through all he bursts his thundering way—
Vain rage! the mantle quits the conynge hand,
Wraps his fierce eye—'tis past—he sinks upon the sand![2]

1. *Idem*, I, 75–7.
2. *Idem*, I, 78. When Byron speaks here of "Matadores" he must be thinking of the footmen known as *chulos*, who keep the bull occupied just before the single matador appears.

In these stanzas Byron, as we have seen, skillfully diverts attention and sympathy successively from the bull himself to the mounted picador whom the bull attacks, from the picador to his staggering horse, and then from the suffering horse to the furious, tormented bull again. But, coming to the final moments when bull and matador face each other for the climactic scene, Byron surprisingly fails not merely to give dramatic emphasis to this last struggle but he does not even make it clear that, with the arena cleared, the matador now faces the raging bull completely alone and dependent upon his own resourcefulness. In Byron's description there is no transition from

> Once more through all he burst his thundering way—

to the immediately following lines:

> Vain rage! the mantle quits the conynge hand,
> Wraps his fierce eye—'tis past—he sinks upon the sand!

It seems surprising that either Byron's memory or his dramatic instinct, so sure and dependable up to this moment, should suddenly fail him at this especially dramatic juncture, when the climax of the struggle has been reached.

One unusually ferocious Andalusian bull was the chief attraction on the Sunday Byron visited the amphitheater. Indeed, Carr had been induced by the fame of this particular animal to visit the arena a second time[3] and Hobhouse exclaimed with horror that "One bull killed three horses, *off his own horns*."[4] Both mention that because of his "peculiar merit" this beast was, contrary to the usual custom, saved for another fight. Byron must have seen this bull in action and it is likely that its spectacular performance inspired to a great extent the lines in *Childe Harold*. It is just possible, too, that there is some connection between the absence of a final act in that one unusually bloody fight and the extremely perfunctory treatment of the slaying of the bull in *Childe Harold*. Especially if, as Hobhouse intimates, he and Byron stayed for only a few of the fights this striking episode that did not involve the matador may, as he looked back, have blurred Byron's impressions of the more usual ritual of the bullfight. The chief drawback to such a theory is, of course, the vivid picture in Stanza 79 of the bull's death throes and its final removal. Byron must have seen at least one bull dispatched by the matador but whether for the reason just mentioned or some other, that last struggle between one man and one beast, the high point of most descriptions of bullfights, did not strongly affect Byron's imagination.

Byron's final emphasis rests upon the cruelty and brutality of Spain's favorite pastime.[5] He links the enthusiasm for this "ungentle

3. *Op. cit.*, pp. 60–1.   4. *P*, II, 522.   5. *Childe Harold*, I, 80.

sport," as have many observers before and after him, with a cruel, vengeful strain in the Spanish character. Hobhouse was in agreement and as illustration of this feeling he tells of the moment when

A gentleman present, observing them [Byron and Hobhouse] shudder and look pale, noticed that unusual reception of so delightful a sport to some young ladies, who stared and smiled, and continued their applause as another horse fell bleeding to the ground . . . An Englishman who can be much pleased with seeing two men beat themselves to pieces, cannot bear to look at a horse galloping round with his bowels trailing on the ground, and turns from the spectacle and the spectators with horror and disgust.[6]

Cadiz itself almost exhausted Byron's superlatives. It was not merely "the most delightful town I ever beheld"—it was "the first spot in the creation" and "a complete Cythera."[7] Nor is it to the discredit of Cadiz that by the time Byron came to write *Don Juan* it had declined in his estimation to "A pretty town, I recollect it well."[8] The situation of Cadiz must have delighted one with Byron's instinctive love of the sea; the city rises at the very tip of a long, narrow peninsula that juts forth into the vast Atlantic and forms the splendid bay of Cadiz. And the balconied, ivory-like houses, the handsome public buildings, and the clean, attractive streets of Cadiz were a joy. Byron was pleased, also, to discover that "The beauty of its streets and mansions is only excelled by the loveliness of its inhabitants."[9]

Here, as at Seville, there was talk of war on all sides; military leaders and government officials, both Spanish and English, were very much in evidence. Byron dined one evening with Admiral Purvis who was in charge of the naval blockade of Cadiz.[1] On another evening he joined Admiral José de Cordova and his family at the opera; Admiral Cordova had commanded the French fleet when it was defeated by the British off Cape St. Vincent in February, 1797.[2] It must have been at Cadiz, also, that a theater performance was suddenly interrupted and the audience, which included Byron, heard a dispatch announcing the defeat of the French at Talavera.[3] Byron was not, however, disposed to join in the rejoicing and, when later he had leisure for correspondence at Gibraltar, he wrote to his mother, "You have

6. *P*, II, 522.   7. *LJ*, I, 229, 234.   8. *Don Juan*, II, 5.   9. *LJ*, I, 234.
1. *LJ*, I, 242. Admiral John Child Purvis was from 1806 until 1810 "chiefly employed at the blockade and defence of Cadiz, where he distinguished himself much by his zeal and good judgment." William R. O'Byrne, *A Naval Biographical Dictionary* . . . (London, 1849).
2. *LJ*, I, 239–40. Also *Recollections*, I, 11–12.
3. In a manuscript note for his *Recollections* Hobhouse wrote that the despatch came at Seville. Churchman (*op. cit.*, XI, 133 and n.) accepts this statement. But Byron and Hobhouse must have left Seville before the battle of Talavera took place. And it has already been pointed out that Carr, who was at Seville at the same time, observed that the theater there was closed. Hobhouse's note was probably written late in life.

heard of the battle near Madrid, and in England they will call it a victory—a pretty victory! Two hundred officers and five thousand men killed, all English, and the French in as great force as ever."[4] The victory at Talavera was indeed a costly one for the British arms but Byron was mistaken in his estimate of the fatalities. There were over five thousand British casualties but fewer than a thousand British soldiers were killed.[5] The French fatalities were somewhat fewer than the British but their casualties outnumbered the British. Spanish losses were inconsiderable since the British bore the brunt of the battle.

Byron and Hobhouse both showed irritation that Spanish reports of the battle gave credit for the victory to their general Cuesta and made little mention of Sir Arthur Wellesley and his British troops. In this they were justified, for historians of the Peninsular War have made it clear that Cuesta's part in the victory was small and that his jealousy of Wellesley and his lack of coöperation contributed much to the ineffectualness of the Talavera campaign.[6]

Byron's doubts about the battle persisted in 1811, when in a note to *Childe Harold* he wrote, "Sorely were we puzzled how to dispose of that same victory of Talavera; and a victory it surely was somewhere, for everybody claimed it. The Spanish despatch and mob called it Cuesta's, and made no great mention of the Viscount; the French called it *theirs* . . . and we have not yet determined *what* to call it, or *whose*; for, certes, it was none of our own."[7] History agrees that, more through the fault of others than his own, Talavera was not one of Wellesley's greater achievements. As a result of it, however, Sir Arthur Wellesley became the Duke of Wellington.

On the morning of August 1 a thunderous royal salute, fired by the ships in the bay and answered by the garrison of Cadiz, announced the arrival of Richard Colley, Lord Wellesley, to assume his new duties as British Ambassador to the Supreme Junta of Spain.[8] Byron was among the thousands who lined the shore to witness Wellesley's approach. By careful plan a French flag was so placed on the wharf that the Marquess' first act as he stepped on Spanish soil was to trample on the hated French flag. Byron referred to this ceremony when he wrote of Sir Arthur Wellesley's "Oriental brother, whom I saw charioteering over the French flag, and heard clipping bad Spanish, after listening to the speech of a patriotic cobbler of Cadiz, on

4. *LJ*, I, 241. In the original letter, which I have examined in the Pierpont Morgan Library, Byron wrote "will call" rather than "would call," as Prothero renders it.
5. Oman, *op. cit.*, I, 555–6.   6. *Idem*, pp. 463–82.   7. *P*, II, 89.
8. *Recollections*, I, 11. In Lady Knighton's *Memoirs of Sir William Knighton* (London, 1838), I, 95–6, 98–102, there is a detailed description of Wellesley's arrival at Cadiz. Sir William Knighton (1776–1836) went to Spain as medical attendant to Lord Wellesley.

the event of his own entry into that city, and the exit of some five thousand bold Britons from this 'best of all possible worlds.' "[9] Among those who came with Wellesley from England were another brother, Henry Wellesley, who was to be secretary of the Embassy; his nephew William Wellesley; and a young friend Henry Gally Knight, whom Byron had known at Cambridge.[1] The latter two joined Byron and Hobhouse in Cadiz shortly after they disembarked.[2]

Even the stern realities of war did little to disturb the pleasant social routine of Cadiz. Here, as at Seville, festivities went on apace; the theaters and gaming houses were thriving, intrigue was "the business of life."[3] His experience in Cadiz led Byron to play in *Childe Harold* with the fancy that when Paphos fell, Aphrodite had fled to Cadiz.[4] His admiration for the women of Spain increased. Byron found Cadiz "full of the finest women in Spain, the Cadiz belles being the Lancashire witches of their land."[5] But in comparing them with Lancashire witches Byron did not mean to imply that English beauty was the supreme standard of comparison, for the loveliness and fascination of the Spanish women quickly led him to confess that "the women of Cadiz are as far superior to the English women in beauty as the Spaniards are inferior to the English in every quality that dignifies the name of man."[6] This judgment persists in two lines of *Childe Harold* which have, perhaps, more conviction than they have poetic merit:

> Who round the North for paler dames would seek?
> How poor their forms appear! how languid, wan, and weak![7]

The charm of Spanish women led Byron to forgive their apparent want of education and information. Their minds were concerned only with intrigue; that, Byron insisted, was "strictly and literally true."[8] In *Childe Harold* he sings of

> . . . Andalusia's maids,
> Nurst in the glowing lap of soft Desire.[8a]

---

9. *P*, ɪɪ, 88–9.
1. In the second of the rejected stanzas ridiculing Sir John Carr's inevitable book of travels, Byron referred satirically (*P*, ɪɪ, 79) to the numerous Wellesleys who embarked for Spain "As if therein they meant to colonize." There were actually four Wellesleys in Spain in the summer of 1809. Sir Arthur had, of course, come to the Peninsula in the spring and three more Wellesleys now arrived from England. Richard Colley, Marquess Wellesley, the eldest of the brothers, had served earlier as Governor-General of India. When the Marquess returned to England in the fall of 1809 to serve as Foreign Secretary, Henry Wellesley, who had originally come as Secretary, took his brother's place as Ambassador. William Wellesley Pole Wellesley, an exact contemporary of Byron's, is called by Prothero (*LJ*, ɪɪ, 78, n.) "one of the most worthless of the bloods of the regency."

2. *Recollections*, ɪ, 11.   3. *LJ*, ɪ, 239. See also Carr, *op. cit.*, pp. 10–11, 28–9.
4. *Childe Harold*, ɪ, 66.   5. *LJ*, ɪ, 239.   6. *LJ*, ɪ, 234.
7. *Childe Harold*, ɪ, 58.   8. *LJ*, ɪ, 240.   8a. *Childe Harold*, ɪ, 64.

Byron's emphasis upon laxity of morals among the women of Spain has aroused the indignation of many Spaniards, the most vocal and eloquent of whom is Emilio Castelar who protests, not without some justice, against the superficiality of Byron's judgment:

But why did not Lord Byron—who showed himself so keenly sensible of the valor of the Spaniards—why did he not also appreciate the virtue of Spanish women? . . . The virtues of women are hidden in the home, in the sanctuary of the family; one must seek them as pearls in the shells, in the depths of the ocean. A traveler passes some days in a foreign town—he sees all things superficially, finds vice and vicious pleasures easy of attainment, and generalizes his emotions . . . Byron should not have been contented to behold the fire stolen from heaven by the black eyes of our Andalusian ladies, the passion which flashes from under their silken lashes, the long tresses of rich hair which twine over their shoulders like serpents—among so much beauty he should have discovered the delicacy and the loveliness of the soul.[1]

One is inclined to feel that Castelar makes rather excessive demands of a twenty-one-year-old Englishman spending a short time in a foreign country of whose very language he is ignorant. It is hardly likely that Byron could have had access to the "sanctuary of the family" had he so desired. But the point needs to be made; these *are,* of necessity, superficial judgments.

Byron met at Cadiz one young lady who especially attracted him and who offered to remedy at least his *linguistic* deficiencies. This was the daughter of Admiral Cordova. With Señorita Cordova, Hobhouse reports, Byron "contrived to fall in love at very short notice."[2] She it was who "commanded" that Byron be seated next to her at the theater and after the performance conferred upon him "the honour of attending her to the admiral's mansion." Byron had reluctantly to decline her offer to tutor him in the intricacies of the Spanish language, expressing regret that "I quitted Cadiz too soon to permit me to make the progress which would doubtless attend my studies under so charming a directress."[3]

Señorita Cordova was an excellent example of that Spanish style of beauty which Byron so admired and which, in speaking of this particular young lady, he defined in one enthusiastic sentence: "Long black hair, dark languishing eyes, *clear* olive complexions, and forms more graceful than can be conceived by an Englishman used to the

---

1. *Life of Lord Byron and Other Sketches* (New York, 1876), pp. 66–7. This translation, by Mrs. Arthur Arnold, of Castelar's book should be used with extreme caution. This particular passage is accurately translated but on p. 74, where the author speaks of Byron's stay in Malta, there appears the fantastic rendering of "Primero encontró en su travesía á la bella Florencia, escapada dos veces á los persecuciones de Napoleon" as "The first happened during his stay at beautiful Florence, where he twice escaped the persecutions of Napoleon." The reader should compare any passage in the translation with *Vida de Lord Byron* (Habana, 1873).
2. Recollections, I, 12.   3. *LJ*, I, 240.

drowsy, listless air of his countrywomen, added to the most becoming dress, and at the same time, the most decent in the world, render a Spanish beauty irresistible."[4] The exuberant stanzas entitled "The Girl of Cadiz," which Byron originally intended to include in *Childe Harold*, must owe more than a little of their origin to this attractive daughter of a Spanish admiral.

There is every reason to believe that "The Girl of Cadiz" reflects Byron's dominant mood during his stay at Cadiz more faithfully than do the melancholy lines, "To Inez," which he substituted for them in *Childe Harold*.[5] The complete contrast in tone furnishes a striking example of the duality of gaiety and gloom that was so characteristic of Byron. The excitement and novelty of his experiences in Spain and Portugal seem at least temporarily to have diminished the mood of melancholy in which he left England. "The Girl of Cadiz" was doubtless written in Spain while impressions were still very fresh; it is entirely otherwise with "To Inez," which Byron wrote at Athens on January 25, 1810. As was the case with "The Girl of Cadiz," it seems unlikely that "To Inez" was written primarily for inclusion in *Childe Harold*. The poem has, indeed, a ring of sincere emotion that is in a different key from the very artificially somber stanzas that precede it in the poem as finally published. Byron doubtless wrote it in low spirits at Athens; later, sensing the inappropriateness of "The Girl of Cadiz," he seems to have given the young lady addressed in Athens a Spanish name and substituted this later poem for "The Girl of Cadiz."

The memory of Cadiz was still vivid in Byron's mind when he wrote the second canto of *Don Juan*. In fact he seemed to take an active pleasure in leading his new hero along his own course from Seville to Cadiz and on toward the mosques, the minarets, and the harems of Constantinople. In *Don Juan* there is a pleasing nostalgia in all those stanzas that treat of places Byron had known in his own travels. Those that deal with Juan's departure from Cadiz are especially exhilarating:

> I said that Juan had been sent to Cadiz—
>   A pretty town, I recollect it well—
> 'Tis there the mart of the colonial trade is
>   (Or was, before Peru learned to rebel),
> And such sweet girls!—I mean, such graceful ladies,
>   Their very walk would make your bosom swell;
> I can't describe it, though so much it strike,
> Nor liken it—I never saw the like.[6]

· · · · · · · · ·

4. *LJ*, I, 239.
5. "To Inez" appears between Stanzas 84 and 85 of Canto I. The rejected "Girl of Cadiz" stanzas have always been published in Byron's works as an independent poem. See *P*, III, 1, n.
6. *Don Juan*, II, 5.

Juan embarked—the ship got under way,
   The wind was fair, the water passing rough;
A devil of a sea rolls in that bay,
   As I, who've crossed it oft, know well enough;
And, standing on the deck, the dashing spray
   Flies in one's face, and makes it weather-tough.[7]

Byron himself departed from Cadiz in a British ship of war, the *Hyperion,* on August 3.[8] Admiral Purvis offered the travelers passage on the frigate bound for Gibraltar. There they arrived the following day and there they remained for about two weeks, waiting first for Fletcher and the other servants to arrive from Lisbon and then for a packet that would take them on to Malta.[9] Except for the fortifications there was little of interest at Gibraltar and at "this cursed place"[1] for the first time since he left England Byron found the days hanging heavily on his hands. Cadiz must have seemed even more delightful than ever by comparison. Here at Gibraltar there was ample time for a long, leisurely letter to his mother, in which he hymned the praises of Seville and especially of Cadiz.[2] Byron told Hodgson of his determination to return to Spain before seeing England again, "for I am enamoured of the country."[3]

The lack of such pleasing sights and diversions as had filled the preceding days led Byron even to seek out the garrison library. It was there on a very sultry August day that the Scottish traveler John Galt, who was also shortly to sail on to Malta, had his first glimpse of Byron. Galt observed that

His physiognomy was prepossessing and intelligent, but ever and anon his brows lowered and gathered; a habit, as I then thought, with a degree of affectation in it, probably first assumed for picturesque effect and energetic expression; but which I afterwards discovered was undoubtedly the occasional scowl of some unpleasant reminiscence: it was certainly disagreeable—forbidding—but still the general cast of his features was impressed with elegance and character.[4]

For a time at Gibraltar Byron had some hope of crossing the straits to Africa but contrary winds made this impossible. He did, however, visit Algeciras across the bay and there at the residence of Lady Westmorland met the renowned General Francisco de Castaños, who had won the first great Spanish victory against the French at Baylen the summer before. Byron dined with the General several days later and found him "pleasant and, for aught I know to the contrary, clever"[5] —a rather noncommittal judgment for so decided a person as Byron! When Castaños had failed to repeat the success of Baylen the Spanish

7. *Idem,* II, 11.   8. *Recollections,* I, 12.   9. *LJ,* I, 242.   1. *LJ,* I, 239.
2. *LJ,* I, 236–42.   3. *LJ,* I, 236.   4. Galt, p. 63.   5. *LJ,* I, 242.

Government retired him to his home at Algeciras, where he was living as something of a martyr when Byron saw him. Five months later, however, when the French were pouring through the passes of the Sierra Morena, the Junta frantically recalled Castaños.[6]

Visiting Lady Westmorland with Byron and Hobhouse was Sir William Drummond, who had but recently retired as British Ambassador at Naples. Sir William's very unambassadorial imprudence of tongue greatly surprised his companions. When Byron assured him that the passengers were in no danger during their rather rough crossing to Algeciras, Drummond startled him by replying, "It is well for you who think that if you are drowned you will go to another world, but, I who have no such belief, would rather remain a little longer where I am." Later at Lady Westmorland's Sir William boasted of having refused a large bribe when he was Ambassador at Constantinople, appealing, with notable lack of diplomacy, for congratulation to Castaños, who had lately been accused of taking bribes from the French.[7]

From Gibraltar Joe Murray and Robert Rushton were sent back to England, since neither the advanced age of the one nor the extreme youthfulness of the other seemed to fit him for further travel into what might prove to be rough surroundings. In a second postscript, dated August 15, to the long letter to his mother, Byron said that he was about to depart for Malta on the morrow but it is unlikely that he actually sailed on the *Townshend* packet until three or four days later.[8]

V. *Byron and the Peninsular War*

It has been suggested throughout that the Peninsular War made a deep impression upon Byron's consciousness. There now remains to consider and to gauge, if possible, the extent to which his closeness to the war in Portugal and Spain affected both the poet and the man.

6. Jacob, *op. cit.*, p. 382.

7. Hobhouse describes the incidents in the British Museum MSS. *op. cit.*, 36445 ff., 584–5, quoted by Churchman, XI, 83.

8. *LJ*, I, 242. Hobhouse remarks in his *Journey* (I, 37) that he and Byron were held up three weeks at Gibraltar, waiting for baggage they had sent by water from Lisbon. His entries in the *Recollections* (I, 13–14) suggest, however, that the Gibraltar stay was nearer to two weeks in extent than three. In this case the latter evidence is the more dependable, for from Galt's *Life of Byron* one can establish August 19 as the probable date of departure for Malta. Galt does not give the date explicitly but he says (p. 62) that it was on a Sunday that the *Townshend* reached Cagliari, the capital of Sardinia. Sunday could have been no other than August 27, since the 20th would have been too early and September 3 too late to coincide with other evidence. Galt mentions (p. 65) that on that Sunday "we had been eight days together." From this testimony it seems safe to assume Saturday, August 19, was the date of departure. As so often, Byron's own expectations of sailing were disappointed.

As Byron traveled in the Peninsula, he gained those impressions from which he drew when he wrote the first canto of *Childe Harold;* some of the more immediate of these have already been mentioned. But there are other more general and accumulative impressions that cannot be connected with any one particular moment or place. Such are the stanzas in which Byron exhorts Spain to rise against her French oppressors, those that deal with the battle of Talavera, and the reflections on warfare that follow; and close to the end of the canto come six stanzas that comprise Byron's farewell to Spain.

Biographers have been in the habit of passing over Byron's six weeks in Spain and Portugal with a few exuberant quotations from his letters, thus giving the impression that the period there was a delightful, carefree lark, and nothing more.[9] To some extent it was that, to be sure, but the engaging accounts Byron wrote to his mother and his friend Hodgson must not be taken as the whole story. Thirty-nine of the ninety-three stanzas in the first canto of *Childe Harold* refer to the Peninsular War; and the greater number of these are wholly concerned with that struggle. Yet Galt has criticized Byron on the grounds that "Considering the interest which he afterward took in the affairs of Greece, it is remarkable that he should have passed through Spain, at the period he has described, without feeling any sympathy with the spirit which then animated that nation."[1] And much the same objection is voiced in Watkins' biography of the poet.[2] Such complaints as these must arise either from misunderstanding or from neglect of the full evidence. They surely betray insufficient attention to the first canto of *Childe Harold.*

It is vain, however, to look for any completely consistent attitude toward the war in *Childe Harold,* for the first canto is a loosely connected series of reflections representing opinions held at several distinct times during a period of over two years—two of the most impressionable years of Byron's life. We have, it is true, little record of Byron's immediate reactions as they came to him directly on the very spot; he kept no journal and the only direct reference to the war in his four letters from the Peninsula is the caustic remark regarding Talavera, written about two weeks after he had heard news of the battle. *Childe Harold* was begun nearly three months after Byron had left Spain, with the result that most of the first impressions came, and events occurred, about four months before they were given poetic

---

9. Moore, by his complete dependence upon the letters, was probably largely responsible for this deficiency. Neither Miss Mayne nor Drinkwater mentions the fact that the Peninsular War was in progress. Maurois and Miss Richter mention it only in passing.

1. Galt, p. 61.

2. John Watkins, *Memoirs of the Life and Writings of the Right Honorable Lord Byron* (London, 1822), pp. 102–03.

expression.[3] Byron has said that he was in low spirits when he began *Childe Harold;*[4] thus it is very possible that, even when they are not the exaggerated reactions of a shadowy misanthrope created in his own darkest image, Byron's animadversions in retrospect in November and December were of a gloomier cast than his immediate impressions in July and August.

There is, then, a step from the immediate experience to *Childe Harold* as Byron first wrote it. A much longer and more significant step is that from *Childe Harold* as it was originally written to the poem that appeared in March, 1812. For when Byron returned to England in 1811 he not only omitted stanzas from the original manuscript but he also added seven new ones dealing with Spain and the Peninsular War.[5] The mood of these later stanzas differs markedly from those written two years earlier.

Yet even within the 1809 stanzas there are marked inconsistencies. It is now necessary to look at those stanzas with some care. We have seen that in the part of the poem dealing with Portugal Byron showed his condemnation of Napoleon and his scorn for the Convention of Cintra. In the much more extensive section on Spain—the bulk of the canto—he begins with an apostrophe to Spain, in the light of her glorious past, to rise against her attackers. Where, Byron asks, is that spirit which over a thousand years ago drove the Moorish invaders from the land? That great achievement, he says, now survives only in song, only in the "peasant's plaint." Today in the roar of the cannon Spain's ancient goddess Chivalry calls more loudly than ever:

> Awake, ye Sons of Spain! awake! advance![6]

Such a prose paraphrase as this must inevitably set off the fine energy of Byron's lines. Everywhere had been the sights and sounds of war. These Byron expresses in stanzas that are stirring in their sheer animation and rhetorical power:

> Hark!—heard you not those hoofs of dreadful note?
> Sounds not the clang of conflict on the heath?
> Saw ye not whom the reeking sabre smote,
> Nor saved your brethren ere they sank beneath
> Tyrants and Tyrants' slaves?—the fires of Death,
> The Bale-fires flash on high:—from rock to rock
> Each volley tells that thousands cease to breathe;
> Death rides upon the sulphury Siroc,
> Red Battle stamps his foot, and Nations feel the shock.[7]

3. The poem was begun in Albania, October 30, 1809. See *P*, II, xvi.

4. In 1815 Byron told the American traveler George Ticknor of the "impressions of extreme discontent" under which he wrote the poem. *Life, Letters, and Journals of George Ticknor* (Boston, 1876), I, 67.

5. These stanzas were I, 43, 85-7, 88-90.   6. *Childe Harold*, I, 35-7.

7. *Idem*, I, 38.

The conception, which he proceeds to develop, of Battle as a giant standing upon a mountain is overelaborate and artificial yet it is not without its grandeur and imaginative appeal. Before this terrible giant, with his blood-red tresses and his scorching eye, his fiery hands and feet of iron, now "three potent Nations" offer sacrifice.[8]

But even as he senses the grim dramatic appeal of such a scene Byron cannot restrain himself from looking behind the gleaming façade of even his own creation. The four stanzas on the battle of Talavera are the melancholy record of what he professes to find there.[9] It is not surprising that these stinging lines have lingered longer in the memories of most readers than have other passages in *Childe Harold* that deal with the war. Nor can it be denied that in themselves the stanzas constitute one of the most bitter and sardonic pronouncements on war in all poetry. Indeed, if this passage were Byron's *only* commentary on the war, Galt's criticism of his attitude would be highly pertinent.[1]

It is not Byron's only comment, however. Only a moment before he had been urging Spain to rise against the French and shortly afterward he was expressing compassion for the Spanish peasant threatened by war, lamenting the apparent futility of the efforts of "the young, the proud, the brave,"[2] speaking of "Her [Spain's] fate, to every freeborn bosom dear."[3] How are we to account for what appears to be a serious inconsistency in Byron's attitude? What are we to make of a poet who exhorts the people of Spain to deliver themselves and then in almost the same breath implies that all who engage in warfare are "Battle's minions," that they can do nought but "fertilise the field that each pretends to gain"?[4]

It will not be enough to say that Byron was never a consistent person nor a thoroughly consistent thinker. The first point to observe is that in these stanzas he is speaking of one particular battle although he appears to go on to generalize from the specific instance. Among the most significant words in the passage are Byron's designation of England as

. . . the fond ally
That fights for all, but ever fights in vain.[5]

Talavera was one of the most widely acclaimed but actually one of the most indecisive and costly battles of a military campaign in which, as

---

8. *Idem*, I, 39.   9. These are Stanzas 40–2, 44.
1. See above, p. 43. One "A. H." in a poem in the *Gentleman's Magazine* (LXXXIII [1812], 566) indignantly protested "No, Byron, no!" The *Edinburgh Review* (XIX [1812], 467) remarked of the sentiments expressed in *Childe Harold* that they "are not only complexionally dark and disdainful, but run directly counter to very many of our national passions, and most favoured propensities."
2. *Childe Harold*, I, 53.   3. *Idem*, I, 63.   4. *Idem*, I, 41.   5. *Ibid*.

an Englishman and more especially as a Whig, Byron did not believe and in whose success he had little confidence. We have noted also that he greatly overestimated the losses. Byron came to Spain opposing the conduct of the war; thus he was only too ready to seize upon Talavera as the supreme example of military vanity and futility. Those who died at Talavera were "Ambition's honoured fools"; they were the "broken tools" of tyrants.[6] Let these favorites of battle, these "blest hirelings" barter breath for fame if they like—had they lived they might have proved their country's shame![7]

Byron's failure to distinguish between the motives of "The Foe, the Victim, and the fond Ally"[8] betrays more spleen and partisan rancor than it does judgment; some of the lines, moreover, are examples of that sophomoric bad taste that Byron never completely outgrew. Yet there is something rather admirable here, too. One wishes Byron had omitted the last of the four stanzas on Talavera, had not let his destructive spirit run away with him. For the first three, lacking though they are in restraint, offer a salutary antidote to the conventional glorification of war; they show one of Byron's chief sources of strength, his ability to see through the external appearances of things. Unfortunately he oversteps the mark and the political and philosophic elements are not entirely distinguishable.

It would be convenient to believe that in the third of these stanzas Byron was thinking mainly of the French invaders. In itself the stanza is a strong indictment of those wars of conquest Byron was always to despise. The scorn here is not so much for the "broken tools" as it is for the "Tyrants" themselves, who

> . . . dare to pave the way
> With human hearts—to what? a dream alone.[9]

The truth is that Byron's scorn for Talavera and his observations on the vanity of military glory did not keep him from feeling real sympathy for the cause of the Spaniards. The former attitude was to a large extent something he brought with him from England; he was looking upon the war from the point of view of a skeptical Englishman whose concern had been more with the success or failure of British arms than it had been with the plight of the Spanish and Portuguese. The latter feeling, however, grew more directly from experience on the Peninsula; its basis was genuine human feeling, evoked by what he saw and heard round about him.

Byron never glorified war. In 1820 he wrote from Italy, "The worst of it all is, that this devoted country will become, for the six thousandth time, since God made man in his own image, the seat of war. I recollect Spain in 1808 [*sic*], and the Morea and part of Greece in

6. *Idem*, I, 42.   7. *Idem*, I, 44.   8. *Idem*, I, 41.   9. *Idem*, I, 42.

1810–1811."[1] And the satirical treatment of military fame in the eighth canto of *Don Juan* had its roots in Byron's own belief and experience. When in 1814 it was Napoleon who was on the defensive, Byron wrote of the French emperor that "He has my best wishes to manure the fields of France with an *invading* army. I hate invaders of all countries."[2] That hatred for invaders was first actively aroused in Portugal and Spain; there in 1809 Byron directed it at Napoleon himself and his French armies.

The personality and career of Napoleon never ceased to fascinate Byron.[3] A familiar story is that of his boyhood enthusiasm for Napoleon and his fight at Harrow for the preservation of Napoleon's bust.[4] With one exception something of this hero worship was to persist throughout Byron's life, though mingled at times with scorn and abuse.[5] The exception was on the Peninsula. Here, where Byron may be said to have come closest to immediate contact with Napoleon, significantly enough his opinion of the French emperor sank to its lowest ebb. Seeing at first hand the anguish and destruction caused by Napoleon's armies Byron could find no good to say of "Gaul's unsparing lord,"[6] the despoiler of weak Portugal and Spain. And in Spain for the first time—and the last—Byron saw Napoleon through the eyes of those very people whose land he was destroying, people who led good lives in good surroundings. In such a land Napoleon was not the inheritor of the principles of the French Revolution but the invading despot; he was "Gaul's Vulture" and "the Scourger of the world."[7] There is no word of admiration or even of toleration for Napoleon as Byron sees him through the eyes of the sturdy Spanish peasant.

Yet Byron feels that Napoleon's power is too great even if Spain defends herself valiantly. And English assistance has availed but little. In fact, by implication at least, Byron seems to look upon the deliverance of Spain as Spain's *own* task, much as he was later to insist that by Greeks alone could Greece be freed. But this task is a hopeless one:

> Ah! Spain! how sad will be thy reckoning-day,
> When soars Gaul's Vulture, with his wings unfurled,
> And thou shalt view thy sons in crowds to Hades hurled.[8]

---

1. *LBC*, II, 163. 2. *LJ*, III, 17.

3. Byron's relationship to Napoleon is fully discussed in Paul Holzhausen's *Bonaparte, Byron, und die Briten* (Frankfurt, 1904) and Gerhard Eggert's *Lord Byron und Napoleon* (Weimar, Leipzig, 1933).

4. "Ever since I defended my bust of him at Harrow against the rascally time-servers, when the war broke out in 1803, he has been a *Héros de Roman* of mine—on the Continent; I don't want him here." *LJ*, II, 323–4.

5. A graphic example is the strident "Ode to Napoleon Bonaparte," written in April, 1814.

6. *Childe Harold*, I, 16.   7. *Idem*, I, 52.   8. *Ibid.*

His dire predictions bring Byron no pleasure. On the contrary, his sense of their doom quickens his concern and sympathy for the people of Spain. He looks upon "the rustic—with his trembling mate" and exclaims:

> Ah, monarchs! could ye taste the mirth ye mar,
> 　Not in the toils of Glory would ye fret;
> The hoarse dull drum would sleep, and Man be happy yet![9]

Of the doomed sons of Spain he protests:

> And must they fall? the young, the proud, the brave,
> 　To swell one bloated Chief's unwholesome reign?
> 　No step between submission and a grave?
> 　The rise of Rapine and the fall of Spain?
> 　And doth the Power that man adores ordain
> 　Their doom, nor heed the suppliant's appeal?
> 　Is all that desperate Valour acts in vain?
> 　And Counsel sage, and patriotic zeal—
> The Veteran's skill—Youth's fire—and Manhood's heart of steel?[1]

Of the eleven stanzas Byron added to *Childe Harold* after his return to England in 1811 six serve as a kind of postlude to the section on Spain and the war. The difference between these later stanzas and those we have been discussing is very striking. The 1811 stanzas are much more hopeful in spirit. Where in 1809 Byron wrote,

> Ah! Spain! how sad will be thy reckoning-day[2]

in 1811 he wrote,

> Nor yet, alas! the dreadful work is done.[3]

Though the main turning point of the war had not yet come, the success of Wellington's Torres Vedras strategy in the winter of 1811 gave some reason for optimism.[4] Byron by no means changed his mind about the Peninsular operations in 1811 but at least he did adopt a somewhat more hopeful view.[5] The added stanzas are less occupied with predicting Spain's certain downfall than they are with lamenting that her day of deliverance is not nearer at hand. The assumption now is that that day will eventually come.

The stanzas begin with a farewell to Cadiz. Byron can now praise

---

9. *Idem*, i, 47.　　1. *Idem*, i, 53.　　2. *Idem*, i, 52.　　3. *Idem*, i, 89.

4. Wellington drew up vast defensive works, known as the "Lines of Torres Vedras," north of Lisbon from the Tagus to the sea. Massena was unable to penetrate them and retreated into Spain.

5. "The late exploits of Lord Wellington have effaced the follies of Cintra. He has, indeed, done wonders . . . Massena's retreat is a great comfort; and as we have not been in the habit of pursuing for some years past, no wonder we are a little awkward at first. No doubt we shall improve; or, if not, we have only to take to our old way of retrograding, and there we are at home." *P*, ii, 86, 89.

Cadiz for withstanding the long siege of the French.[6] It is significant that the words "Liberty" and "Freedom" appear. After his added experience of tyranny and oppression in Greece Byron now sees freedom as a concept:

> Fall'n nations gaze on Spain; if freed, she frees
> More than her fell Pizarros once enchain'd.[7]

In imagery that anticipates the famous picture of Freedom in Canto IV of *Childe Harold*[8] he exclaims:

> When shall her Olive-Branch be free from blight?
> When shall she breathe her from the blushing toil?
> How many a doubtful day shall sink in night,
> Ere the Frank robber turn him from his spoil,
> *And Freedom's stranger-tree grow native of the soil!*[9]

But the task is Spain's, not England's. Byron's Whig orthodoxy remained as strong as ever. In his speech for the Catholic Bill as late as April 21, 1812, he spoke with scorn of the results "of those extraordinary expeditions, so expensive to ourselves, and so useless to our allies; of those singular inquiries, so exculpatory of the accused, and so dissatisfactory to the people; of those paradoxical victories, so honourable, as we are told, to the British name, and so destructive to the best interests of the British nation."[1]

6. *Childe Harold*, i, 86.   7. *Idem*, i, 89.   8. *Idem*, iv, 98.
9. *Idem*, i, 90.   1. *LJ*, ii, 443.

II

Western Mediterranean and Albania

THE passage from Gibraltar to Malta was a slow one since winds were neither strong nor favorable. Byron gives little information about the voyage, merely observing that "I have touched at Cagliari in Sardinia, and at Girgenti in Sicily."[1] For details we must turn to Hobhouse and to John Galt. During the first few days at sea Byron kept himself aloof from his fellow passengers; his behavior gave the impression of sullenness and petulance but his shipmate Galt eventually decided that this was mere capriciousness. About the third day Byron put aside his "rapt mood" and entered playfully into the life of the ship. Yet, according to Galt's recollection, he spent only one evening in the cabin with his companions; his extreme self-absorption and hypochondria could hardly have been expected to attract the favorable regard of the other passengers. Galt, however, found his own interest and curiosity aroused by the unusual deportment of this young lord.[2]

One greatly wishes Galt had written down his first impressions of Byron immediately, rather than over twenty years later, for today it is hard to tell how much his well-known description of Byron on shipboard, written in 1830, was colored even unconsciously by his knowledge of the later career and fame of Byron and perhaps by his own instinct as a creative writer. But even if we allow for some romanticizing of his immediate impressions it still seems obvious that Galt was one of the first to feel something of that spell that Byron could even thus early exert over those who observed him. Of Byron as he saw him on the *Townshend* between Gibraltar and Sardinia Galt wrote:

When the lights were placed, he made himself a man forbid, took his station on the railing between the pegs on which the sheets are belayed and the shrouds, and there, for hours, sat in silence, enamoured, it may be, of the moon . . . He was often strangely rapt—it may have been from his genius; and, had its grandeur and darkness been then divulged, susceptible of explanation; but, at the time, it threw, as it were, around him the sackcloth of penitence. Sitting amid the shrouds and rattlins, in the tranquillity of the moonlight, churming an inarticulate melody, he seemed almost apparitional, suggesting dim reminiscences of him who shot the albatross. He was as a mystery in a winding-sheet, crowned with a halo.[3]

1. *LJ*, I, 246.   2. Galt, pp. 61-3.   3. Galt, pp. 62-3.

By comparison with this romantic evocation Byron's own correspond-ing stanzas in the second canto of *Childe Harold* seem rather pale and insufficient![4]

The passengers finally landed at Cagliari, the capital of Sardinia, on August 27, a Sunday. There, as they dined and attended the theater together, Byron and Galt began to get along harmoniously. Mr. Hill, the Ambassador, invited them to dinner at his residence and after-wards the whole company went to the theater; since it was the occa-sion of some special court festival the royal family were present for the opera. In deference to his rank the Ambassador led Byron to a special private box near the royal group. Later in the evening Byron's ceremonious manner as he parted from the Ambassador was a source of some amusement to both Galt and Hobhouse.[5]

The account of Cagliari in Hobhouse's *Recollections* is a confusing combination of what seems immediate detail and vague reminiscence. Hobhouse's statement that "We dined one day with Mr. Hill, the English Minister" betrays a hazy memory[6] for it is clear from Galt's account that the travelers spent only one day and evening ashore at Cagliari. On the other hand, there are in the *Recollections* many details in the present tense which sound like immediate impres-sions:

Byron, coming back from a ride in the country, describes it as neither agree-able nor attractive, having seen nothing worthy of notice but three heads nailed to a gallows . . . One gentleman the other day, after being con-victed of sixteen murders, cut the throat of the son of a neighbor in whose house he had been brought up as a child, and on being outlawed for this crime was seen arm-in-arm with one of the Queen's equerries.[7]

Hobhouse found the island still in a state of barbarism. The gentry would often steal their neighbors' flocks or shoot their horses and no man traveled outside a town without being armed. In Cagliari, a fortified town, with narrow, "tolerably clean" streets, the people of the higher classes whom they met were attired in court dress, those of the lower classes in leather garments over which they threw a short piece of shaggy goatskin, with two holes for the arms.[8]

On Monday, August 28, the *Townshend* proceeded toward Sicily and Malta. Byron was indisposed and did not appear until late that evening but the next day as they sailed along the shores of Sicily he was in the highest spirits, "overflowing with glee and sparkling with quaint sentences." Galt tells us that "the champagne was uncorked and in the finest condition." The mail was landed at Girgenti, on the southwest coast of Sicily; the ruins of the ancient city, which he saw

---

4. Stanzas 23–6.   5. Galt, pp. 65–6; *LBC*, II, 11.   6. *Recollections*, I, 12.
7. *Recollections*, I, 12–13.   8. *Ibid.*

by moonlight, made a lasting impression on Byron.[9] At noon the following day the ship reached Malta. Galt, who from the beginning had been amused and perhaps somewhat nettled by what he felt to be Byron's undue sense of his rank, took obvious pleasure in the discomfiture of his new acquaintances when, upon arriving in the Grand Harbor at Malta, they waited in vain for the salute from the batteries which Byron assumed was his due.[1]

Malta, long the island stronghold of the famous Knights of St. John of Jerusalem, had been captured by Napoleon on his way to Egypt in 1798 but was delivered from French control by the British in 1800. When Napoleon insisted that the British evacuate Malta they had declared a renewal of the war with France in May, 1803. Since that time the island, very strategically located and strongly fortified, had been under British administration with Sir Alexander Ball as Governor.[2] Malta's position as a vital link between western Europe and the Near East made it of great importance both militarily and commercially.

Byron found the inhabitants of Malta hospitable and pleasant.[3] On the day after their arrival the Governor provided the English travelers with a house in the upper part of the capital city Valetta and this served as their pleasant headquarters for almost three weeks.[4] It is clear from the fact that Byron soon began to take lessons in Arabic that he still had the intention of traveling into Asia. At Valetta there was talk of Napoleon and of the powerful Turkish pashas who controlled the Balkan Peninsula from Albania south to the Peloponnesus. And one evening Byron and Hobhouse dined with General Oakes, who had been next to Nelson when he lost his eye.[5]

Hobhouse also noted that Byron was "of course, very popular with

9. Thomas Medwin, *Conversations of Lord Byron: Noted during a Residence with His Lordship at Pisa, in the Years 1821 and 1822* (London, 1824), pp. 12–13.

1. Galt, pp. 66–7. This would indicate they reached Malta on the 30th. In the *Recollections* Hobhouse, however, gives the date as August 31. There is a letter from Malta to Hanson, dated August 31 (*LJ*, VI, 443–4); this is additional evidence that they had arrived by that date. Elsewhere Byron wrote to Hanson that "It has been my custom to write to you from every seaport on my arrival and previous to my departure." *LJ*, VI, 449.

2. Sir Alexander J. Ball (1757–1809) had been in charge of the blockade of Malta from 1798 to 1800. He was a distinguished naval officer, rising to the rank of rear admiral, and was a close friend of Lord Nelson. During the period of his administration of the island he was adored to an extraordinary degree by the people of Malta and he was to a large extent responsible for the good relations that existed between Malta and England. Sir Alexander died at Malta, greatly lamented, less than a month after Byron left the island. For further details see the *Dictionary of National Biography*.

3. *LJ*, I, 243.   4. Galt, p. 68.

5. *Recollections*, I, 13–14. Major-General Hildebrand Oakes (1754–1822), who served with Cornwallis in the American Revolution and was with Nelson in Corsica in 1794, had been in command of the British troops at Malta since March, 1808. He was later knighted and raised to the rank of lieutenant general.

all the ladies, as he is handsome, amusing, and generous; but his attentions to all and singular generally end . . . in *rixae feminae*."[6] Byron did, however, fix his particular attentions upon one young lady, the attractive and already somewhat renowned Mrs. Spencer Smith who was, he wrote to his mother, his almost constant companion at Malta.[7] The appeal of Mrs. Spencer Smith was by no means lessened by the highly romantic story of her life. Born in Constantinople, daughter of the Austrian Ambassador, she had married the British Minister at Stuttgart and in Byron's words "her life has been from its commencement so fertile in remarkable incidents, that in a romance they would appear improbable."[8] When Constance Spencer Smith was seized by the French in Italy in 1806, the gallant Marquis de Salvo had not merely rescued her in as thrilling a manner as the imagination could devise—employing disguise, ladder, swift horses, and even two boats —but he had also proceeded to give a graphic account of the adventure in a book published in 1807.[9] Almost the whole of Byron's one letter from Malta to his mother was devoted to Mrs. Spencer Smith and he took obvious relish in communicating the information that "Buonaparte is even now so incensed against her, that her life would be in some danger if she were taken prisoner a second time."[1]

The tone of the stanzas on "fair Florence" in the second canto of *Childe Harold* has misled several biographers into assuming that Byron was never really attracted to Mrs. Spencer Smith.[2] Yet we have not only Byron's own word that "I was seized with an *everlasting passion*" but also Hobhouse's firsthand observation that "My friend Byron fell in love with her."[3] To be sure, the infatuation did not endure and by the following January Byron was writing ungrammatically that "The spell is broke, the charm is flown!"[4] And it is especially significant that it was at this time, after the charm was flown, that he wrote the "Florence" stanzas in *Childe Harold*. But Byron's own statements and the four poems he wrote in the fall of 1809[5] make it clear that, far from displaying a "marble heart," he took Mrs. Spencer Smith very seriously indeed while he was at Malta and for some weeks

6. *Recollections*, I, 13–14.   7. *LJ*, I, 245.   8. *LJ*, I, 245.

9. *Travels in the Year 1806 from Italy to England* (London, 1807). In the fifteenth volume of her *Mémoires* (Paris, 1834) the Duchesse d'Abrantès, wife of the French general Junot, also described at length "l'aventure étonnante de madame Spencer-Smith."

1. *LJ*, I, 246.

2. Moore, surprisingly enough, speaks of Byron's attitude toward Mrs. Spencer Smith as "purest admiration and interest, unwarmed by any more ardent sentiment" (I, 200) and Galt (p. 68) says "he affected a passion for her."

3. *LBC*, I, 77 and n. Byron also refers to his love for Constance Spencer Smith in the diary he kept in 1821. *LJ*, v, 173, 436.

4. See the poem of the same title, written at Athens on January 16, 1810. *P*, III, 12.

5. These were "Lines Written in an Album, at Malta"; "To Florence"; "Stanzas Composed during a Thunderstorm"; and "Stanzas Written in Passing the Ambracian Gulf."

afterward. It is likely that the quarrel which led Byron to challenge Captain Cary, General Oakes's aide-de-camp, was occasioned by his association with Mrs. Spencer Smith.[6]

Byron wrote to Lady Melbourne in 1812 that he and Mrs. Spencer Smith had been all prepared three years before to set off together for Friuli when its occupation by the French prevented them.[7] They finally had to part at Malta but only after promising to meet there again a year later. As for keeping this vow, Byron remarked that "I at the moment had certainly much greater doubts of her than myself." Time changed Byron's feelings, however, as we have noted, and it was not until the spring of 1811 that he returned to Malta.

The recent publication of selections from Mrs. Spencer Smith's letters to Byron sheds some further light on the episode and for the first time presents it from the lady's point of view.[8] Constance Spencer Smith did return to Malta in September of the next year, and apparently waited patiently for Byron until November, when she wrote to him at Athens: "You made me give you my word to keep it in mind and to remember well what you had said to me—and I did. . . . In case your thoughts are still the same as they were on the 16th of September, 1809, then set out for Malta on the very first opportunity, as I cannot stay here longer without injuring my own interests."[9] Failing of any answer, in March she wrote again offering the inducement that "Malta is rather more brilliant than it was, and you would perhaps like it."[1] But still Byron lingered.

It is interesting to consider how different a poem *Childe Harold* would have been if Byron had kept to his original plan of travel—or whether it would ever have been written at all. Most of the first canto as we have it would, of course, not exist, for the trip to Portugal and Spain was an accident. Moreover, if Byron had proceeded directly to the East as he planned to do in June, 1809, the vivid stanzas on Al-

6. The letter of challenge to Captain Cary, previously unpublished, appears in *LBC*, I, 5–6. It begins: "SIR,—The marked insolence of your behaviour to me the first time I had the honour of meeting you at table, I should have passed over from respect to the General, had I not been informed that you have since mentioned my name in a public company with comments not to be tolerated, more particularly after the circumstance to which I allude." Halleck's version of Byron's letter to Drury, May 3, 1810 (*LJ*, I, 262–9), contains an interesting passage which has never to my knowledge appeared elsewhere. The following sentence follows the second paragraph of *LJ*, I, 266: "At Malta I fell in love with a married woman, and challenged an aide-de-camp of General . . . (a rude fellow who grinned at something—I never rightly knew what)—but he explained and apologized, and the lady embarked for Cadiz, and so I escaped murder and crim. con."

7. *LBC*, I, 77.

8. George Paston and Peter Quennell, *"To Lord Byron" Feminine Profiles Based upon Unpublished Letters 1807–1824* (New York, Charles Scribner's Sons, 1939).

9. *Idem*, pp. 12–13.   1. *Idem*, p. 14.

bania would never have been written. Indeed it can be said with some truth that most of what was new in *Childe Harold* was occasioned by the accident of travel. There had been poems before on Greece but there had been few on Spain and Portugal and none on Albania.

Byron would doubtless have composed poetry wherever he went. But who can say whether he would have written of the farther East with animation and exhilaration equal to that with which he described the Iberian Peninsula and the Near East? My own inclination is to doubt it, for it seems to me that the extraordinary impact of the first cantos of *Childe Harold* was to a large extent attributable to its combination of the unknown and the known, the remote and the more immediate; intellectually as well as geographically the material of the poem was neither too distant nor too near at hand; it was neither too timely nor too far removed to be able to arouse the imagination of the poet and to engage the excited attention of its readers.

Be this as it may, chance rather than plan led Byron and Hobhouse to Albania. The opening words of Hobhouse's book make this clear:

"My friend and myself, after a stay of three weeks at Malta, and after many hesitations whether we should bend our steps toward Smyrna or some port of European Turkey, were at last determined in favour of the latter, by one of those accidents which often, in spite of preconcerted schemes, decide the conduct of travellers.—A brig of war was ordered to convoy about fifty sail of small merchantmen to Patrass, the chief port on the western side of the Morea, and to Prevesa, a town on the coast of Albania. The Governor of Malta was so obliging as to provide us with a passage in this ship to the later place, whence we resolved to commence our tour."[2]

Hobhouse's *Journey* begins with the departure from Malta; there are only occasional indirect references to the period spent in Portugal and Spain. Before embarking from Falmouth Byron had written to Drury that "Hobhouse has made woundy preparations for a book on his return; 100 pens, two gallons Japan Ink, and several vols best blank, is no bad provision for a discerning public."[3] To Hodgson he wrote gaily, "It has pleased Providence to interfere in behalf of a suffering public by giving him a sprained wrist, so that he cannot write, and there is a cessation of ink-shed."[4] Three weeks later from

2. *Journey*, I, 17.
3. I quote here from the original letter in the possession of Professor Chauncey Brewster Tinker. All editors except Henley have followed Moore in giving the phrase "several volumes *of* best blank." See *LJ*, I, 226. The words as Byron wrote them, "several vols best blank," suggest a facetiousness that is lost in most published versions of the letter. As with so many of Byron's letters, Moore has here also made arbitrary and unnoted omissions. Henley gives the fullest version, including the postscript "We have been badly fleabitten at Falmouth"!
4. *LJ*, I, 230.

Lisbon Byron omitted any detailed account of the sights of Portugal on the grounds that they were "to be heard in my friend Hobhouse's forthcoming Book of Travels."[5]

Hobhouse nowhere explains his silence with regard to the first stages of the journey. Possibly the sprained wrist prevented him during the early weeks from taking down anything beyond the brief notes that were later published in his *Recollections*. A more likely explanation lies, however, in the simple fact that there already existed innumerable travel books dealing with Portugal and Spain; the Near East, particularly Albania, was less well known and would have more appeal for the reading public. Moreover, before leaving England Hobhouse seems to have prepared himself for his undertaking by reading rather extensively in the history and background of Turkey and Greece—something which he did not do for Portugal and Spain since originally he had no intention of going there.

There are two distinct editions of Hobhouse's account of his travels. The first is the work which appeared in 1813 as *A Journey through Albania and Other Provinces of Turkey in Europe and Asia to Constantinople during the Years 1809 and 1810*. Most of the material in this edition is written in the form of letters which Hobhouse sent back to England from time to time. Byron is rarely mentioned by name but is referred to usually as "my companion." In 1855 Hobhouse, then the Right Honorable Lord Broughton, G.C.B., issued a revised edition which he entitled *Travels in Albania and Other Provinces of Turkey in 1809 and 1810*. The main reason for preparing a new edition was, he said, to correct mistakes that appeared in the original volumes. Thus in the *Travels* there is an abundance of learned footnotes; Byron is mentioned by name more frequently, the letter form is dropped, the style is formalized, and many passages of a personal nature are omitted. Where John Cam Hobhouse observed in the *Journey* that "The Turks think that the Christians stink," Lord Broughton in the *Travels* wrote "The Turks pretend they can know a Christian by the smell."[6] To the young man of twenty-three Ali Pasha was "indeed, a very great man"; to the statesman nearing seventy he was only "most remarkable."[7] Indeed what the later volumes gain in correctness they lose in immediacy and freshness. How understandable it is, but also what a shame, that in his later years Hobhouse omitted such a revealing passage as the following: "Properly speaking, the word comfort cannot be applied to any thing I ever saw out of England, which any one in my place, who was not afraid of being taken for a downright prejudiced national blockhead, would confess."[8] And much is lost, in the account of Prevesa, by the deletion of Hobhouse's admis-

5. *LJ*, I, 232.   6. *Journey*, I, 41; *Travels*, I, 27.
7. *Journey*, I, 43; *Travels*, I, 115.   8. *Journey*, I, 47.

sion that "never afterwards during our whole journey, did we feel so disheartened, and inclined to turn back, as at this instant."[9] The early *Journey* is, then, the source to which we turn for the mood as well as the matter. Moore wrote well when he drew attention to "the feeling that Lord Byron is, as it were, present through its pages, and that we there follow his first youthful footsteps into the land, with whose name he has intertwined his own for ever."[1]

On Tuesday, September 19, Byron and Hobhouse left Malta on the *Spider* which was under the command of a Captain Oliver.[2] The inspiration for Stanzas 17–20 of the second canto of *Childe Harold* must have been mainly this voyage rather than the earlier stages of the journey, for the references are to a warship, the "gallant Frigate tight," and its "convoy spread like wild swans in their flight." Also the mention of the "pennant-bearer," the guns, and "the little warlike world within" clearly suggest no mere packet like the *Townshend* but a full-dress naval convoy.[3] Hobhouse, writing of the approach to the Ionian Islands, mentions that "We had not much wind, and were obliged also to wait for the slow sailers of our convoy, so that it was not until seven o'clock in the evening that we were near enough to see Ithaca."[4] This passage would seem to refer to the same incident as Byron's lines:

> Then must the Pennant-bearer slacken sail,
> That lagging barks may make their lazy way

and the accompanying manuscript note: "An additional 'misery to human life!'—lying-to at sunset for a large convoy, till the sternmost pass ahead."[5]

The voyage to Albania was not without incident. In the vicinity of the Ionian Islands, then in the possession of the French,[6] the two English travelers had a taste of naval warfare on a small scale. Close to the Gulf of Corinth on the twenty-fourth the *Spider* captured a currant boat which was swiftly fitted out as a privateer; in this boat, armed with muskets and cutlasses and equipped with a small cannon, nine members of the crew, and Hobhouse and the ship surgeon as volunteers, cruised about among the islands for a day and a half, seizing two other small boats—and, much more exciting, capturing a Turkish brig of seventy tons which fired briskly upon them. Then

9. *Journey*, I, 26. 1. Moore, I, 203.

2. *Journey*, I, 17. Byron (*LJ*, I, 246) writes to his mother that they left on the 21st but it is safer to trust the more exact Hobhouse's explicit statement that "On Tuesday Sept. the 19th, 1809, we left Malta, and on the following Saturday, at nine o'clock in the morning, we were in the channel between Cefalonia and Zante."

3. *Childe Harold*, II, 17–20. 4. *Journey*, I, 18. 5. *P*, II, 112, n.

6. The British took possession of the islands a month later.

on the evening of the twenty-sixth as they sailed on from Patras to Prevesa the *Spider* captured a boat from Ithaca and a Turkish ship from Dulcigno; the latter Byron rummaged but found nothing save some worthless arms.[7]

On September 28, after passing Ithaca and viewing on the southern extremity the famous cliff known as "Sappho's Leap," Byron and Hobhouse reached the shores of Albania. The following day they disembarked at Prevesa, the southernmost point of the region known as Albania.[8]

At that time Albania was probably the least known and least accessible region in Europe. Over a century later it is still unfamiliar to most foreign travelers and many details of its geography remain obscure. No adequate map, no accurate description of the country existed in 1809; this prevailing ignorance doubtless prompted Hobhouse to entitle his volumes *A Journey through Albania and Other Provinces of Turkey,* despite the fact that only about a sixth of his account actually dealt with Albania.[9] A handful of Englishmen and Frenchmen had traveled over the rugged mountains of Albania in the early years of the nineteenth century but only one Englishman had penetrated north of the capital city Janina.[1] Before Byron and Hobhouse there are few records of foreigners traveling there without a specific military or diplomatic purpose.

The origins of the Albanian people are uncertain but there is strong evidence that they are descended from the Illyrians and Thracians of ancient times.[2] Unlike other primitive peoples, however, the Albanians were little affected by foreign influences and retained their independence of character and their language and customs despite the ascendancy of the Greeks, the Romans, and then the Slavs. After a period of native rule Albania first began to come under Turkish control in 1431 when Janina fell to the Ottomans. Resistance on the part of the Albanians was fierce, however, and Giorgio Castrioti,

7. *Recollections,* I, 14–15. Further details of these adventures appear in an extensive footnote to pp. 2–3 of the 1855 *Travels.* It is curious that Byron nowhere refers to these incidents and that Hobhouse did not mention them, at least in print, until 1855. Perhaps, in time of war, such informal naval maneuvers were considered "off the record."

8. *Journey,* I, 19–20. Stanzas 39–41 of the second canto of *Childe Harold* were inspired by this stage of the voyage. "Dark Sappho" and her fate engaged Byron's special attention.

9. Miss Mayne refers to the whole journey, rather misleadingly, as the "Albanian tour." *Byron,* pp. 101, 104.

1. This was Capt. (later Major) William Martin Leake (1777–1860), the British Resident, whom Byron met at Janina. When he was not carrying on diplomatic negotiations with Ali Pasha, Leake traveled widely in the Near East, adding much to existing knowledge of the topography of Albania and Greece. His *Travels in Northern Greece* (London, 1835) contain much valuable material concerning Albania.

2. *Albania:* Handbooks prepared under the direction of the Historical Section of the Foreign Office, No. 17 (London, 1920), pp. 7–8. The Albanians call themselves Skipetars; they are called Arnauts in Turkish.

known to his countrymen as Iskender Bey or Scanderbeg, became a national hero when for years from the mountain fastnesses of northern Albania[3] he led guerrilla warfare against the Turks. By 1478 the Turkish sway was complete and Albania became a part of the vast Ottoman Empire. But though many Albanians abandoned the Christian faith for Mohammedanism the authority of the sultans was never effectively established. And as through the seventeenth and eighteenth centuries the Turkish power waned and a state approaching anarchy resulted in some parts of the empire, strong men seized the opportunity to take the law into their own hands. The most remarkable of these was Ali Pasha who in the early years of the nineteenth century exercised a practically independent sovereignty in Albania.

The Albania of 1809 was a province of European Turkey; it was not, however, defined by any strict boundaries. "Albania" was, indeed, but a rough geographical term which was loosely applied to the region, comprising the ancient Epirus and Illyria, that extended from the northern confines of west Greece to Montenegro and from the Adriatic east to Macedonia and Thessaly, where rugged mountain ranges formed a natural dividing line. The northern part of this area, that part which corresponds approximately to the modern nation, was, however, considered the true Albania and it was there that the greater number of native Albanians dwelt. The southern region, from Delvinaki south to Prevesa and the Gulf of Arta, contained a large Greek population; this was the section of the Balkan Peninsula over which Ali Pasha had most recently gained control and it was considered by many of the people as a southern appendage to Albania proper rather than an intrinsic and genuine part of their country. However Janina, which in 1809 Ali made his chief city, lay within this southern district.[4]

Geographical factors have strongly affected the history of Albania. The extremely mountainous nature of the country has made it so difficult of access that it has been relatively free from foreign influences. Thus the native language and customs have persisted and through the centuries the Albanians have remained a fierce and tenacious mountain people, remote from the affairs of Europe and Asia and fierce in the defense of their mountain stronghold. Geography has long been a factor also in dividing the people of Albania into numerous sectional tribes, each controlled by a native chieftain.

3. Byron hails him in *Childe Harold* (ii, 38) as the modern Alexander:
   And he his namesake, whose oft-baffled foes
   Shrunk from his deeds of chivalrous emprise.
 4. The frontispiece map in Dr. Henry Holland's *Travels in the Ionian Isles, Albania, Thessaly, and Greece* (London, 1815) identifies only the region north of Delvinaki as Albania. Byron calls Delvinaki the "frontier village of Epirus and Albania Proper." *P*, ii, 174.

Even after its conquest of most of Albania the Turkish Government seems to have found it more expedient to keep Albania weak by encouraging rivalry among these clans than by trying to govern the region directly. When, however, the shrewd and ruthless Ali Pasha managed methodically to eliminate his rivals and gain control of most of the Peninsula the old feudal system came to an end. As Vizier of Albania Ali became a threat to the Sublime Porte and a factor to be considered in European politics.

Both the English and the French did pay notice to Ali during the period of the Napoleonic Wars and the Vizier managed cleverly to use now the one country, now the other, to serve his self-interest and to help him maintain his authority.[5] When in 1797 the French occupied the Ionian Islands off the coast of Albania and Napoleon's designs against the Ottoman Empire began to take shape, the French Emperor's representatives did everything they could to encourage the growth of Ali's independent power. At first Ali dealt favorably with the French but in 1798 he decided to support the Sultan against them and drove the French from Prevesa and Butrinto on the Albanian coast. But the consequent Turkish and Russian control of the approaches to Albania pleased Ali no better and in 1803 the imminent renewal of England's war against Napoleon prompted him to seek the support of the English against all three of those troublesome nations. The outcome was the diplomatic visit of William Hamilton, the secretary of the British Embassy at Constantinople, to Janina. During 1803 the young Earl of Aberdeen, Byron's "travelled Thane, Athenian Aberdeen,"[6] visited Ali at his capital, returning to England with 'a friendly letter from Ali to the Prime Minister. And the following year J. P. Morier was dispatched to Albania and its environs as British Resident and Consul-General, with the principal object of keeping Ali from giving aid to the French. Morier seemed to be laying the groundwork for a real understanding but when in 1806 Napoleon, through his agent at Janina, François C. H. L. Pouqueville, began to gain Ali's ear once more Morier returned to England with the feeling that he had failed.[7] However, Ali's disappointment the next year when, by the Treaty of Tilsit, the Ionian Islands were awarded to France led him to turn again to the British. A closer friendship com-

---

5. Ali's relations with England and France are treated fully in John W. Baggally's *Ali Pasha and Great Britain* (Oxford, 1938) and A. Boppe's *L'Albanie et Napoleon* (Paris, 1914).

6. Byron so described Aberdeen in *English Bards*, l. 509. He also refers to him in ll. 1027–32. George Hamilton Gordon, fourth Earl of Aberdeen (1784–1860), traveled widely in Europe and the Levant between 1802 and 1804 and was the founder of the Athenian Society. See the Honorable Sir Arthur Gordon, *The Earl of Aberdeen* (London, 1893), p. 11.

7. See Baggally, "Morier's Mission (1804–1806)," *op. cit.*, chap. ii, pp. 11–28.

menced upon the arrival of Captain William Leake as British representative in the fall of 1807. With the aim of using Ali's assistance against the French in the Ionian Islands, Leake offered naval assistance to Albania in case of attack and held out the seaport town of Parga to Ali as a bribe for his coöperation against the French. But during the next two years Ali's large demands in money and guaranties did not always meet with British approval and in September, 1809, the Vizier showed signs of growing nervous lest England leave him to face a French threat singlehanded. The British occupation of the Ionian Islands which occurred in late October encouraged him, however, and excited his hopes.[8] Thus when Byron visited the country Ali was, for the moment at least, well disposed toward the English.

> Morn dawns; and with it stern Albania's hills,
> Dark Suli's rocks, and Pindus' inland peak,
> Robed half in mist, bedewed with snowy rills,
> Arrayed in many a dun and purple streak,
> Arise; and, as the clouds along them break,
> Disclose the dwelling of the mountaineer:
> Here roams the wolf—the eagle whets his beak—
> Birds—beasts of prey—and wilder men appear,—
> And gathering storms around convulse the closing year.
>
> .   .   .   .
>
> Now he adventured on a shore unknown,
> Which all admire, but many dread to view:
> His breast was armed 'gainst fate, his wants were few;
> Peril he sought not, but ne'er shrank to meet:
> The scene was savage, but the scene was new;
> *This* made the ceaseless toil of travel sweet.[9]

On a dismal rainy morning the Englishmen first set foot on the shores of Albania at Prevesa, the chief seaport of the lower section of the country.[1] In spite of the novelty afforded by the sight of mosques and minarets betokening the romantic East, the wretchedness of the town and the savage appearance of the Turks whom they encountered there combined with the gloom of the day to render first impressions discouraging indeed. Hobhouse even admitted that "had the commander of the brig been very pressing, I believe that we should have consented to go back to Patrass."[2] Had they done so, Byron would have missed some of the most exciting and rewarding experi-

---

8. Baggally, *idem*, p. 40. The foregoing account is based chiefly on Baggally. In Sir Robert Adair's *The Negotiations for the Peace of the Dardanelles* (London, 1845), II, there are some interesting and revealing letters from Adair, the British Ambassador Extraordinary at Constantinople, to Ali Pasha and Leake. See especially II, 217–227, for letters written during the period of Byron's visit to Albania. Ali, the former robber chieftain, is addressed as "Most High, Most Powerful, And Most Illustrious Prince!"

9. *Childe Harold*, II, 42–3.   1. *Journey*, I, 25 ff.   2. *Journey*, I, 26.

ences of his life. But spirits rose as the weather improved and as Byron and Hobhouse found themselves treated in friendly manner by the brother of the absent Vice-Consul, with whom they dined, and the shaggy-looking governor of the town, who offered them the customary Turkish coffee and pipes.

Prevesa had been the scene of one of Ali Pasha's signal triumphs when in 1798 he wrested the town from the French and thus extended his control over the Peninsula. In 1809 Prevesa was a straggling town of three thousand inhabitants, about half of whom were Albanian Turks.[3] A new fortress at the bottom of the harbor and a battery at the end of the town, commanding the entrance of the port, were tangible signs of the might of Ali Pasha.

A ride of less than an hour across a plain and through olive groves took the travelers to the ruins of Nicopolis, the famous city of victory built by Octavius Caesar in honor of his victory over Antony and Cleopatra at Actium.[4] Ruins extended for nearly three miles from sea to gulf and, despite the fact that the buildings had nearly all been constructed of brick and but little of their ancient glory remained, the scene possessed something of a "melancholy grandeur," particularly by contrast with the single shepherd and his flock who were now the sole inhabitants of the once renowned and populous city. The "least dilapidated remain" was a large theater of stone from which there was a fine view of the distant Bay of Actium. Nicopolis inspired Byron to reflect in *Childe Harold:*

> Look where the second Caesar's trophies rose!
> Now, like the hands that reared them, withering:
> Imperial Anarchs, doubling human woes!
> GOD! was thy globe ordained for such to win and lose?[5]

On the following day, October 1, Byron, Hobhouse, Fletcher, and George, the Greek interpreter and factotum whom they had acquired at Patras, sailed twelve miles down the gulf to Salora, the seaport of the inland city Arta, from which they went to set forth to Janina.[6] There was much talk of Ali Pasha, of whom all spoke with great awe

---

3. The inhabitants of Albania were chiefly native Albanians, Turks, and Greeks. Hobhouse and all others who have written of Albania are confusing in their use of these terms. The mixed origin of the inhabitants of Albania has led to much overlapping of nationality, language, culture, and dress. When Hobhouse speaks simply of Albanians, he means all those, either Mohammedan or Christian, who speak the Albanian language and wear the national dress. All who follow the Mohammedan religion, whether they be native Albanians or of Turkish origin, he calls Turks. Fortunately, the term Albanian Turks, referring to those Albanians who are Mohammedans, frequently helps to clarify the picture. But the situation is further complicated by the fact that a great number of the Albanians know Greek as well as their native tongue, while relatively few, even among the Mohammedans, are acquainted with the Turkish language.

4. *Journey,* I, 32–4. See also *Recollections,* I, 15.   5. *Childe Harold,* II, 45.

6. *Journey,* I, 38–43.

as "the Vizier." It was at a barrack recently built at Salora by the Vizier and occupied by a small guard of his Albanian soldiers that the travelers were obliged to spend two nights while they awaited horses to carry them northward. This enforced delay was no misfortune, however, for it gave the Englishmen their first real insight into the way of life of the Albanians.

The captain of the guard at Salora was an unsavory looking fellow named Elmas, who was quick to offer his visitors coffee and pipes and after dinner urged them to spend the evening in his "apartment." As he observed the comings and goings of the Albanians, Byron found their manner of walking "truly theatrical" but he assumed their extraordinary strut was caused not by pride but by the cloaks which hung awkwardly from their shoulders.[7] Elmas so surpassed all others in this respect that the well-clad Englishmen could not help staring at "the magisterial and superlatively dignified air of a man with great holes in his elbows, and looking altogether, as to his garments, like what we call a bull-beggar."[8] Yet Elmas lived on terms of easy familiarity with his men and exercised a perfect control over them. As Englishmen and Albanians sat together smoking, eating grapes, and conversing with the aid of the Greek interpreter, there were congeniality and considerable curiosity on both sides.[9] The watch chains of the visitors enchanted the Albanians and Captain Elmas was so delighted with Byron's fine Manton gun that only the information that the weapon was intended as a gift for the Vizier deterred him from wanting to exchange his own for it. Indeed, by the second evening the group had become quite intimate and those who had seemed mere uncouth Albanians were now "Abdoul" and "Yatchee" and "Zourlos." When the last-named did not respond so cheerfully as the others to the exchange of familiarities, the Englishmen learned to their chagrin that they had been calling him "Blockhead!"

Songs of a monotonous, nasal sort were also sung, both in Albanian and in the modern Greek, or Romaic. One man would normally take the lead, repeating the recitative, to be joined in the chorus by the whole group, all of whom dwelt as long as breath would last on the last note. Hobhouse recorded that "One of the songs was on the taking of Prevesa, an exploit of which the Albanians are vastly proud; and there was scarcely one of them in which the name of Ali Pasha was not roared out, and dwelt upon, with peculiar energy."[1] The Albanian lay which Byron included later in *Childe Harold* was composed from just such songs as these.[2] Thus what had promised to be

7. *P*, ɪɪ, 177. 8. *Journey*, ɪ, 40–1.
9. *Journey*, ɪ, 41–3. 1. *Journey*, ɪ, 43.
2. Note especially the lines:
　　Remember the moment when Prevesa fell,
　　The shrieks of the conquered, the conqueror's yell;

a dreary stay in an uncomfortable barrack among strange and rather terrifying people proved to be both an entertaining and a highly revealing experience. Byron had "never found soldiers so tolerable" and Hobhouse observed that "Notwithstanding, however, their wild and savage appearance, we found them exceedingly mild and good-humoured."[3]

> From the dark barriers of that rugged clime,
>   Ev'n to the centre of Illyria's vales,
>   Childe Harold passed o'er many a mount sublime,
>   Through lands scarce noticed in historic tales.[4]

It was a veritable caravan that set out for Arta and points farther north the following morning. There were ten horses, four of them for Byron, Hobhouse, Fletcher, and George the Greek interpreter, a like number for their weighty baggage, and two more on which rode Albanian soldiers who acted as a guard. The baggage included no less than four large trunks, three smaller ones, a canteen, three beds, bedding, and two bedsteads—all of which were carried in large sacks swinging like panniers from each side of the heavily burdened horses.[5] Byron and Hobhouse had reason to congratulate themselves that they had brought along English saddles and bridles, for the cruder Albanian equipment would have made riding exceedingly difficult.

The journey over the marshes to Arta occupied nearly three hours; the approach to the city was picturesque and agreeable. And Arta itself, even though it had declined since Ali made Janina his capital, proved more attractive than either Prevesa, which had proved a squalid town, or Salora, which had been no town at all. Byron and Hobhouse strolled about Arta until sunset and before dinner took pleasure in treating their host, the Greek collector of duties, to "a dish of tea . . . the best travelling commodity in the world."[6]

Through a part of the hazardous mountain country between Arta and Janina, as protection against robbers, they took an additional guard of four Albanian soldiers who were armed with long guns and sabers. This was a wise and necessary thing to do, for much of Albania was infested with bandits; and the precaution seemed to be justified,

. . . .

Since the days of our Prophet the Crescent ne'er saw
A chief ever glorious like Ali Pashaw.

Shelley, describing a stormy evening on Lake Geneva in the summer of 1816, told of Byron's characteristic challenge to the elements: " 'I will sing you an Albanian song,' cried Lord Byron, 'now be sentimental and give me all your attention.' It was a strange, wild howl that he gave forth, but such as, he declared, was an exact imitation of the savage Albanian mode,—laughing, the while, at our disappointment, who had expected a wild Eastern melody." Moore, II, 24.

3. *LJ*, I, 254; *Journey*, I, 40.   4. *Childe Harold*, II, 46.
5. *Journey*, I, 36–7, 44–5.   6. *Journey*, I, 50.

farther along, by the sudden report of a gun and the appearance of a ferocious and uncouth-looking creature armed with pistols, a large knife, and a long gun. But to the amazement and relief of the travelers this stalwart fellow proved to be merely a shepherd whose flocks were feeding on the mountainside.[7] The umbrellas of the Englishmen must have been a curious sight to the hardy mountaineer.

The road was "very mountainous and romantic." To Byron this was "a country of the most picturesque beauty."[8] They had probably traveled thirty miles from Arta when they finally reached the han of St. Dimetre, a rough sort of hostel where they shared a small room for the night with four Albanian Turks and a priest. These wayfarers proved to be of some interest, since they were engaged on a mission from the Vizier to the French general at Corfu. It was not especially reassuring that night to observe that all but three of the company slept with pistols by their heads.

From the road the next noon the travelers had their first view of Janina and the lake which it borders. This was a thrilling sight, as Hobhouse's description shows:

The houses, domes, and minarets, glittering through gardens of orange and lemon trees, and from groves of cypress—the lake spreading its smooth expanse at the foot of the city—the mountains rising abruptly from the banks of the lake—all these burst at once upon us, and we wanted nothing to increase our delight, but the persuasion that we were in sight of the Acherusian lake, of Pindus, and the Elysian Fields.[9]

It was but one of the many sharp contrasts of this new land that they also saw, as they entered Janina, the arm and part of the side of a human being hanging from a tree along the road. This they later discovered to be a portion of the remains of a robber who had been beheaded a few days before.

Word of the Englishmen's approach had preceded them to Janina, with the result that a comfortable house was ready for them when they reached the city.[1] And scarcely had they arrived when a secretary of the Vizier and the Greek Primate of the city called to make them welcome. Th.. former bore the flattering news that Ali Pasha had ordered them to be provided for in Janina and had urged that, since he was engaged in a "petite guerre" farther north, they should avail themselves of the escort he supplied and travel north to see him at the town of his birth, Tepelini.[2]

7. *Journey*, 1, 53.   8. *Journey*, 1, 56; *LJ*, 1, 249.   9. *Journey*, 1, 56–7.
1. A drawing of this "modern Greek mansion," the home of Signore Nicolo Argyri, appears opposite p. 438 of the first volume of Thomas S. Hughes' *Travels in Sicily, Greece and Albania* (London, 1820).
2. *Journey*, 1, 57. Ali's army was besieging Ibrahim Pasha in the castle of Berat, farther north.

Byron and Hobhouse spent six agreeable days at Janina before proceeding northward. Though the Vizier was away they did have opportunity to visit two of his grandsons. Byron found them "totally unlike our lads," with "pink complexions like rouged dowagers, large black eyes, and features perfectly regular."[3] He paid the young Albanians the compliment of calling them "the prettiest little animals I ever saw." The dignity and bearing of the boys impressed their English visitors particularly. Hussein Bey, the ten-year-old son of Mouchtar Pasha, received them in his father's palace with perfect composure and did not allow even his natural boyish delight at Byron's handsome sword to disturb his perfect self-control. When Hobhouse attempted to touch a charm, sacred to St. Nicolo, which hung from his neck, little Hussein drew himself back, making "a curious display of Greek Christianity in a Mussulman."[4] Hussein's cousin Mahmout, two years older, was already a pasha in his own right. Byron was especially pleased with this young Albanian lord and observed to his own mother that "we are friends without understanding each other, like many other folks, though from a different cause."[5] Mahmout's knowledge was surprisingly wide; he amazed Byron by asking to which of the English Houses of Parliament he and his friend belonged.[6] And the homage which the young pasha received as he rode through the streets made as deep an impression upon his visitors as did the poise with which he accepted it.

Janina was at this time one of the leading towns of European Turkey; its importance was, of course, enhanced by the fact that it served as the chief headquarters of Ali Pasha. Although Janina served as Ali's capital it was predominantly a Greek city; Greeks far outnumbered the native Albanians and in 1809 Janina was reputed to surpass even Athens in its cultural enlightenment and wealth.[7] Not only were there an extensive and showy main street and many handsome buildings but schools flourished as well. On a triangular peninsula jutting out into the beautiful lake was the Vizier's principal residence; and Ali also maintained a sybaritic summer house in the suburbs.[8]

It soon became apparent to Byron and Hobhouse that they were visiting Janina at a very special time, for on the third day after their arrival the annual fair opened. Shops in town were closed and local

---

3. *LJ*, I, 257. I have, however, substituted the word "pink," which appears in the original letter in the Morgan Library, for "painted."

4. *Recollections*, I, 15. Also *Journey*, I, 59–60.   5. *LJ*, I, 257.

6. *P*, II, 206. Hughes met Mahmout Pasha three years later and mentioned that "This is the little fellow of whom Lord Byron speaks so favourably in his notes to Childe Harold, and certainly not more than he deserves." *Op. cit.*, I, 458–9.

7. "Joannina in Epirus is universally allowed, amongst themselves (the Greeks), to be superior in the wealth, refinement, learning, and dialect of its inhabitants." *P*, II, 189.

8. *Journey*, I, 68–72.

merchants as well as traders from distant lands set up booths on a plain to the southeast of the city. A piece of ground was also set aside for cattle, sheep, and horses, and several plots of grass were reserved for parties of dancers. This fair coincided with the beginning of the Ramazan, the Mohammedan Lent, which started with the rising of the moon on the evening of October 8. As the moon rose that evening many guns were fired and the minarets of all the mosques were illuminated. A distinctive feature of the Ramazan was the circumstance that, though strictest abstinence was observed during the day, the hours after sunset were given over to feasting and entertainment which went on far into the night.

The young British Resident, Captain Leake, proved a valuable adviser and friend at Janina. In his intercourse with his fellow countrymen far from their native land Leake could not help noticing how Byron from time to time "turned aside from the contemplation of nearer objects and from the conversation of those about him to gaze with an air distrait and dreamy upon the distant mountains."[9]

One is tempted to wonder whether the inaccessibility of the young ladies of this new region, in marked contrast to his experience elsewhere on his travels, had anything to do with Byron's mood. As an example of the care with which the young ladies of Janina were sheltered we are told that the custom of the country kept the Englishmen from having even a glimpse of the unmarried sister of their host at Janina; Byron and Hobhouse presented some Venetian silks to the young lady, who "sent word to us, that she regretted, that not being married, she could not kiss our hands in person, but begged that it might be done by proxy by our dragoman, who brought the message."[1]

Athanasius Psallida, the schoolmaster at Janina and a leading Greek scholar, was the only Greek the travelers met in Albania or later in Greece itself who had what could be called a library; and his was a very small one.[2] It was largely because of Psallida's influence, Byron later felt, that the Greek spoken at Janina was, with the exception of that spoken in the Phanar, the Greek quarter in Constantinople, the purest he heard anywhere.[3] Hobhouse recalled that "Psallida, . . . on my reading to him the first few lines of Homer, talked with much contempt of the presumption of those who, coming from a remote corner of the north, from regions absolutely unknown to their ancestors, pretend to teach, in *Greece*, the descendants of *Greeks*, how to pronounce the *Greek*, their mother tongue."[4]

9. J. H. Marsden, *A Brief Memoir of the Life and Writings of the Late Lieutenant-Colonel William Martin Leake* . . . (London, 1864), p. 31. Byron, meeting Leake in London two years later, told Hobhouse "he is grown less taciturn, better dressed, and more like an (English) man of the world than he was at Yanina." *LBC*, I, 47.

1. *Journey*, I, 409.
2. *Journey*, II, 35.
3. *P*, II, 202.
4. *Journey*, II, 15.

On the Vizier's horses, which were courteously put at their disposal, Byron and Hobhouse rode across the plain where the fair was in progress. From the surrounding country the beauty of Janina was especially striking. In the neighborhood of a village called Cherco-vista, about four hours south of Janina, they came upon some impressive ruins.[5] In a stanza added to the second canto of *Childe Harold* in 1811 Byron asked

> Oh! where, Dodona, is thine aged Grove,
> Prophetic Fount, and Oracle divine?[6]

Hobhouse also, after dismissing the conjectures of others regarding the site of the ancient Dodona and concluding that "We must be content to know what Homer has told us," proceeded to describe the "magnificent ruin of Chercovista," remarking that it would probably be futile to try to assign to it a classical name.[7] Ironically enough, that spot was determined upon in 1876 as the very site of Dodona by the excavations of M. Constantin Carapanos, a native of Arta.[8] Byron himself, in an unpublished letter written in November, 1811, mentioned the amphitheater at Chercovista as the only discovery "worthy of remark" that he and Hobhouse made in the Levant; but he went on to say that the credit really belonged to the British Resident, Captain Leake, who first investigated the site in the company of the Italian Lusieri. "With the exception of these two Gentlemen," Byron wrote, "I question whether it had been seen by previous travellers to ourselves. The amphitheatre in question is in Sr. Lusieri's opinion the largest and most perfect in the Levant or Italy, and far superior to a similar ruin at Epidaurus. No trace remains of the city to which it belonged."[9]

> He passed bleak Pindus, Acherusia's lake,
>   And left the primal city of the land,
>   And onwards did his further journey take
> To greet Albania's Chief, whose dread command
> Is lawless law; for with a bloody hand
> He sways a nation, turbulent and bold:
> Yet here and there some daring mountain-band
> Disdain his power, and from their rocky hold
> Hurl their defiance far, nor yield, unless to gold.[1]

5. *Journey*, I, 66.   6. *Childe Harold*, II, 53.
7. *Journey*, I, 65–7.   8. See *P*, II, 132, n.
9. This letter, addressed to the Reverend Dr. Valpy on November 19, 1811, is in the possession of the Library of the University of Texas. I quote it through the courtesy of Miss Fannie Ratchford, Director of the Rare Books Collections at the University of Texas. A biographical sketch of Giovanni Battista Lusieri appears on p. 94.
1. *Childe Harold*, II, 46.

On October 11 the travelers left Janina.[2] A thrilling episode during the short journey over the mountains to Zitza was the direct inspiration for one of Byron's most spontaneous short poems. When a fierce storm descended upon them a few miles from Zitza, Byron and several of the attendants, who had fallen behind the others, had lost their way in the dark and in Hobhouse's words, "after wandering up and down in total ignorance of their position, had, at last, stopped near some Turkish tomb-stones and a torrent, which they saw by the flashes of lightning." They were exposed to the elements for nine long hours and the guides, instead of assisting, "only augmented the confusion, by running away, after being threatened with death by George the dragoman, who, in an agony of rage and fear, and without giving any warning, fired off both his pistols, and drew from the English servant [Fletcher] an involuntary scream of horror; for he fancied they were beset by robbers."[3] Amid this experience Byron kept himself sufficiently calm to be able to compose a seventy-two-line poem, "Stanzas Composed during a Thunderstorm," in which the progressive excitement of the dark and stormy night was made dramatically real; less than half way through, the "stanzas" became a love poem, addressed to "Sweet Florence," the thought of whom

> . . . has still the power
> To keep my bosom warm.[4]

The "fatigues and disasters of the night" determined the pilgrims to pause for a day at Zitza to dry and refit their luggage.[5] Virtue was made of necessity, however, for the tiny hillside village delighted both Byron and Hobhouse beyond all expectations. Byron, indeed, found the situation of Zitza "the most beautiful (always excepting Cintra, in Portugal) I ever beheld";[6] and, despite his statement that "no pencil or pen can ever do justice to the scenery," he devoted five stanzas of *Childe Harold* to the village, its lofty white-walled monastery, and the glorious landscape where

> Rock, river, forest, mountain, all abound.[7]

2. *Journey*, I, 76.   3. *Journey*, I, 79–80.
4. Matthew Arnold included this poem in his selected *Poetry of Byron*, which first appeared in London in 1881.
5. *Journey*, I, 80.   6. *LJ*, I, 249.
7. *Childe Harold*, II, 48. See also *P*, II, 174. Captain J. J. Best, visiting the monastery at Zitza in 1838, noted (after paying tribute to the accuracy and beauty of Byron's description) that "The principal, an old man, who did not recollect whether he was sixty or seventy years old . . . told us he remembered Lord Byron, and inquired of us if it were true that Lord Byron had written concerning the convent." *Excursions in Albania* (London, 1842), p. 113. Ten years later Edward Lear visited at Zitza a priest who recollected well Byron's stay in 1809. *Journal of a Landscape Painter in Albania, Illyria, etc.* (London, 1851), p. 327.

From Zitza, which they left on the thirteenth of October, it turned out to be a week's journey to Tepelini. The travelers had already had occasion to realize that inadvertently they had chosen the rainy season for visiting Albania. This fact became even more apparent during the journey north from Zitza, for not only did they encounter considerable rain but they were also held up by the effects of previous storms. In some places the mountain roads were almost impassable; in several spots they had been completely washed away by the torrents of rain that swept down the mountain sides. Thus the journey was a slow and difficult one, much of it over steep, rugged country.[8] Byron was surprised to observe that the Albanians whom he encountered mending the roads were all women; indeed, "the most beautiful women I ever beheld, in stature and in features, we saw *levelling* the *road* broken down by the torrents between Delvinaki and Libochabo."[9] It was at first startling to find Albanian women engaged in heavy labor while the men were occupied with warfare and the chase but Byron concluded that even strenuous physical activity was no great hardship in such a delightful climate.[1]

Eggs, fowls, and grapes constituted the unvarying bill of fare as the Englishmen traveled on and accommodations proved less and less adequate as they proceeded north. But, far from complaining of the hardships encountered in the interior of a rugged, undeveloped country, Byron rejoiced in his ability to endure the rigors of travel cheerfully. In retrospect he later mentioned, "Now, my friend Hobhouse, when we were wayfaring men, used to complain grievously of hard beds and sharp insects, while I slept like a top, and to awaken me with his swearing at them."[2] Unlike his comrade, Byron insisted that he "could sleep where nought but a *brute* could, and certainly where *brutes did;* for often have the *cows*, turned out of their apartment, *butted* at the door all night, extremely discomposed with their unaccountable ejectment. Thus we lived—one day in the palace of the Pacha, and the next perhaps in the most miserable hut of the mountains."[3] If there is something of bravado and even egotism in Byron's rather frequent reference, often at Hobhouse's expense, to his own surpassing fortitude, this can be partially excused as the exuberance of a young man enjoying the test of his own vigor and endurance.

Byron's chief scorn was reserved for the Leporello-like servant Fletcher, whose "perpetual lamentations after beef and beer, . . .

8. *Journey*, I, 83–8.

9. *P*, II, 177. In his answer to Bowles in 1821 Byron made the point that a few women possessed all the beauty that the ideal of sculpture could require and then went on to give as an example "the head of an Albanian girl, who was actually employed in mending a road in the mountains." *LJ*, v, 549.

1. *LJ*, I, 253.   2. *LJ*, v, 115.   3. *LBC*, I, 176.

stupid, bigoted contempt for everything foreign, and insurmountable incapacity of acquiring even a few words of any language, rendered him, like all other English servants, an incumbrance."[4] But the spectacle of the conventional English servant in such un-English surroundings amused Byron as often as it annoyed him. Years later he reminded Hobhouse with delight of the incongruous figure Fletcher had cut "in Albania in 1809 during the autumnal rains in his jerkin and umbrella. As Justice Shallow says, 'Oh the merry days that we have seen!' "[5]

The wild mountain scenery in the vicinity of Delvinaki was irresistibly beautiful. Here, too, the travelers began to see native Albanians in much greater numbers than before. Now the prevailing dress was the picturesque Albanian kilt rather than the loose woolen garments of the Greeks which they had previously seen most frequently.[6] Indeed, this striking change in costume seemed to bear out the notion that the true and indigenous Albania began at Delvinaki and extended to the north. After Delvinaki they proceeded laboriously to Libohavo, a town that seemed to hang from the steep side of the mountain, and finally on by way of Cesarades and Ereneed to Tepelini, which they reached at sundown on October 19. The sight that confronted Byron as he arrived at Tepelini so appealed to his imagination that it is necessary to quote his own description:

I shall never forget the singular scene on entering Tepaleen at five in the afternoon, as the sun was going down. It brought to my mind (with some change of dress, however) Scott's description of Branksome Castle in his *Lay,* and the feudal system. The Albanians, in their dresses (the most magnificent in the world, consisting of a long *white kilt,* gold-worked cloak, crimson velvet gold-laced jacket and waistcoat, silver-mounted pistols and daggers), the Tartars with their high caps, the Turks in their vast pelisses and turbans, the soldiers and black slaves with the horses, the former stretched in groups in an immense open gallery in front of the palace, the latter placed in a kind of cloister below it, two hundred steeds ready caparisoned to move in a moment, couriers entering or passing out with the despatches, the kettle-drums beating, boys calling the hour from the minaret of the mosque, altogether, with the singular appearance of the building itself, formed a new and delightful spectacle to a stranger.[7]

Here are practically all those vivid details that formed the basis for Byron's highly colored stanzas, beginning "The Sun had sunk behind vast Tomerit," in *Childe Harold.* Especially abundant and fresh with the excitement of a new world is the poetic treatment of the scene, described above in rapid prose, in the court of the Vizier's palace:

4. *LJ,* I, 308.
6. *Journey,* I, 88.

5. *LBC,* II, 155.
7. *LJ,* I, 249–50.

Richly caparisoned, a ready row
  Of arméd horse, and many a warlike store,
  Circled the wide-extending court below;
  Above, strange groups adorned the corridore;
  And oft-times through the area's echoing door
  Some high-capped Tartar spurred his steed away:
  The Turk—the Greek—the Albanian—and the Moor,
  Here mingled in their many-hued array,
While the deep war-drum's sound announced the close of day.

The wild Albanian kirtled to his knee,
  With shawl-girt head and ornamented gun,
  And gold-embroidered garments, fair to see;
  The crimson-scarféd men of Macedon;
  The Delhi with his cap of terror on,
  And crooked glaive—the lively, supple Greek
  And swarthy Nubia's mutilated son;
  The bearded Turk that rarely deigns to speak,
Master of all around, too potent to be meek,

Are mixed conspicuous: some recline in groups,
  Scanning the motley scene that varies round;
  There some grave Moslem to devotion stoops,
  And some that smoke, and some that play, are found;
  Here the Albanian proudly treads the ground;
  Half-whispering there the Greek is heard to prate;
  Hark! from the Mosque the nightly solemn sound,
  The Muezzin's call doth shake the minaret,
"There is no god but God!—to prayer—lo! God is great!"[8]

Since word of their approach had been sent ahead from Janina
Byron and Hobhouse found accommodations awaiting them in the
Vizier's palace. Upon their arrival Ali, regretting his inability to see
them directly, sent a congratulatory message and ordered them provided with sherberts, sweetmeats, and fruits from his own harem.
Through the night they were disturbed by the perpetual noise in the
court outside, by the drum, and by the long, piercing cry of the boy
calling the hour of prayer.

The following noon one of the most exciting episodes in Byron's life
took place—his first interview with Ali Pasha, the powerful and infamous Vizier of Albania, the self-willed tyrant whom Napoleon had
twice offered to make king of Epirus. Ali was probably in his late
sixties when Byron met him. His control, gained by the methodical and
unscrupulous suppression first of rival chieftains, then of rival pashas,

8. *Childe Harold*, II, 57–9. Thomas S. Hughes, a later firsthand observer, remarked of
these stanzas, "There cannot be a more lively or faithful representation of that mixed
assemblage which appears in the court of the Albanian Pasha." *Op. cit.*, I, 444.

extended over most of the southern part of the Balkan Peninsula; it reached from northern Albania south into Greece and east into Macedonia and Thessaly. For his son Veli Pasha Ali had gained control of the Morea. And at the moment he was himself in the process of enlarging his own northern dominions.

But far from playing the role of melodramatic villain Ali received his English visitors in a mood of high good humor and comradeship. In the large, marble-paved room where they met he first paid his guests the compliment of standing as he greeted them. And then, after asking Byron why he had left his own country at so early an age, Ali pleased him greatly by praising his appearance and referring to his small ears, curling hair, and little white hands as certain signs that he was of noble birth. Byron found it singular that the Turks, who had no hereditary dignities of their own, should pay so much attention to pedigree in others. Ali also desired that his respects be sent to Byron's mother and indeed seems to have taken special interest in his handsome young guest.[9]

Byron, in turn, found the Pasha "very fat, and not tall, but with a fine face, light blue eyes, and a white beard; his manner is very kind, and at the same time he possesses that dignity which I find universal among the Turks." Both Englishmen were surprised by Ali's mildness of manner and friendliness as they took pipes, coffee, and sweetmeats with him. Byron wrote to his mother that "He has the appearance of anything but his real character, for he is a remorseless tyrant, guilty of the most horrible cruelties, very brave, and so good a general that they call him the Mohammedan Bonaparte."[1]

And in *Childe Harold* the same contrast is emphasized, in lines which foreshadow a salient feature in the characterization of several of Byron's fictitious heroes:

> Ali reclined, a man of war and woes
> Yet in his lineaments ye cannot trace,
> While Gentleness her milder radiance throws
> Along that aged venerable face,
> The deeds that lurk beneath, and stain him with disgrace.[2]

9. *Journey*, I, 101–4. Byron himself wrote (*LJ*, I, 250–1) that the Vizier "expressed himself pleased with my appearance and garb. He told me to consider him a father whilst I was in Turkey, and said he looked on me as his son. Indeed, he treated me like a child, sending me almonds and sugared sherbet, fruit and sweetmeats, twenty times a day. He begged me to visit him often, and at night, when he was at leisure."

1. *LJ*, I, 252. The artist, Charles R. Cockerell, meeting Ali several years later, noted that "he laughed with so much *bonhomie*, his manner was so mild and paternal and so charming in its air of kindness and perfect openness, that I, remembering the blood-curdling stories told of him, could hardly believe my eyes." *Travels in Southern Europe and the Levant, 1810–1817*, S. P. Cockerell, ed. (London, 1903), p. 236. For further information regarding Cockerell see below, p. 135.

2. *Childe Harold*, II, 62.

Ali's conversation gave his visitors a very favorable impression of his intelligence and abilities. On this occasion and in the course of their three further visits, they had occasion to talk with him of war and politics. Ali pointed out to his visitors, who could scarcely have failed to observe it, a mountain howitzer that was lying in his apartment and took care to apprize them of the fact that he also had several large cannon. His visitors had an example of the Vizier's constantly increasing domination over Albania when, handing them an English telescope, he bade them look at a party riding along the river toward Tepelini. "That man whom you see on the road," Ali smilingly told them through his interpreter, "is the chief minister of my enemy, Ibrahim Pasha, and he is now coming over to me, having deserted his master to take the stronger side." Englishmen who had been close to the war on the Peninsula could not keep from smiling at this Albanian war in miniature when, during a visit the next evening, Ali sent a long weapon "looking like a duck-gun" to help remedy the need for ordnance in his army besieging Berat.

It is clear that the Vizier's cordiality was in no way made the less by the fact that the British had but recently seized four of the Ionian Islands off the Albanian coast from the French; he took occasion to congratulate his visitors on this achievement. Ali seems to have been at pains to leave Byron and Hobhouse with the impression that he had always been friendly to England and hated the French and that he was confident now that the British were his neighbors that they would not treat him as the French had done.[3] Surely Byron can be pardoned for taking the shrewd Ali's remarks at their face value and writing rather naively that Ali "prefers the English interest, and abhors the French, as he himself told me."[4] Yet prominently displayed in Ali's palace was a gun presented to him by Napoleon and less than six months after he had talked with Byron he was threatening to break with England in favor of the French. The truth is that Ali Pasha pursued a course of completely politic and realistic behavior, encouraging each nation as it served his interest. For the time being the English were in ascendancy but by 1812 Ali was again delicately balanced between a French and an English alliance. Shortly after, the decline of Napoleon determined him in England's favor.

Ali was already becoming a legendary figure when Byron visited the pasha's native land. Songs celebrating his military exploits and his ruthless cruelty were familiar to the common populace of the Levant as well as to the warriors of Albania. One of these ballads was especially prevalent; in Janina, and later in Athens and elsewhere, Byron heard "many a Romaic and Arnaout ditty" telling of the fate of the fair young Phrosine who, though guiltless, was drowned along with a dozen or so other eligible young ladies in the lake at Janina when Ali Pasha discovered that his son Mouchtar's affections had strayed from his wife.[5] Byron mentions this incident in a note to *The Giaour*.[6] The episode was especially immediate and poignant to Byron and Hobhouse because their Albanian attendant Vasilly said he was one of the soldiers who had carried out the Vizier's orders on that melancholy occasion.

Ali was undoubtedly selfish and unscrupulous; though there are obviously inaccuracy and exaggeration in many accounts of his behavior it is manifest that he was a harsh man who did not hesitate to resort to treachery and murder to attain his ends. Yet it is clear, too, that he fell short of being a complete monster and that, as is not infrequently the case with dictators, he brought some benefits along with the terror that his name and actions inspired. Hobhouse is not alone in insisting that, granted Ali was a man of "ferocious and sanguinary disposition," the fact remains that on the whole the country was better for his rule: "He builds bridges, clears the country of all robbers except himself, and to some extent even polices the towns. Every other pasha would have been as despotic and as powerful; perhaps hardly any one would have mitigated his villainy by Ali's reforms." [7] And his recent biographer echoes Hobhouse's point that "It is not fair to appreciate the merits of any man without a reference to the character and customs of the people among whom he is born and educated. In Turkey the life of man is held exceedingly cheap, more so than any one, who has not been in the country, would believe. . . . You may, therefore, transfer your abhorence of Ali to the Turkish nation."[8]

5. The story appears in several different versions. Indeed, the details seem to be as different as the tellers. Hobhouse (*Journey*, I, 111–12) divides it into two distinct anecdotes. The name of the unfortunate victim is variously given as Phrosine (Byron), Zofreni (Hobhouse), and Euphrosyne (Cockerell). Henry Gally Knight, whom Byron met in Spain and Greece, in *Phrosyne, a Grecian Tale* (London, 1817), gave poetic treatment to the incident. Four years earlier, hearing the rumor that Byron was at work on a similar subject, Knight had written him: "My story is one which I dare say you heard, as I did, in Albania—the adventures of a certain Miss Phrosyne, whom Ali Pasha wish'd to get into his Haram, but her relations put her to death, to save her from infamy. The said Ali's cruelties have given rise to so many tragedies that very likely you have chosen another." *LJ*, III, 59, n.

6. *P*, III, 144–5, n.

7. *Recollections*, I, 17. Dr. Henry Holland concluded that "notwithstanding all the faults and evils of despotism, it [Ali's rule] is beneficial rather than otherwise." *Op. cit.*, pp. 194–5.

8. *Journey*, I, 110–11. William Plomer, in his *Ali the Lion* (London, Jonathan Cape, Ltd., 1936), says that "He was selfish and cruel on a gigantic scale, a thief and a liar, jealous, vindictive, miserly, and mad with ambition. His faults cannot be overlooked or explained away, but they can be to some extent accounted for, and are to some extent set off by his good qualities . . . It must be remembered that he had been brought up to be ambitious and rapacious, and that to such a man any display of good faith would seem a weakness . . . By any standards whatsoever one cannot but admire his extraordinary courage, and even in his wicked adroitness there is a curious fascination, for the

Eventually Ali overreached himself and in 1822 he came to a violent end at the hands of the supporters of the Sultan, whose power he had challenged.[9] But his fame lived on after him; Edward Lear, traveling in Albania in 1848, noted that "Even now, after the lapse of so many years, a foreigner perceives that the awful name of Ali Pasha is hardly pronounced without a feeling akin to terror."[1] And today Ali Pasha is not entirely forgotten, especially in that embattled part of the world where he had his spectacular day.[2]

The powerful personality of Ali Pasha moved Byron profoundly. The spectacle of a willful human being who could rise above his fellows always fascinated him. We have seen how he looked upon Napoleon with mingled admiration and contempt; and here was a remarkable being who, though no Augustus or Tiberius, Sulla or Timon,[3] had nevertheless the inestimable advantage of being seen and known at first hand. There was, to begin with, a great deal that was appealing in the primitive power and passions of Ali, the very enormity of his egoism and ambition. All these characteristics, especially when set in remote, highly dramatic surroundings, were deeply impressive.

But the vivid contrasts in his character made the spell of Ali most irresistible to Byron's imagination. Here was a cruel tyrant whose manner was mild and charming, a luxury-loving sensualist who in a moment could leave his exotic surroundings for the rigors of mountain warfare. Here, too, was a strong man who was bound by none of the restraints of the society Byron knew; who, when he acted, acted directly and ruthlessly; who lived fully and extremely and with all the senses. It is no wonder that even four years after he left Albania Byron

sardonic smile that lurked in his beard was not the smile of a fool. Let us admit that he admired talent, that he was not intolerant of religious differences, and that he understood the value of education . . . And there is no denying the fact that Jannina, in Ali's time, became the most civilized town in Greece, superior even to Athens" (pp. 82–3).

9. After resisting for two years, the aged ruler was finally forced to sue for terms and was stabbed in the back as he left the tent of his conqueror at Janina.

1. *Op. cit.*, pp. 270–1.

2. Ali Pasha is treated in detail not only by several travelers but he is also the subject of numerous biographies. An anonymous life in English appeared in 1823, the year after his death, and another by R. A. Davenport was published in 1837. Then there was a gap of almost a century until the appearance of Plomer's very readable *Ali the Lion.* Stefan Cristowe's *The Lion of Janina* (New York, Modern Age Books, 1941) is a less substantial work. Ali also appears in imaginative literature as the main character in John Howard Payne's melodramatic play, *Ali Pacha; or, the Signet-Ring* (London, 1823), and Mór Jókai's novel, *The Lion of Janina* (1898). There is a long and highly romantic account of his death in Dumas' *Count of Monte Cristo*, narrated by the Vizier's Dumas-invented and Byron-inspired daughter Haydée. Finally, mention should be made of an undated pamphlet, probably appearing shortly after Ali's death, entitled "The Atrocious Life of the Despot Ali Pacha Vizier of Epirus; Detailing the Most Horrid Instances of Cruelty, Murder and Oppression, Without Parallel in the Annals of the World."

3. See *LJ*, v, 189, 404–6, for some of Byron's reflections on the great men of history.

wrote to Moore with excitement that "Yesterday I had a letter from *Ali Pacha!*"[4]

Except for the portrait in *Childe Harold,* Byron never pictured Ali Pasha directly in his poetry. Ali was, however, undoubtedly the model from which Byron drew several of the most remarkable attributes of his poetic characters. The conception of the cruel and treacherous Pasha Giaffir in *The Bride of Abydos* owes much to Ali and Byron observed that in real life Ali had removed a rival from his path in exactly the manner attributed to Giaffir in Canto I of *The Bride* and afterward had married his daughter.[5] Byron heard about the fate of Ali's unfortunate rival while he was in Albania. It is interesting that the name of Ali's victim was Giaffir; in his poem Byron borrowed the name of the victim and attached it to his pasha. Byron's portrait of Giaffir Pasha merits quotation:

> Begirt with many a gallant slave,
> Appareled as becomes the brave,
> Awaiting each his Lord's behest
> To guide his steps, or guard his rest,
> Old Giaffir sate in his Divan:
>   Deep thought was in his agéd eye;
> And though the face of Mussulman
>   Not oft betrays to standers by
> The mind within, well skilled to hide
> All but unconquerable pride,
> His pensive cheek and pondering brow
> Did more than he was wont avow.[6]

Conrad, in *The Corsair,* has more of Byron in his make-up than he has of Ali Pasha. Yet there is some reminiscence of Ali in the empha-

4. *LJ,* II, 262–3. The letter, beginning "Excellentissime *nec non* Carissime," was brought back from Albania by Dr. Henry Holland. It ends characteristically "about a gun he wants made for him." Byron mentions a new atrocity committed by Ali since 1809: the murder of a large part of the inhabitants of a town where his mother and sisters had been maltreated forty-two years before! Byron did send a "splendid pistol" to Ali by George Ticknor in 1815 but Ticknor never reached Albania to deliver the gift. The American traveler suggested the enduring impression Ali Pasha and his empire made upon Byron when he recorded that Byron gave him "more information on this subject than all I have before gathered from all the sources I have been able to reach, and did it, too, with so much spirit, that it came to me as an intellectual entertainment as well as a valuable mass of instruction." *Life, Letters, and Journals of George Ticknor,* I, 179.

5. *P,* III, 189, n.

6. *The Bride of Abydos,* I, 20–31. Harold S. L. Wiener, "The Eastern Background of Byron's Turkish Tales" (Ph.D. dissertation, Yale University, 1938), p. 182, is of the opinion that Ali "is unmistakably the original of Giaffir, the villain of the piece. Aged and outwardly dignified in bearing, he was at heart cruel and scheming. He had fought against Paswan at Widdin and poisoned a rival at Sophia. He married off his children to powerful landholders in order to strengthen his own position. Giaffir's career matches this in every respect; and finally, it seems more than accidental that Giaffir should bear the same name as Ali's victim."

sis upon the very terror inspired by Conrad's name and the contrast
between his exterior calmness and the "feelings fearful" within:

> But who that CHIEF? his name on every shore
> Is famed and feared—they ask and know no more.
>
> .   .   .   .
>
>   What is that spell, that thus his lawless train
> Confess and envy—yet oppose in vain?
> What should it be, that thus their faith can bind?
> The power of Thought—the magic of the Mind.
>
> And oft perforce his rising lip reveals
> The haughtier thought it curbs, but scarce conceals.
>   Though smooth his voice, and calm his general mien,
> Still seems there something he would not have seen.[7]

It has been suggested that the exploits of Lambro Katzones and
other Greek pirates about whom Byron heard during his stay in the
East may have suggested some of the material for *The Corsair*.[8] In
Don Juan the corsair-chief is actually named Lambro. This can hardly
be accidental. Yet Galt states categorically that Ali Pasha is the original of Byron's Lambro, basing his remark solely upon the Vizier's
compliment to Byron on the smallness of his hands and the reference
in *Don Juan* to the delicacy of the hands of Lambro and his daughter
Haidee.[9] The truth probably is that Byron's Lambro has some of the
qualities of both Lambro Katzones and of Ali Pasha but that also a
good deal of Byron's own creative instinct and sense of humor have
gone into the portrait of his Lambro, the "sea attorney." The following are some of the passages in the characterization of Lambro that
are most reminiscent of Ali Pasha:

> He was the mildest manner'd man
> That ever scuttled ship or cut a throat;
> With such true breeding of a gentleman,
> You never could divine his real thought.[1]
>
> .   .   .   .
>
> High and inscrutable the old man stood,
> Calm in his voice, and calm within his eye—
> Not always signs with him of calmest mood:
> He looked upon her, but gave no reply.[2]
>
> .   .   .   .
>
> He was a man of a strange temperament,
> Of mild demeanour though of savage mood.[3]

7. *The Corsair*, ll. 61–2, 179–82, 205–08.   8. *P*, III, 219.   9. *P*, VI, 195, n.
1. *Don Juan*, III, 41.   2. *Idem*, IV, 39.   3. *Idem*, III, 53.

Finally, there is a hint of one side of Ali's nature in Byron's characterization of Sardanapalus, the luxurious but courageous Assyrian monarch who all too late shook off his sloth and pleasures. The resemblance here in Byron's play is only superficial, however, for the essential nature of Sardanapalus is closer to a Richard II or even in some respects a Hamlet than it is to so galvanic a human being as Ali.

After three days in Tepelini the travelers began the return trip to Janina and Prevesa on October 22. The Vizier had provided them with orders to his several military posts for guards and transportation[4] and also with a letter to his son Veli, the pasha of the Morea; Ali also allowed them to take Vasilly, their Albanian attendant, on into Greece and Turkey. Since the weather had improved, the journey back to Janina took but four days; en route they stayed overnight in the towering monastery at Zitza and reached Janina on the twenty-sixth. There they lingered a week, sailing on the lake, strolling about the town, riding in the country, and visiting some of the acquaintances they had made three weeks before. A Greek marriage procession and a puppet show attracted some interest. From Janina Byron sent back his rifle as a present for Ali Pasha.

Byron, ever attracted by the colorful and bizarre, had by now acquired some "magnifique" Albanian costumes which, he enjoyed pointing out, contained so much gold that in England they would have cost four times the fifty guineas he paid for them.[5] In describing the dress of the Albanians Hobhouse noted a line from Spenser, "of which my friend put me in mind," referring to a "huge capoto Albanese-wise."[6] This would seem to suggest not only that Spenser was in Byron's mind while he was in Albania but also that he must have known the Faerie Queene well to have remembered, even inaccurately, such a single isolated passage.[7] In another place Hobhouse records at about the same time that "Byron is all this time engaged in writing a long poem in the Spenserian stanza."[8] From his own testi-

---

4. In the Appendix to the first volume of his Journey Hobhouse gives, in Albanian and then in English, the contents of Ali Pasha's directive on behalf of Byron and himself to "My beloved Jacob Bey Ali and whichever of my Bolu-bashees is to be found at Vrachore" (pp. 487–8).

5. LJ, I, 256.   6. Journey, I, 121.

7. The correct lines, from Bk. III, canto XII, stanza 10, read:

> Next after him went Doubt, who was yclad
> In a discolour'd cote, of straunge disguyse,
> That at his backe a brode Capuccio had,
> And sleeves dependaunt Albanese-wyse.

The Faerie Queene, "The Works of Edmund Spenser" (Variorum ed., Baltimore, Johns Hopkins Press), Bk. III, 1934, p. 170. The extent of Byron's inaccuracy suggests that he was speaking from memory and probably did not have the Faerie Queene with him in Albania.

8. Recollections, I, 19.

mony, it was on the fifth day at Janina, October 31, that Byron began to write *Childe Harold*.[9] The Albanian mountains, as he said, took him "back to Morven"[1] and it was not to the scenes about him but to his own earlier youth that his thoughts now turned as he began his poem:

Whilome in Albion's isle there dwelt a youth.[2]

As he traveled on to Arta and Prevesa, and then to Delphi and Athens, we must imagine Byron's mind to have been occupied not only with new sights and experiences but also with himself, his youth in England, the crossing to Portugal, and his impressions of Portugal and Spain.[3]

The journey to Prevesa offered nothing that was especially new. Byron's and Hobhouse's accounts of the sail from Salora to Prevesa are, however, an agreeable reminder of the intimacy with which the two travelers shared experiences and observations. Byron wrote to his mother that "Today I saw the remains of the town of Actium, near which Antony lost the world, in a small bay, where two frigates could hardly manoeuvre," while Hobhouse recorded in his journal that "We sailed down the Gulf in which was fought the battle of Actium—not big enough for the manoeuvres of two of our modern frigates!"[4]

Since the province of Acarnania, lying south of the Gulf of Arta, was reputedly infested with robbers, two days later the travelers took advantage of Ali Pasha's generosity and set forth for Patras by sea, on board an armed galiot manned by forty men.[5] Scarcely were they out of the harbor when a storm drove them off their course northward; soon the nautical ineptitude of the Turkish crew almost led to disaster. Byron gives a vivid description of the near-shipwreck that followed:

Fletcher yelled after his wife, the Greeks called on all the saints, the Mussulmans on Alla; the captain burst into tears and ran below deck, telling us to call on God; the sails were split, the main-yard shivered . . . and all our chance was to make Corfu, which is in possession of the French, or (as Fletcher pathetically termed it) 'a watery grave.' I did what I could to console Fletcher, but finding him incorrigible, wrapped myself up in

9. The original manuscript is so dated. See *P*, ii, xvi.

1. *P*, ii, 174. "The Arnaouts, or Albanese, struck me forcibly by their resemblance to the Highlanders of Scotland in dress, figure, and manner of living: Their very mountains seemed Caledonian, with a kinder climate. The kilt, though white; the spare, active form, their dialect, Celtic in its sound; and their hardy habits, all carried me back to Morven."

2. In the published text, this verse begins the second stanza, since Byron added the invocation to the Muse after his return to England in 1811. Despite the immediacy of many passages, Byron's indications imply that none of the Albanian stanzas were written on the spot but rather in Athens during the winter.

3. Most of the first canto of *Childe Harold* had been written by the time Byron reached Athens on Christmas Day.

4. *LJ*, i, 251–2; *Recollections*, i, 20. 5. *Journey*, i, 162–3.

my Albanian capote (an immense cloak), and lay down on deck to wait the worst. I have learnt to philosophize in my travels; and if I had not, complaint was useless.[6]

Fortunately the wind finally abated and by substituting two small staysails it was eventually possible to steer across to the mainland of Albania, many miles north of Prevesa. After a harrowing afternoon and night at sea the voyagers managed to land there the following morning at Phanari, near Parga, and thence they proceeded to a village called Volondorako for the night.[7] The hospitality of the native Suliotes, who might well have been expected to be hostile to Turks and foreigners,[8] made a strong impression on Byron; after leading the survivors to safety, feeding them and lodging them, the Suliotes also sent several of their number along with them to Prevesa as guides. And the chief of the village refused compensation from Byron with the disarming words, "I wish you to love me, not to pay me."[9] It is indicative of Byron's admiration of the Albanians that he devoted three stanzas of *Childe Harold* to a direct and almost literal account of this episode and in those stanzas he laid emphasis not upon his own exciting adventure but upon the admirable generosity and good will of the Albanians.[1]

A two-day ride on horseback brought them once more to Prevesa on November 12. There, on that very day, Byron not only wrote to his mother one of the longest and most exhilarating letters he ever penned, dealing with his exciting weeks in Albania, but he also wrote to his lawyer Hanson requesting information about his financial affairs, declaring that he now intended to proceed to Athens "to study the modern Greek" and expected to spend a year in Greece before entering Asia. In addition he insisted with great emphasis that "I never will revisit England if I can avoid it; it is possible I may be obliged to do so lest it should be said I left it to avoid the consequences of my Satire, but I will soon satisfy any doubts on that head, if necessary, and quit it again, for it is no country for me."[2]

Deciding now to proceed by land across the province of Acarnania in spite of the threat of robbers, the travelers provided themselves the next day, by the governor's assistance, with thirty-seven Albanian soldiers and sailed safely across the Gulf of Arta, or Ambracian Gulf, to Vonitza, on the northern shore of Acarnania.[3] As they sailed on the next day to Utraikee, farther east on the gulf, over waters where

---

6. *LJ*, I, 253–4.   7. *Journey*, I, 163–5. Also *Recollections*, I, 20.
8. The inhabitants of the district called Sulli, who were Greek Christians but "have a much greater resemblance to the Albanian warrior than the Greek merchant," were finally conquered by Ali Pasha after thirteen years of intermittent warfare. *Journey*, I, 151.
9. *LJ*, I, 255.   1. *Childe Harold*, II, 67–9.   2. *LJ*, VI, 445–6.
3. *Journey*, I, 166 ff.

. . . for Egypt's queen,
The ancient world was won and lost,

Byron's thoughts returned again to his own fair "Florence." The "Stanzas Written in Passing the Ambracian Gulf" close with the impassioned vow that

I cannot *lose* a *world* for thee,
But would not lose *thee* for a *World*.

At Utraikee a band of robbers had appeared only five days before Byron arrived there, and had murdered a Greek and a Turk. It was at this disquieting place that the travelers spent their first night on Greek soil. Sitting in the open air before a great fire in the evening, they watched and listened with wonder to their Albanian guard as

. . . bounding hand in hand, man
linked to man,
Yelling their uncouth dirge, long daunced the kirtled
clan.[4]

The Englishmen admired also

. . . as the flames along their faces gleamed,
Their gestures nimble, dark eyes flashing free,
The long wild locks that to their girdles streamed.[5]

Hobhouse mentions that almost all the songs celebrated robbing exploits and that it did not diminish his and Byron's pleasure to know that all of this group had been robbers themselves, some until very recently. Byron describes this Albanian ritual vividly in poetry; Hobhouse's prose description is also worth repeating:

. . . the greater part of them assembled round the largest of the fires, and . . . danced round the blaze of their own songs . . . with astonishing energy . . . One of them, which detained them more than an hour, began thus—"When we set out from Parga, there were sixty of us:" then came the burden of the verse,

"Robbers all at Parga!
Robbers all at Parga!"

. . . and, as they roared out this stave, they whirled round the fire, dropped, and rebounded from their knees, and again whirled round, as the chorus was again repeated. The rippling of the waves upon the pebbly margin where we were seated, filled up the pauses of the song with a milder, and not more monotonous music. The night was very dark, but by the flashes of the fires we caught a glimpse of the woods, the rocks, and the lake, which, together with the wild appearance of the dancers, presented

4. *Childe Harold*, II, 71.   5. *Idem*, II, 72.

us with a scene that would have made a fine picture in the hands of such an artist as the author of the Mysteries of Udolpho.[6]

Hobhouse could hardly have realized as he wrote that the scene was soon to make a fine picture in the hands of the author of *English Bards and Scotch Reviewers!*

The song Byron gives in *Childe Harold* is not a robbers' song but a more national song which he composed from several different versions he heard.[7] This animated Albanian war song is a dramatic example of the rich and abundant poetic material and coloring which Byron was beginning to find everywhere about him in the East. His poetry was never to be quite the same again. Here is a new and authentic accent; Byron would never need to turn again to Ossian or to manufacture Oscars of Alva. In time, to be sure, this new Oriental manner came all *too* easily. But its first notes are fresh and exciting.

It had been something more than a thrilling adventure—this trip of a young man of twenty-one "very high up into Albania, the wildest province in Europe, where few Englishmen have ever been."[8] It had also been a very revealing experience. Byron found that those who had at first seemed uncouth savages were, despite their ferocious habits, essentially goodhearted human beings. These mountain people lived according to their own mores, brutal though those mores often were. They preferred open force to fraud, robbed but did not steal, had "several vices but no meannesses." Vasilly, the servant assigned to him by Ali Pasha, he found "brave, rigidly honest, and faithful."[9] Indeed, the rugged, warlike impulsive Albanians, attired in their pic-

6. *Journey*, I, 170. There is also a brief account in *Recollections*, I, 21.

7. In his article, "Byron und die Albanologie," *Seminar za arbanasku filologi ju Arkiv za arbanasku starinu*, III, Pts. I–II (Belgrade, 1926), 176–204, Karl Treimer notes the influence of Albanian folk poetry, with its habitual end rhyme, upon Byron's war song. See also (*P*, II, 183–4) the Albanian choral love songs, with English translations, which were copied for Byron by a native of Athens familiar with the Albanian language. Treimer points out, apropos of these poems, that, despite the fact that Byron knew little Albanian himself, he was one of the first Europeans to present an Albanian text and in so doing was a stimulating force toward the greatly increased interest in Albanian philology during the nineteenth century, exemplified in the work of such scholars as Xylander, Hahn, and Gustav Meyer. Treimer gives (p. 185) his own corrected version of Byron's faulty phonetical text of the Albanian choral songs. Gustav Meyer, in his discussion of these songs ("Die Albanischen Tanzlieder in Byrons Childe Harold," *Anglia*, XV [1893], 1–8) points out that they belong to a popular type of small two-lined improvisations. Noting several previous attempts at restoration, Meyer gives in seventeen consecutive couplets his version of the text of the songs, differing in several details from Treimer's. Albanian was almost completely an unwritten language when Byron and Hobhouse visited the country; the absence of material on the subject led Hobhouse to include fragments from the Albanian and a study of its grammar in the Appendix to his *Journey* (I, 466–84). A more important early contribution to study of the Albanian language appeared in William M. Leake's *Researches in Greece* (London, 1814); chap. ii, pp. 237–362, is devoted entirely to Albanian; other chapters deal with modern Greek, Wallachian, and Bulgarian.

8. *LJ*, VI, 451.   9. *LJ*, I, 252.

turesque native costume, many of them strikingly handsome, ever armed, came to stand in Byron's mind as an antithesis to the hypocrisy he all too frequently detected among his more "civilized" fellow Englishmen. The extremes and the striking contrasts in their natures, their restlessness, their furious likes and dislikes—these inevitably appealed to a temperament that was in some degree akin. It did not displease Byron that these people had no undue reverence for an established church, that many were not Christians yet showed themselves good men, nor that the Albanians subordinated their women to a level of inferiority.[1]

In directness of impression Albania affected Byron more than any country he ever visited. He was captivated by the wild natural beauty of the mountain country, where dangers lurked and where there were "places without a name, and rivers not laid down in maps."[2] And it is not purely accidental that in this inspiriting country he began to write *Childe Harold*.

1. Hobhouse (*Journey*, I, 120–40) notes these characteristics of the Albanians. Apropos of the debasement of Albanian women, Hobhouse implies darkly (*Journey*, I, 130) but does not say outright that homosexuality was widespread among the Albanians. Rejected verses in *Childe Harold* bear this out (*P*, II, 138, 147). Moreover, Gen. Guillaume de Vaudoncourt, in his *Memoirs of the Ionian Islands . . . , including the Life and Character of Ali Pacha, the Present Ruler of Greece* (London, 1816), remarks of Ali Pasha that "he is almost exclusively given up to Socratic pleasures, and for this purpose keeps up a seraglio of youths, from among whom he selects his confidants, and even his principal officers" (p. 278).

2. *LJ*, I, 264–5. J. Hoopes, in a review of K. Treimer's *Byron und die Albanologie* (*Englische Studien*, LXI [1926–27], 297) observes that "Aber stärker noch als Griechenland hat den Dichter auf seiner levantinischen Reise das wildromantische, weltentlegene Albanien beeindruckt."

III

Greece, Asia Minor, Constantinople

THE journey south to Missolonghi through the thick forests and desolate plains of Acarnania occupied six days.[1] Although its population was almost entirely Greek, this district of northern Greece was under Ali Pasha's jurisdiction; Albanian soldiers were quartered in the towns to assert the Vizier's control and also to protect the people against the bands of robbers which frequented the region. The travelers were thankful for the Albanian guard accompanying them. Fortunately they met with none of the feared marauders but as they passed through the forest the Albanian soldiers pointed out three newly made graves with the words, "Sir, the robbers!"[2]

On November 20 Byron and Hobhouse and their formidable entourage arrived at "a town called Messalonge"[3] on the northern side of the gulf of Patras. Missolonghi was a town of some five thousand inhabitants, most of whom were dependent upon fishing for their livelihood. There the English travelers dispensed with their military escort, keeping only one of the Albanian soldiers as a companion for Vasilly, the attendant assigned to them at Tepelini by Ali Pasha. In the ceremonies of farewell as the Albanian soldiers took leave of their comrade Dervish the Englishmen witnessed another example of the gentler feelings that existed beneath the outer ferocity of the Albanians: "At parting with him, all his companions embraced him, and accompanying him to our boat, fired off their guns as a last salute to the whole party."[4]

After three days at Missolonghi the company, now reduced to six members, made the crossing in a small vessel to Patras, on the north shore of the Peloponnesus.[5] Byron and Hobhouse had first set foot on Greek soil at Patras almost two months earlier, en route to Prevesa; on that occasion, however, they had had time only for a short walk in some currant grounds to the north of the town.[6] Now there was opportunity for a more extensive acquaintance with this important seaport.

Patras was the most flourishing town in southern Greece in 1809. Moreover, its beautiful situation on the mountain slope rendered it "one blooming garden of orange and lemon plantations, of olive-

---

1. *Journey*, I, 170–7. 2. *Journey*, I, 173. 3. *Journey*, I, 177.
4. *Journey*, I, 180. 5. *Journey*, I, 180–1. 6. *Journey*, I, 19.

groves, vineyards, and currant-grounds."[7] Yet Patras was not a desirable place to live in, for it was frequently visited by fevers and pestilence. Hobhouse noted that the old Turkish fortress above the town was "perfectly useless, and is, so said the Greeks, put in a state of defence, by being white-washed at the beginning of every war."[8] When, however, the Greek revolution broke out at Patras in 1821, the Turks, confined to the citadel, managed to hold out for seven years.

Byron and Hobhouse had determined earlier to pause at Patras for reoutfitting and repairs. And Hobhouse hinted at another very understandable reason for their lingering as long as a week and a half, following the arduous journey to Tepelini and back again, when he mentioned that "After a long disuse of chairs and tables, we were much pleased by those novelties."[9] Samuel Strané, the Greek-born English Consul, and Mr. Paul, the Imperial Consul, entertained the visitors handsomely during their stay at Patras. There was the opportunity, also, for several rides into the neighboring countryside.

Refurbished and somewhat rested, the travelers left Patras to proceed toward Athens on the fourth of December.[1] A multilingual Greek, Andreas by name, accompanied them in place of George, whose crafty behavior during the Albanian journey led Hobhouse to reflect that, "When we had him we thought it would be impossible to do without him; when he was gone, we wondered how we had ever done with him."[2] A leisurely two-day journey eastward over bad roads brought them to Vostizza, on a tongue of land extending into the gulf. Much of the route had been close to the shore; they had a glimpse of Lepanto and there was impressive mountain scenery on the other side of the Gulf of Corinth. Parnassus, capped with snow, loomed far above the other peaks in the distance.[3]

Vostizza, a town of several thousand inhabitants, and its district were governed by a Greek "codja-bashee" or elder. Here it was a singular sight for the travelers to see, for the first time, a native Greek in power in a country under Turkish domination. And this "elder," surrounded by countless visitants, clerks, and claimants, was doubly remarkable in that he proved to be less than twenty years of age. Andreas Londos was the son of Veli Pasha's chief minister, and at his house Byron and Hobhouse stayed during the nine days they spent at Vostizza. The young codja-bashee's residence was one of the finest in the Morea; during their sojourn there the travelers became sincerely attached to their host, who was quick to put aside his official gravity and reveal himself as both lively and good-humored—in Hobhouse's words, "a merry playful boy." Such was Londos' enthusiasm, indeed, that he was easily prevailed upon to "throw off his robes and

7. *Journey*, I, 183.   8. *Ibid.*   9. *Journey*, I, 182–3.
1. *Journey*, I, 189.   2. *Journey*, I, 36.   3. *Journey*, I, 192.

cap, tuck up his sleeves, and attempt several feats of agility, such as jumping over chairs, tumbling, and sparring."[4]

This young Greek was well educated and read Herodotus in the original ancient Greek.[5] He was also, in spite of the fact that he held high position in the Turkish Government, an ardent Greek patriot. Londos told the Englishmen with enthusiasm of the efforts of the poet and nationalist, Rhigas, to organize a revolution of the Greeks twenty years before.[6] One evening, upon hearing the name of Rhigas as he was playing chess with Hobhouse, Londos "jumped suddenly from the sofa, threw over the board, and clasping his hands, repeated the name of the patriot with a thousand passionate exclamations, the tears streaming down his cheeks."[7] The famous Greek war song of Rhigas, which Londos recited with great passion, so impressed Byron that when later he had learned something of the Romaic he translated the poem into an English version, beginning:

> Sons of the Greeks, arise!
> The glorious hour's gone forth . . .[8]

Andreas Londos was to be one of the first to take a leading part in the Greek War of Independence.[9] At Missolonghi in January, 1824, three months before his death, Byron was pleased to receive a letter from Londos.[1] In reply he wrote:

Greece has ever been for me, as it must be for all men of any feeling or education, the promised land of valour, of the arts, and of liberty; nor did the time I passed in my youth in travelling among her ruins at all chill my affection for the birthplace of heroes. In addition to this, I am bound to yourself by ties of friendship and gratitude for the hospitality which I experienced from you during my stay in that country, of which you are now become one of the first defenders and ornaments. To see myself serving, by your side and under your eyes, in the cause of Greece, will be to me one of the happiest events of my life.

From Vostizza Londos took his English guests on several sporting expeditions into the country.[2] A touching passage in Byron's 1814

4. *Journey*, I, 193.   5. *Recollections*, I, 22.

6. Constantine Rhigas (1760–98) was the founder of the Hetaireia, a society whose purpose it was to organize Greek nationalistic sentiment and to provide the Greeks with the money and arms necessary for rising against the Turks. Rhigas was killed by the Turks in 1798 but after his death his patriotic songs, written in the modern Greek, were an important factor in eventually arousing Greece to rebellion.

7. *Journey*, II, 46.

8. Byron's poem is entitled "Translation of the Famous Greek War Song." For Hobhouse's translation of the same work see *Journey*, II, 47.

9. George Finlay, *History of the Greek Revolution* (London, 1861), II, 35.

1. *LJ*, VI, 320–1. The letter first appeared, in Byron's original Greek, in Count Gamba's *Narrative of Lord Byron's Last Journey to Greece*, p. 147. Prothero prints the English version above from Moore, II, 729.

2. *Journey*, I, 195.

Journal is a reminiscence of one of these excursions: "The last bird I ever fired at was an *eaglet*, on the shore of the Gulf of Lepanto, near Vostitza. It was only wounded, and I tried to save it, the eye was so bright; but it pined, and died in a few days; and I never did since, and never will, attempt the death of another bird."[3]

It was the desire to see Delphi that determined the travelers to cross the Gulf of Corinth rather than proceed by land along the northern shore of the Morea and cross the isthmus to Athens. On December 14, therefore, when favorable winds permitted, they were transported in a large ten-oared rowboat across the gulf to the port of Salona where—sharp contrast to their experience of comfort at Vostizza—they spent the night in a room that was already nearly filled with onions! The following day they rode to the small town of Chrisso, located at the very roots of Parnassus.[4]

Through these early weeks in Greece Byron was, of course, proceeding with his "long poem in the Spenserian stanza." On this particular day, as he completed his tribute to the Maid of Zaragoza and challenged Greece to match the "dark-glancing daughters" of Spain, Mount Parnassus itself rose majestically before him, no longer in the remote distance but now near at hand. The emotion aroused in Byron by the immediate sight of the classic mount caused him suddenly to interrupt his remarks on Spain and in defiance of order and poetic illusion humbly to pay his homage:

> Oh, thou Parnassus! whom I now survey,
> Not in the phrensy of a dreamer's eye,
> Not in the fabled landscape of a lay,
> But soaring snow-clad through thy native sky,
> In the wild pomp of mountain-majesty![5]

Despite the small size of Chrisso the village boasted a bishop. That gentleman was kind enough to "lend" the travelers a copy of Meletius' *Geography*[6] which, however, Byron still had in his possession when he returned to England in 1811.[7] The bishop obviously had need of his geography book, too, for he shocked Hobhouse by asking him if Spain, where the English were fighting, was in the Baltic.[8]

The following day, riding from Chrisso up to Castri on the site of Delphi, Byron saw a flight of eagles in the air. The number of birds rather than the species excited his attention[9] and, since he had written

3. *LJ*, II, 404.   4. *Journey*, I, 202–5.   5. *Childe Harold*, I, 60.
6. Meletius of Janina (1661–1714) published in Venice in 1728 his *Ancient and Modern Geography*. See *P*, II, 198, n.
7. *LBC*, I, 41. Byron mentions "Meletius' Geography (we stole it from the Bishop of Chrysso)."   8. *Journey*, II, 42, n.
9. There is conflicting evidence with regard to the exact number. In 1814 Byron wrote in his Journal (*LJ*, II, 404) that there were six. Seven years later, however, the six had increased to twelve! *LJ*, V, 450.

his lines to Parnassus the day before, he "seized the Omen" and "had a hope that Apollo had accepted my homage."[1]

As they climbed the steep, craggy path up the mountainside from Chrisso, in several places the travelers noticed the remains of sepulchers hewn in large rocks along the way.[2] Their guide's remark that one of these was the sarcophagus of a king who broke his neck hunting led Byron to observe that "His majesty had certainly chosen the fittest spot for such an achievement."[3]

Delphi was a rather disappointing sight in 1809. One must remember, however, that the excavations which laid bare the extensive ruins of the ancient shrine were not undertaken until late in the nineteenth century.[4] Thus Byron and Hobhouse merely saw, scattered about here and there in a small, dirty town, occasional masses of stones, pillars, and sections of walls. They could make out rows of seats belonging to the ancient Pythian stadium but otherwise there was little to suggest the ancient glory of Delphi except the dramatic situation on the steep side of Mount Parnassus and, trickling from a deep gorge in the mountainside, the waters of the famous Castalian spring. A cave of immense depth was pointed out as the seat of the Delphic oracle but its authenticity seemed doubtful. The magnificent theater, the foundations of the Temple of Apollo, the handsome little Treasury of the Athenians—such rewarding sights as these could exist only in the mind's eye in 1809 and Byron could not realize how far he was from the truth when he said he "saw all that Delphi retains."[5]

There were several ancient inscriptions; but almost as interesting to Englishmen who had not seen a fellow countryman in many weeks were two marble pillars bearing the names "H. P. Hope, 1799" and "Aberdeen, 1803." To these Byron and Hobhouse added their own names.[6] Byron records that they drank of half a dozen streamlets before discovering the "true Castalian" and even that had "a villainous twang, probably from the snow, though it did not throw us into an epic fever."[7]

On the following day the travelers set out again with the heights of Parnassus rising high above them.[8] As they journeyed over Parnassus an incident took place that impressed Byron once more with the virtues of the rugged Albanians; this time he had reason to notice the touching loyalty of his newest servant Dervish. When, during a dispute about the baggage, the impetuous Fletcher pushed Dervish, the

1. *Ibid.*   2. *Journey*, I, 206; *Recollections*, I, 22.   3. *P*, II, 84.

4. Until 1891 when the French Government bought the site of Delphi, it had been occupied by the village of Castri. In 1892 the inhabitants were removed to a new situation a few miles away and the excavations began which soon revealed the remains of many of the ancient wonders of Delphi.

5. *LJ*, I, 263.   6. *Recollections*, I, 23.   7. *P*, II, 189.

8. *Journey*, I, 213–4.

Albanian interpreted the gesture as a blow. But, instead of retaliating, Dervish sat down silently with his head upon his hands. His surprising reply to Byron's attempts at explanation was: "I *have been* a robber; I *am* a soldier; no captain ever struck me; *you* are my master, I have eaten your bread, but by *that* bread! (a usual oath) had it been otherwise, I would have stabbed the dog, your servant, and gone to the mountains."[9]

At Arakova the people of the village displayed as a sort of wonder a boy who had been to Malta, which they evidently looked upon as Ultima Thule. And when, not far from Distomo, the road met two others, one from Chaeronea and one from Livadia, it was impossible not to think of the fateful murder of Laius of Thebes by his son Œdipus.[1] At Livadia, a town of some size, a halt was made for three days.[2] Here the chief sight was another of the famed oracles of antiquity, the cave of Trophonius; to the skeptical Byron, however, it was but the "nominal" cave of Trophonius. Indeed, Byron found more remarkable a freethinking Greek bishop who did not hesitate to deride his own religion with great intrepidity.[3] During the stay at Livadia Byron and Hobhouse rode a few miles north to Caperna, which occupies part of the site of ancient Chaeronea. They found little remaining of the ancient city but looked with some awe upon the vast, barren plain where two of the great battles of antiquity had been fought.[4]

From Livadia the travelers went out of their way to visit Scripoo, seven or eight miles north on the site of Orchomenus. The remains of the ancient city were not extensive but again there was a *modern* wonder in the shape of an extraordinarily fat Greek shepherd who was in the habit of passing the hottest hours of the summer up to his neck in the nearby river in order to endure the heat![5]

At Mazee, a wretched village in the hills, they paused overnight before continuing on the last stage of the journey to Thebes. Here they found poverty at its worst and its most ludicrous. The people were able to afford little to eat and yet what money the women could acquire many of them strung on their hair, since the scarcity of husbands required a thousand piaster dowry from every prospective wife.[6] In these difficult circumstances Byron displayed his resourcefulness by cutting off the head of a goose which, along with pigs and cows, shared their apartment; "and thus," in Hobhouse's words, "we got an excellent roast."[7]

Late the following afternoon the pilgrims galloped into Thebes in

9. *P,* II, 177.   1. *Journey,* I, 215–6.
2. *Journey,* I, 221.   3. *P,* II, 188–9.
4. *Journey,* I, 223–5. In 338 B.C. the Athenians and Thebans were defeated there by Philip II and Alexander of Macedon. In 86 B.C. Sulla, the Roman general, defeated the army of Mithradates VI near Chaeronea.
5. *Journey,* I, 225–7.   6. *Journey,* I, 228–9.   7. *Recollections,* I, 24.

a downpour of rain.[8] There was little to detain them in the insignificant hamlet that was the modern Thebes; Byron indeed seems to have left sight-seeing entirely to Hobhouse,[9] who visited the Church of St. Luke and the house of Pindar and "resolving," as Byron said, "to be at once cleanly and classical,"[1] bathed in the fountain of Dirce. At Thebes Byron busied himself with *Childe Harold;* he was writing the satirical passage on the English Sabbath and probably some of the stanzas on the Spanish bullfight.[2]

After some difficulty in obtaining horses Byron and Hobhouse, with their attendants, were off again for Athens on the twenty-fourth of December. Christmas Eve was passed at the half-deserted village of Scourta in "the worst hovel of which we had ever been inmates."[3] Neither Byron nor Hobhouse mentions the singular appropriateness of spending Christmas Eve among the cows and pigs in a place where "there were racks and mangers, and the appurtenances of a stable."[4] On Christmas Day from the rugged heights near Fort Phyle Byron had his first view of Athens; it was a glorious sight as the plain of Athens, Pentelicus, Hymettus, the Ægean, and the Acropolis "burst upon the eye at once."[5] At eight-thirty in the evening he and Hobhouse arrived in Athens and took lodgings at the home of Madame Tarsia Macri, the widow of the late English Vice-Consul.[6]

Byron's early impressions of Greece, and of Athens, are to be derived chiefly from the stanzas of the second canto of *Childe Harold* that he wrote in the winter of 1810 and from a few of the notes to the poem; most of the latter, however, were written in 1811 and will be considered later with relation to Byron's longer stay in Athens. In fact most of Byron's more extended judgments on Greece belong to his second visit in 1810–11. It is rather surprising that no letters have come to light, beyond a brief business note to Hanson,[7] from Byron's first period in Athens; the answer probably lies in his admission that "Indeed the further I go the more my laziness increases, and my aversion to letter-writing becomes more confirmed."[7a] There is, then,

---

8. *Recollections,* I, 24.

9. Hobhouse, in describing the sights of Thebes (*Journey,* I, 234–8), speaks in the first person singular. This is unusual enough to indicate that Byron was not accompanying him.

1. *P,* II, 189.   2. *P,* II, 93.   3. *Journey,* I, 239.

4. Miss Mayne has drawn attention to this point and adds further (*Byron,* p. 113) that none of Byron's biographers sensed the dramatic significance.

5. *P,* II, 189; *Journey,* I, 240.

6. *Journey,* I, 241–4. Hobhouse makes a double mistake in his identification of Madame Macri as Theodora Macri, the *daughter* of the Vice-Consul. C. G. Brouzas points out that a sister Theodora, who spoke English, was the real manager of the Macri estate. "Teresa Macri, the Maid of Athens," *West Virginia University Bulletin, Philological Papers,* v (1947), 3.

7. *LJ,* VI, 448. The letter is dated March 3, 1810.   7a. *LJ,* I, 258.

a gap of over four months in the correspondence, from November 12, 1809, when Byron wrote the long letter to his mother from Prevesa, to March 19, 1810, when he wrote more briefly from Smyrna.

Byron wrote fifteen stanzas on Greece as "a kind of dramatic prologue"[9] to the second canto of *Childe Harold*. There were minor revisions within the stanzas, one was drastically revised,[1] and two were omitted before the publication of the poem in 1812.[2] Two stanzas were, however, added before publication,[3] so that the length of the opening section remained the same as it had been in manuscript. Of the twenty-six supplementary stanzas on Greece that now appear at the conclusion of the canto, it would appear that only ten were written in 1810.[4] Seven Byron added before publication and nine more appeared in the seventh edition in 1814. Thus in seeking out Byron's first impressions of Greece we have to do with twenty-five stanzas, fifteen preceding and ten following the long middle section on the Mediterranean and Albania. It should be added that in the opening stanzas Byron temporarily catches up with his scene. He is writing of Athens as he sees it before him at the moment.

Contrary to the case in Albania, Byron was but one of numerous Englishmen to visit Greece. Travel to the Near East and especially Greece had been stimulated in the early nineteenth century by increased interest in classical architecture and archaeology and, more immediately, by Napoleon's control over most of the continent of Europe.[5] Through the latter half of the eighteenth century, indeed, the architectural magnet had been veering sharply away from Rome in the direction of Greece. The significant activities in England of such scholars as Sir William Jones in Oriental languages and literature and Richard Porson in Greek were matched abroad by the firsthand investigations of James Stuart and Nicholas Revett, Richard Pococke, Edward Dodwell, Richard Chandler, and Edward D. Clarke. The researches and writings of these and other men, many of them undertaken with the support of the Society of Dilettanti, laid the foundations for the relatively modern science of Greek archaeology.[6] Yet it was not until the beginning of the nineteenth century that, in the

9. *P*, II, 99, n.
1. The view of immortality expressed in the present eighth stanza is a greatly softened version of the original stanza. See *P*, II, 103–5, n. For a summary of omissions and insertions in the second canto see *P*, II, xix–xx.
2. *P*, II, 108–9, n.   3. These are the present Stanzas 9 and 15.
4. The Stanzas are 73–6, 84–7, 91–2.
5. Adolf Michaelis, *Ancient Marbles in Great Britain* (Cambridge, 1882), p. 129. See also Wallace Cable Brown's articles, "Byron and English Interest in the Near East," *Studies in Philology*, XXXIV (1937), 55–64, and "The Popularity of English Travel Books about the Near East, 1775–1825," *Philological Quarterly*, XV (1936), 70–80.
6. Lionel Cust, *History of the Society of Dilettanti* (London, 1898), pp. 68–106, 125–36.

words of Hobhouse, others than "a few desperate scholars and artists ventured to trust themselves amongst the barbarians, to contemplate the ruins of Greece."[7] When the Napoleonic Wars closed most of Europe to European travelers Greece, as a part of neutral Turkey, attracted greater attention than ever before. The overthrow of French power in Egypt and the consequent British dominance in the Near East encouraged not only the scholar and the artist but also the less specialized traveler to visit Greece. Thus in 1809 an abundance of travelers, most of them English, were pouring into Greece—in such numbers that there was even talk of providing Athens with its first tavern.[8]

But since Athens as yet boasted no hotels or inns it was necessary for Byron and Hobhouse to find lodgings in private houses. Three or four of the leading families were in the habit of taking in foreigners who came to Athens. Such accommodations were not, however, offered entirely in the spirit of hospitality; though there was no regular charge travelers were expected to pay according to their inclination. These establishments, with a dozen or so foreign families resident in Athens, constituted the "Frank society" of the town. At the house where Byron stayed there still stood the tall flagpole on which the Union Jack had flown during the lifetime of Madame Macri's husband, the Greek-born English representative in Athens. During the ten weeks in Athens Hobhouse occupied an adjoining house and thus the Englishmen were able to enjoy more comfort than the ordinary accommodations would have offered.[9]

In 1810 Athens was a squalid Turkish provincial town of about ten thousand inhabitants under the protective custody of the Kislar Aga in Constantinople, to whom an annual tribute of thirty thousand crowns was paid. The Turkish governor of Athens was a representative of the Kislar Aga's known as the Waiwode. The ill-built houses and narrow streets of Athens extended to the north and east of the lofty Acropolis and were, with the Acropolis, surrounded by a ten-foot wall. The size of Athens in the early nineteenth century is indicated by the fact that Hobhouse found it possible to walk briskly around the walls in forty-seven minutes.[1]

Greeks and Turks lived side by side in Athens, although there was

7. *Journey*, I, 252.

8. William Miller's lecture, *The English in Athens before 1821* (London, Anglo-Hellenic League, 1926), gives interesting details. For information concerning the French, see Emile Malakis, *French Travellers in Greece (1770–1820): An Early Phase of French Philhellenism* (Philadelphia, 1925).

9. *Journey*, I, 243–7.

1. *Journey*, I, 245. To Galt Athens looked "as if two or three ill-built villages had been rudely swept together at the foot of the north side of the Acropolis, and enclosed by a garden wall, three or four miles in circumference." *Letters from the Levant* (London, 1813), pp. 112–13.

a minimum of intercourse between the sullen Athenians and the "domiciliated military"[2] who were their masters. Turks and Albanians together outnumbered native Greeks. Another group, small but influential, was the foreign colony, which consisted of a dozen or so families, chiefly French, who were engaged in lending money to the Greeks and in small-scale exportation of oil. The French Consul, M. Fauvel,[3] who had been in Athens for many years, enjoyed a position of high esteem in the city whose inhabitants, in the words of Hobhouse, "for some time, felt a lively interest in everything relative to the affairs of France."[4] Yet international differences did not prevent Fauvel and his countryman, the merchant Phokion Roque,[5] from giving assistance to Byron and Hobhouse and accompanying them on most of their explorations in and about Athens. Roque was the brother-in-law of Byron's hostess in Athens, Tarsia Macri, who was also related to another French family, the Massons.

Shortly after their arrival in Athens Byron and Hobhouse were visited by the British Vice-Consul, Spiridion Logotheti; and soon afterward Don Tita Lusieri, the Italian painter serving Lord Elgin, called and "had much to say about the Elgin marbles and the French."[6] In the company of Logotheti and Lusieri the Englishmen

2. The phrase is Galt's. *Idem,* p. 140.
3. This distinguished Frenchman is mistakenly referred to in the published texts of Byron's letters (*LJ,* I, 307, n.; *LBC,* I, 14) as "Fauriel." Louis François Sebastian Fauvel (1753–1838) was born in Burgundy and received an art education in France before traveling to the Near East in the interests of Count Choiseul-Gouffier, the French Ambassador to Constantinople, in 1787. Fauvel gathered material and prepared illustrations for his patron's *Voyage Pittoresque de la Grèce,* the first volume of which appeared in Paris in 1787, the second in 1809. He settled shortly afterward in Athens, where he became the French Consul and continued his archaeological and artistic pursuits. Byron refers to Fauvel as one "to whose talents as an artist, and manners as a gentleman, none who have known him can refuse their testimony." *P,* II, 190. Scarcely a traveler who visited Greece in the early nineteenth century fails to mention Fauvel's courteous assistance and his extensive knowledge of Athens, ancient and modern. A plan of Athens by Fauvel appears facing p. 480 in Walpole's *Travels in Various Countries of the East* (London, 1820), Vol. I. A biography by Ph.-E. Legrand was published in *Revue Archaeologique,* Ser. 3, xxx (1897), 41–66, 185–201, 385–404; xxxi, 94–103, 185–223.
4. *Journey,* I, 251.
5. Phokion Roque de Carcassone was "a French merchant of respectability long settled in Athens." *P,* II, 190. Roque married the eldest of the five daughters of Mina Macri and was thus the uncle of Byron's "Maid of Athens," Teresa Macri. His daughter Dudu was called by Hughes (*Travels in Sicily, Greece and Albania,* I, 250) "the most accomplished girl" in Athens.
6. *Recollections,* I, 25. Giovanni Battista Lusieri, known to his friends as Don Tita was an eminent Neapolitan painter whom Sir William Hamilton, the antiquary and British envoy at Naples, had employed in 1799 to make topographical studies for him in the Near East. When Lord Elgin began his investigations of Athenian sculpture, he first engaged Lusieri to do extensive drawings in the Greek capital. So vastly did the enterprise grow, however, that when Byron came to Athens Lusieri had already been there for ten years as Elgin's "agent of devastation." Lusieri's drawings became of secondary importance as Elgin's activities broadened in scope but the Italian was accordingly put in charge of the dismantling campaign in the Acropolis. Lusieri was an ac-

paid their respects to the Waiwode, the Turkish governor of the town.[7]

Since it was impossible to visit the Acropolis until one had sent a present of tea and sugar to the Turkish commandant and awaited his consent, Byron and Hobhouse first turned their attention to the sights of the town clustered about the ancient citadel.[8] These included the remarkably well preserved Temple of Theseus, within five minutes' walk of their lodgings, and the hills of the Areopagus, the Pynx, and the Muses, which were also within easy reach. Close by the Acropolis they inspected the remains of the Odeum and Theater of Dionysius and the Monument of Lysicrates. To the east were the ancient Arch of Hadrian, the sixteen imposing columns of the Temple to Olympian Zeus, and the scanty remains of the Stadium.[9] Most interesting of all, however, when they finally were allowed to climb to the lofty Acropolis, were the ruins of the Propylæa, the Erectheum, and especially the Parthenon.[1]

The sight of these ancient glories of Athens in a state of decay was sufficient to inspire melancholy and, in one with Byron's bent of mind, to arouse the gloomy thoughts with which he began the second canto of *Childe Harold.* As Byron wrote, "We can all feel, or imagine, the regret with which the ruins of cities, once the capitals of empires, are beheld."[2] Here he was beholding one of the supreme cities of the world, once the home of great philosophers, artists, statesmen, and soldiers. Byron could not restrain the thought:

> Ancient of days! august Athena! where,
> Where are thy men of might? thy grand in soul?[3]

The sight of modern Athens and its ruined temples to the gods stirred him also to the cheerless reflection that

> Even Gods must yield—Religions take their turn:
> 'Twas Jove's—'tis Mahomet's—and other Creeds
> Will rise with other years, till Man shall learn
> Vainly his incense soars, his victim bleeds;
> Poor child of Doubt and Death, whose hope is built on reeds.[4]

The skull of the ancient hero, once the "Dome of Thought, the Palace of the Soul," was now, like the marble temple on the Acropolis, but a shattered cell, a lonely tower.[5]

complished landscape painter as well as a topographical draftsman. There is a critical analysis of his work in H. W. Williams' *Travels in Italy, Greece and the Ionian Islands* (Edinburgh, 1820), II, 331–3. Lusieri married the sister of Byron's young French friend Nicolo Giraud and was still in Athens as late as 1817. He is mentioned frequently in Byron's letters.

7. *Journey*, I, 244.   8. *Ibid.*   9. *Journey*, I, 257–71.
1. *Journey*, I, 278–91.   2. *P*, II, 165.   3. *Childe Harold*, II, 2.
4. *Childe Harold*, II, 3.   5. *Childe Harold*, II, 5–7.

Byron had earlier insisted that he preferred the doctrines of Socrates to those of St. Paul;[6] now in what remained of Socrates' own city he declared again his agreement with the Athenian philosopher's conclusion that "All that we know is, nothing can be known." And Byron went a step further to reassert not merely his uncertainty but his skepticism regarding immortality with the words:

> . . . I
> Look not for Life, where Life may never be.[7]

The great men of Athens had long since passed to their graves. Now, as one paused among the remaining columns of the Temple of Zeus, it was impossible to visualize the magnificent shrine the "grand in soul" of Athens once knew. The modern Greek passed by unmoved.[8] Yet the indifference of the modern Greek aroused less of Byron's scorn than did the "devastation"[9] of the modern Scot. As he looked upon the Parthenon and the Erectheum, in addition to evidences of the saddening process of decay there were unmistakable signs of the activity of the agents of Lord Elgin, who since 1801 had been systematically removing ornaments from the mouldering monuments of Athens with the purpose of preserving them against the ravages of time and probable war.

Hobhouse has recorded that during the stay in Athens "a war more than civil, was raging on the subject of my Lord Elgin's pursuits in Greece, and had inlisted all the Frank settlers and the principal Greeks on one or the other side of the controversy."[1] It is hardly surprising, then, that as soon as he had seen something of Athens Byron joined vigorously in this controversy and expressed with even more than usual force his condemnation of the activities of Lord Elgin.

Byron had already indicated what side he would take when, shortly before leaving England, he added some lines on Lords Elgin and Aberdeen to *English Bards:*

> Let Aberdeen and Elgin still pursue
> The shade of fame through regions of Virtù;
> Waste useless thousands on their Phidian freaks,
> Misshapen monuments and maimed antiques;
> And make their grand saloon a general mart
> For all the mutilated blocks of art.[2]

In a note to this passage Byron added, "Lord Elgin would fain persuade us that all the figures, with and without noses, in his stoneshop, are the work of Phidias! 'Credat Judaeus!' "[3]

It is worth noting that in 1809 Byron said nothing about the

6. *LJ*, I, 173.   7. *P*, II, 103, n.   8. *Childe Harold*, II, 10.
9. *P*, II, 170.   1. *Journey*, I, 244.   2. *English Bards*, 11. 1027–32.
3. *P*, I, 378, n.

methods of Elgin but limited himself to scorn for the works of art themselves; he shared the view, fashionable in London at the time, that the marbles Elgin transported there had but little artistic value.[4] Byron was always willing to admit that he had no special feeling or aptitude for art and it is natural enough that he should have accepted the adverse judgment of those among whom he moved. English taste, conditioned to the more graceful and familiar Greco-Roman art, was slow to recognize the rougher, more realistic beauties of ancient Greek sculpture.[5] Richard Payne Knight, whose authority in matters of artistic taste was questioned by few, denounced the marbles even before he had seen them[6] and, despite the enthusiasm of a few perceptive individuals like Benjamin Robert Haydon, Knight's was the orthodox view in 1809.

But now in Greece, as Byron beheld the actual buildings from which the "Iris" and the "Ilissos," the "Theseus" and the "Fates" had been taken, he saw the whole Elgin controversy from a new point of view, from that of the Greeks themselves, whose temples he felt were being ruthlessly despoiled. The methods employed by Lord Elgin now put the question of artistic value of the sculpture into the background. As Byron looked upon the Parthenon and the Erectheum he experienced not merely the regret that comes from viewing the deterioration of any work of great beauty but even more a strong indignation that a foreigner to Greece—and a Scotsman at that—should be responsible, as he felt, for hastening the natural process of decay.

In 1799 when Thomas Bruce, Lord Elgin, was named Ambassador to Turkey he had made the resolution, in the interests of English art, to take advantage of his years in the Near East and have drawings and casts made of as much Athenian sculpture as possible.[7] When he failed to interest the Government in this proposition, Elgin undertook to carry out the plan at his own expense. The artistic guidance of his project Elgin entrusted to Don Tita Lusieri, a Neapolitan painter of distinction, and he had his secretary, W. R. Hamilton, secure other painters and architects to assist with the work in Athens. At first Elgin's agents were allowed only to make drawings but when English prestige in Turkey rose with victories in Egypt, Elgin gained permission to erect scaffolding and to take plaster casts.

4. Stephen A. Larrabee, *English Bards and Grecian Marbles* (New York, 1943), pp. 151–8.

5. *Ibid.* See also John Steegman, *The Rule of Taste from George I to George IV* (London, 1936), pp. 136–7.

6. Michaelis, *op. cit.*, pp. 138–9. In his introduction to the Dilettanti Society's *Specimens of Ancient Sculpture* (London, 1809), Knight insisted that the Elgin sculptures were the work of inferior artists.

7. This brief account is based upon A. H. Smith's exhaustive monograph, "Lord Elgin and His Collection," *Journal of Hellenic Studies*, xxvi (1916), 163–372, and Michaelis, *op. cit.*, pp. 132–51.

As the work went on it became increasingly apparent that the buildings were rapidly deteriorating and that many of their artistic treasures were in danger of being lost to the world forever. His awareness of this disturbing possibility led Elgin to interpret his permit with some latitude and to begin removing some of the statues and friezes for shipment to England; for these the Turkish Government was willing to accept payment. In 1802 a large shipment of these Athenian marbles arrived in England but since Elgin was not on hand to attend to them they lay for some time untouched in English harbors. The following year Elgin was recalled from Constantinople but on his way home had the misfortune to be captured and detained by the French for three years. Thus the fate of the sculpture, which was stored, unopened, in London, remained unsettled until its owner was able to return to England in 1806. Once he was at liberty Elgin set about finding a home for his treasures. In 1807 he was able to engage a house in Park Lane and there the marbles were placed on display; to the Park Lane Museum visitors came for the next few years, some to admire but more to scoff.[8]

At Athens in 1810 Byron did more than merely scoff. In his most vehement *English Bards* manner he lashed out against Lord Elgin and his works:

> Cold as the crags upon his native coast,
> His mind as barren and his heart as hard,
> Is he whose head conceived, whose hand prepared,
> Aught to displace Athenae's poor remains.[9]

And in notes to the violent lines in *Childe Harold* Byron exclaimed, "Sylla could but punish, Philip subdue, and Xerxes burn Athens; but it remained for the paltry antiquarian, and his despicable agents, to render her contemptible as himself and his pursuits."[1] And again, "When they carry away three or four shiploads of the most valuable and massy relics that time and barbarism have left to the most injured and most celebrated of cities; when they destroy, in a vain attempt to tear down, those works which have been the admiration of ages, I know no motive which can excuse, no name which can designate, the perpetrators of this dastardly devastation."[2]

Later in their stay at Athens Byron and Hobhouse went to the Parthenon one day with John Galt and observed that two large pieces of the bas-reliefs had fallen since their last visit.[3] It may be interesting, in this connection, to compare the reactions of his two companions to Elgin's pursuits with Byron's own. Galt wrote, "At first, as every

8. A sketch by Charles R. Cockerell of the Elgin marbles as they appeared at Park Lane is reproduced in A. H. Smith, *op. cit.*, p. 299.
9. *Childe Harold*, II, 12.   1. *P*, II, 166.   2. *P*, II, 170.
3. *Recollections*, I, 27.

traveller who comes to Athens must be, I was greatly vexed and disappointed by the dilapidation of the temple of Minerva; but I am consoled by the reflection, that the spoils are destined to ornament our own land, and that, if they had not been taken possession of by Lord Elgin, they would probably have been carried away by the French."[4] And Hobhouse, after a careful presentation of the arguments on each side of the architectural civil war in Athens, concluded:

It is pretty evident, that an infinitely greater number of rising architects and sculptors must derive benefit from these studies, if they can be pursued in a museum at London or Paris, than if they were to be sought in the Turkish territories; and surely, we can hardly complain, if they are to be found in our capital. Present travellers may feel a little mortification, and those who are utterly incapable of appreciating the merit of the remains in question, wherever they may be fixed, will join in the fashionable clamour of the day.[5]

Byron's low opinion of the Elgin marbles was to be discredited within his own lifetime. After 1810 more and more men of distinction in the world of art, including the great Canova himself, proclaimed their tremendous value and in 1816 the British Government bought the marbles for thirty-seven thousand pounds. They have remained among the chief glories of the British Museum ever since. Moreover, responsible opinion has agreed that, in the light of conditions at Athens, Elgin had good justification for removing the sculptures for preservation and that not merely England but the artistic world in general has benefited from his efforts.[6] Byron's feeling that the marbles belonged in their rightful Greek home is perfectly understandable and laudable; in his sense of outrage at the state of decay in which he found the chief monuments of Greece he was at first actuated by the very best impulses. But the dilapidation of the shrines of Athens resulted from the continued neglect of the Turks and the Greeks themselves, not from the activities of Lord Elgin. Byron's failure to ascertain the facts and to consider the larger implications of the question and his descent to mere scurrilous abuse combine to make his attack upon Elgin one of the less creditable episodes in his literary career.

During the stay in Greece the travelers did not restrict themselves to Athens alone. In Byron's words they "topographised Attica."[7] The mildness of the winter weather permitted almost daily rides among the gardens and olive groves of the surrounding countryside.[8] They also rode west to Eleusis and the island of Salamis, east to Mount Hymettus and to Mount Pentelicus, where a huge cave showed how

4. *Letters from the Levant*, p. 112.   5. *Journey*, I, 287, n.
6. Smith, *op. cit.*, pp. 345–8; Michaelis, *op. cit.*, pp. 148–51; *P*, II, 454–6.
7. *LJ*, I, 263.   8. *Journey*, I, 292–8.

much marble had been quarried for the public buildings of Athens.[9]
On a trip to the Piræus they saw "an Hydriote merchant vessel, of
about two hundred tons, anchored in the port, for the purpose of
carrying off the Elgin marbles, and she seemed too big for the station."[1] And as later they circled the peninsula of Munychia they had
difficulty in ascertaining the site of the supposed tomb of Themistocles.[2] The loud murmur produced by the tumbling of the waves on
the pebbly shore of the bay at Phalerum led Byron to conjecture that
this might have been the famous resort of Demosthenes.[3]

Byron and Hobhouse undertook one rather ambitious expedition
during the period at Athens. On January 19 they set off on horseback,
with servants and baggage, and rode south in the direction of Sunium,
the rocky promontory at the southern extremity of Attica.[4] They spent
the first night at Vari, close to the southwestern shore, and the following day reached Keratea, where rain held them up for two days. Taking advantage of a few hours of sunshine during the stay at Keratea,
they climbed up the nearby Mount Parne in search of a cave about
which they had heard wondrous tales. Arriving there with some difficulty they lit pine torches and proceeded to explore the interior of
the cavern, which proved to be a vast and intricate labyrinth of under-
ground chambers. When they had been wandering aimlessly from
one grotto to another for some time their guide suddenly revealed the
disquieting information that he had lost his bearings; and at the same
time the torches began to flicker and fail. A few minutes of stark terror followed. Only extraordinarily good fortune brought the explorers
to the entrance again just as the last torch burned out; and it was
frightening to think what might have been their fate had either light
or luck deserted them a few moments earlier.[5] According to Galt,
Byron often told the story of this adventure "with spirit and humour,"
describing his own anxiety "as a species of excitement and titillation
which moved him to laughter."[6]

Finally on the twenty-third they were able to reach "Sunium's
marbled steep"[7] and admire the imposing remains of the ancient
Temple of Poseidon[8] and the dramatic outlook over the islands of the
Ægean. Sunium was ever to remain one of Byron's favorite scenes;[8a]
in a note to *Childe Harold* he wrote:

9. *Journey*, I, 305–18, 319–29; *P*, II, 186.   1. *Journey*, I, 299.
2. *Journey*, I, 300.   3. *Journey*, I, 301–2.   4. *Journey*, I, 330–41.
5. *Journey*, I, 338–9.   6. Galt, p. 113.
7. Byron so describes it in the poem, "The Isles of Greece," inserted between Stanzas
86 and 87 in the third canto of *Don Juan*.
8. Byron and Hobhouse, like all travelers in their time, considered this the Temple
of Minerva. An inscription found in 1898 revealed it, however, to be dedicated to
Poseidon.
8a. See also the lines in *Childe Harold*, II, 86, and *The Giaour*, ll. 7–22. The modern
name is "Colonna" or "Colonni" but "Sunium" has persisted.

In all Attica, if we except Athens itself and Marathon, there is no scene more interesting than Cape Colonna. To the antiquary and artist, sixteen columns are an inexhaustible source of observation and design; to the philosopher, the supposed scene of some of Plato's conversations will not be unwelcome, and the traveller will be struck with the beauty of the prospect over "Isles that crown the Aegean deep"; but, for an Englishman, Colonna has yet an additional interest as the actual spot of Falconer's shipwreck.[1]

The same afternoon they returned to Keratea and the next day traveled north by the commodious port of Raphti and Mount Penteli-cus to Marathon.[2] There in the dusk they at first passed by the famous plain and barrow of the Athenian heroes without realizing they had reached their goal. After lodging overnight in a cottage nearby, Byron and Hobhouse devoted the following morning to examining their historic surroundings and attempting to revisualize the great battle of antiquity.[3] The extent to which Byron was moved by the sight of Marathon can be determined by the frequency of his allusions to it both in poetry and prose. The fifth stanza of the second canto of *Childe Harold*, with its mention of

> . . . the vanished Hero's lofty mound;
> Far on the solitary shore he sleeps,

must surely refer to Marathon. And in two of the stanzas added in 1814 Byron reminded the modern Athenian of

> The Battle-field, where Persia's victim horde
> First bowed beneath the brunt of Hellas' sword.[4]

In a note to the latter passage he added:

"Siste Viator—heroas calcas!" was the epitaph on the famous Count Merci; —what then must be our feelings when standing on the tumulus of the two hundred (Greeks) who fell on Marathon?

The whole historic plain, Byron exclaimed, was offered him for sale at the equivalent of about nine hundred pounds![5]

In early February Byron was detained at Athens when Hobhouse made a five-day trip to Negroponte. The experience of journeying without Byron led Hobhouse to pay a handsome tribute to his fellow

1. *P*, II, 169. William Falconer's popular poem, *The Shipwreck*, was first published in 1762.
2. *Journey*, I, 347–50.   3. *Journey*, I, 350–5.   4. *Childe Harold*, II, 89.
5. *P*, II, 186–7. In "The Isles of Greece" occur the well-known lines:
> The mountains look on Marathon—
>   And Marathon looks on the sea;
> And musing there an hour alone,
>   I dreamed that Greece might still be free;
> For standing on the Persians' grave,
> I could not deem myself a slave.

traveler: "You will attribute any additional defects in the narration of this short tour, to the absence of a companion, who, to quickness of observation and ingenuity of remark, united that gay good humour which keeps alive the attention under the pressure of fatigue, and softens the aspect of every difficulty and danger."[6]

The friendship of Byron and Hobhouse was, however, one of those lasting relationships that are sustained not only by similar interests and mutual stimulus but also by rather striking differences in temperament. Hobhouse's more conservative and matter-of-fact nature was sometimes an annoyance but oftener a support to his mercurial companion. This close friendship was to persist, with minor dislocations, through the remainder of Byron's life and Harold Nicolson writes well when he refers to it as "the keel and ballast of Byron's errant boat."[7] The contrast between the impulsive, volatile Byron and the meticulous, academic Hobhouse is as evident throughout their travels as is their respect and affection for one another. Byron demonstrated the strength and nature of their friendship when, after Hobhouse's return to England, he wrote to him, "After all, I do love thee, Hobby, thou hast so many good qualities, and so many bad ones, it is impossible to live with or without thee."[8]

A few days after Hobhouse's return from Negroponte a spell of sultry, oppressive weather was followed by a mild earthquake. The description in the *Journey* of this phenomenon has a freshness and immediacy that make it worthy of full quotation:

At half after eleven at night, as I was writing the substance of this letter in our little sitting-room at Athens, and my fellow-traveller, better employed, was sitting opposite to me, a noise like the rushing of a torrent, suddenly roused our attention; the dead stillness of the night rendered every sound more unexpected and more distinct; the branches of the lemon-trees, in the court-yard shook "without a wind"; and instantly afterwards the door of our chamber swung open, and the whole building began to totter. At this moment one of the servants rushed into the room, and exclaimed, that the house was falling! The shaking, however, was but gentle, and did not last more than two seconds, having been more alarming in its approach than dangerous in its consequences.[9]

During these weeks Byron saw more of the Greeks than he had of the inhabitants of any other country he visited. He was boarding with a Greek family and seems also to have had some contact with other natives both in an official and in a social way.[1] Byron said him-

---

6. *Journey*, I, 360.
7. *Byron: The Last Journey* (New ed. London, Constable & Co., Ltd., 1940), p. 294.
8. *LBC*, I, 17.   9. *Journey*, I, 396–7.
1. Hobhouse's remarks on the balls and parties in Athens suggest that the Englishmen took part in such activities to which "the principal Greeks are invited." *Journey*, I, 250. Contacts with officials in Athens were inevitable and, despite the Turkish control, some of these were Greeks.

self, "I have lived a good deal with the Greeks, whose modern dialect I can converse in enough for my purposes."[2] In appearance the modern Greeks still suggested their illustrious forebears: "All are beautiful, very much resembling the busts of Alcibiades; the women not quite so handsome."[3]

After three weeks in Athens Byron wrote what are probably his lines of valediction to Constance Spencer Smith.[4] Whether some Greek maiden supplanted "fair Florence" in his affections at this time it is impossible to say. The legend that the famous poem, "Maid of Athens, Ere We Part," was written in passionate devotion to Teresa, the eldest of the attractive Macri daughters, is somewhat marred by Byron's offhand remark, "I almost forgot to tell you that I am dying for love of three Greek girls at Athens, sisters. I lived in the same house. Teresa, Mariana, and Katinka, are the names of these divinities —all of them under fifteen."[5] Yet there was indication that Byron had at least given the appearance of being attracted to Teresa when he mentioned to Hobhouse in August that "the old woman, Teresa's mother, was mad enough to imagine I was going to marry the girl."[6] Moreover, three years later Byron made indirect reference in his journal to the attractiveness of Teresa.[7]

There seems little reason to interpret the "Teresa episode" as anything more than a passing romantic and, to some extent, literary flourish. Such a view is supported by evidence that Teresa was not the eldest daughter of Tarsia Macri but the youngest; she had, in fact, at the time of Byron's visit barely attained the age of twelve.[8] Teresa was undoubtedly an attractive child; that Byron should have appreciated her girlish beauty and should, indeed, have made an exhibition of his admiration for the youthful daughter of his hostess is perfectly understandable. Such exaggeration, primarily but not

2. *LJ*, I, 271.   3. *LJ*, I, 267.
4. "The Spell Is Broke, the Charm Is Flown!" See above, p. 53 and n. 4.
5. *LJ*, I, 269.   6. *LBC*, I, 16.   7. *LJ*, II, 349.
8. On the basis of his investigations in Athens, Shirley C. Atchley (*Bios kai drasis tou Byronos en Helladi* [Athens, 1918], p. 29, n.) reports that Teresa was born on November 16, 1797. Mariana was three years older and Katinka nearly two years older. Neither Byron nor Hobhouse mentions the relative ages of the three girls. The originator of the tradition that Teresa was the eldest daughter appears to have been H. W. Williams, who visited Athens in May, 1817, and, obviously inspired by Byron's already famous poem to the "Maid of Athens," described the three sisters in some detail; Williams (*op. cit.*, II, 290) spoke of Teresa as "the eldest celebrated for her beauty, and said to be the subject of those stanzas by Lord Byron." When, over ten years later, Moore came to write his biography of Byron, he quoted without question the passage from Williams and thus established the tradition, which has persisted ever since, that Teresa was the eldest daughter of Tarsia Macri. I have been unable to discover any other firsthand account in which Teresa is referred to as the eldest daughter. On the other hand, William Turner, who stayed next door in 1813, calls her the youngest. Turner perhaps sheds some light on the Byron episode, too, when he observes that "it is considered a sort of duty for English travellers to fall in love with one of the daughters." *Journal of a Tour in the Levant* (London, 1820), I, 322.

entirely playful, is thoroughly characteristic of his temperament. And the fragile innocence of childhood, so easily idealized, always had an irresistible appeal for him.

Hobhouse has nothing to say about the Macri sisters. The only first-hand observer of Byron in Athens at this time who expresses any opinion on the matter is John Galt. And Galt, after describing Teresa unenthusiastically as a "pale and pensive-looking girl, with regular Grecian features," goes on to say that he much doubts that Byron had any sincere attachment to her. Galt's rather matter-of-fact final judgment might seem incongruous did we not know it is of the mercurial Byron that he speaks when he says, "I believe his passion was equally innocent and poetical, though he spoke of buying her from her mother."[9]

Later travelers' descriptions of the "Maid of Athens" are untrustworthy because most had already fallen under the spell of the Byronic legend and because it is always difficult to judge which of the daughters is being described. There is the further complication that the time element obscures the picture; for example, H. W. Williams, whose description of the sisters is most frequently quoted, did not see them until over seven years after Byron. All three girls, however, had probably gained some education from Greek tutors and were also at least acquainted with the English, French, and Italian languages. They were trained, too, in domestic skills and in music and dancing.[1]

Moore recollects rather hazily Byron's telling him, in connection with one of the Macri girls, that he "had recourse to an act of courtship often practised in that country—namely, giving himself a wound across the breast with his dagger."[2] The gesture, according to Moore, was but coolly received. Such an incident is given prominence in D. G. Kampouroglou's *Attikoi Erotes,* published at Athens in 1921, a curiously interesting work in which romance and melodrama are mingled with accurate information, some of it unavailable elsewhere, regarding Byron's activities in Athens.[3] In telling his story Kampouroglou

---

9. Galt, p. 119.   1. Williams, *op. cit.*, II, 290–1.   2. Moore, I, 224, n.

3. In the opening scene of Kampouroglou's book Suleiman Aga, the Turkish Governor of Athens, is interrupted in conversation with his friend the Cadi of Thebes by the arrival at the Acropolis of two Englishmen, Byron and Hobhouse. When Hobhouse enters the Aga's house to discuss antiquarian details, Byron is left alone to look with romantic melancholy upon the ruins of the Parthenon. The next scene, at the home of the Macris, is prefaced by genealogical details and a description of the household that includes the grandmother Mariana Macri and the aunt Theodora, as well as Tarsia Macri and her three daughters. Byron and Hobhouse shortly arrive with their attendants to take up lodgings and the stage is set for the melodramatic scene a few days later in which Byron not merely threatens to stab himself for love of Teresa but goes to the extreme of signalizing his infatuation by firing his pistol impetuously into the air! When Teresa later admits with some pride to her family that the handsome young Englishman embraced her, it is deemed prudent to send her for a visit to the family of her uncle Phokion Roque. There we see the last of Teresa as a human being; by the time Byron

draws equally upon such obvious sources as Byron's letters and Hobhouse's *Journey,* his own original investigations, and legendary material current in Athens. For want of corroborative evidence this picturesque episode must be classed among the latter.

It was noted long ago that Byron's choice of the name Katinka for one of the attractive young ladies of the sultan's harem in the sixth canto of *Don Juan* was undoubtedly a reminiscence of his stay with the Macris in 1809–10. Also interesting is the fact that "Dudu," the name of the girl most fully delineated in those *Don Juan* stanzas, was the name of the daughter of Phokion Roque. Yet on the basis of Kampouroglou's revelation that Dudu was also the pet name of Mariana Macri, and that Teresa herself was familiarly known as Lolah,[4] it is possible to go further and suggest that the device of singling out from the members of the harem an intimate group of three, Lolah, Katinka, and Dudu, for association with Don Juan was suggested to Byron by his own acquaintance with the three Macri sisters in Athens. In the details of description there are, however, no grounds for any closer identification.

Byron's only explicit judgment on the Greeks before he returned to live longer among them was the statement: "I like the Greeks, who are plausible rascals,—with all the Turkish vices, without their courage."[5] But, though he might like the Greeks as individuals, as a race and particularly in the light of their glorious past Byron felt it necessary to look upon them as

> The helpless warriors of a willing doom,[6]

who

> . . . idly rail in vain,
> Trembling beneath the scourge of Turkish hand,
> From birth till death enslaved; in word, in deed unmanned.[7]

Liberty and freedom had disappeared; changed in all but appearance these modern Greeks dared not face their oppressors alone but sighed for foreign aid.

departs from Greece she has become to him an idealized symbol of love rather than a reality; and the book ends on a highly romantic note with Byron reciting his "Maid of Athens" lines on the deck of his Malta-bound ship.

4. In an article written for the Byron centenary (*Le Messager,* No. 220, Special Suppl. [Athens, April 19, 1924]), Kampouroglou stated that as a child he had known the former Teresa Macri, then the wife of an officer in the British Army and member of the consular service with the prosaic name James Black. It is an interesting coincidence that Teresa Macri's English husband also died at Missolonghi, forty-four years after Byron. When as a distant relative of the Macris Kampouroglou visited Teresa after her husband's death, he noted in her home a lithograph representing Byron as Don Juan in the grotto of Haidée; it was evident to Kampouroglou that through her life Teresa took pride in and gained considerable satisfaction from the linking of her name with Byron's.

5. *LJ,* I, 267.   6. *Childe Harold,* II, 73.   7. *Idem,* II, 74.

> Hereditary Bondsmen! know ye not
> *Who* would be free *themselves* must strike the blow?
> By their right arms the conquest must be wrought?
> Will Gaul or Muscovite redress ye? No!
> True—they may lay your proud despoilers low,
> But not for you will Freedom's Altars flame.
> Shades of the Helots! triumph o'er your foe!
> Greece! change thy lords, thy state is still the same;
> Thy glorious day is o'er, but not thine years of shame.[8]

Not until Grecian mothers again gave birth to men, Byron insisted, could Greece be restored.[9]

Yet it is clear that Greece had already begun to exert its spell over Byron. As he looked back upon the land from Smyrna he felt that "Greece, particularly in the vicinity of Athens, is delightful;—cloudless skies and lovely landscapes."[1] In *Childe Harold* he wrote:

> And yet how lovely in thine age of woe,
> Land of lost Gods and godlike men, art thou!
> Thy vales of evergreen, thy hills of snow,
> Proclaim thee Nature's varied favourite now.
>
> .   .   .   .
>
> Yet are thy skies as blue, thy crags as wild;
> Sweet are thy groves, and verdant are thy fields,
> Thine olive ripe as when Minerva smiled,
> And still his honied wealth Hymettus yields;
> There the blithe Bee his fragrant fortress builds,
> The free-born wanderer of thy mountain-air;
> Apollo still thy long, long summer gilds,
> Still in his beam Mendeli's marbles glare:
> Art, Glory, Freédom fail, but Nature still is fair.[2]

John Galt arrived at Athens on February 20 and accompanied Byron and Hobhouse on several trips. Galt has noted that during those latter weeks in Athens the travelers were "full of their adventures in Albania" and that Byron was writing the Albanian section of *Childe Harold.*[3] Of his English friends Galt wrote, "One may travel long enough, and come many times even to Athens without meeting with any company equal to theirs."[4] Galt also had a few words to say about Byron's growing affection for Greece: "When I saw him at Athens, the spring was still shrinking in the bud. It was not until he returned from Constantinople in the following autumn, that he saw the climate and country with those delightful aspects which he has delineated with so much felicity in *The Giaour* and *The Corsair.*"[5]

---

8. *Idem,* II, 76.   9. *Idem,* II, 84.   1. *LJ,* I, 258.
2. *Childe Harold,* II, 85, 87.   3. Galt, pp. 111, 122.
4. *Letters from the Levant,* p. 231.   5. Galt, p. 127.

On March 4 Captain Ferguson of the *Pylades,* a sloop of war, offered Byron and Hobhouse a passage to Smyrna. With great reluctance they left Athens the following day, galloping toward the shores
of the gulf, according to Hobhouse, "at a quick pace, in order to rid
ourselves, by the hurry, of the pain of parting."[6] The young Dr. Francis Darwin and a friend had been cruising for several weeks aboard
the *Pylades* and they now returned with their countrymen to Smyrna.[7]
The *Pylades* reached its destination on the afternoon of the sixth and
after dining aboard the *Salsette* frigate, which they found in port,
Byron and Hobhouse went to the mansion of the Consul, Mr. Francis
Werry; there they were treated in most hospitable fashion during the
five weeks they spent in Smyrna.[8]

Smyrna, the chief city of Asia Minor and at that time the commer-
cial capital of the Turkish Empire, had, in addition to its Turks,
Greeks, and Armenians, a considerable population of western Europeans. Numerous Englishmen, Frenchmen, Germans, Dutchmen, and
Italians, most of whom were engaged in trade, lived apart in a district
of Smyrna known as "Frank Town." Unfortunately in 1809 the har-
mony of this international colony was disturbed by national feuds re-
flecting the hostilities on the European continent.[9]

Smyrna itself offered little of special interest. On the thirteenth
Byron and Hobhouse, accompanied by Suliman, a Turkish Janizary,
and some attendants for their horses, set out to visit the ruins of
Ephesus.[1] They passed first through fertile, cultivated country but
late in the day came to a marshy region where the croaking of frogs
was almost deafening. Occasional camel caravans passed them on the
way. After spending the night at a han, they proceeded the next day
on past a marshy lake and over a dreary, extensive plain, where several
cemeteries with tombstones and cypresses were the only indication
that the region had ever been inhabited. At the village of Aiasaluk,
near the sight of ancient Ephesus, they stopped for the night and
spent the evening exploring a ruined mosque and other remains. The
next day, upon the site of Ephesus a mile or so to the southwest, they
were able to make out the vestiges of a theater and some arches and
shafts of columns but little that suggested the famous Temple of
Diana. Byron, in fact, had to admit that "the Temple has almost perished, and St. Paul need not trouble himself to epistolize the present
brood of Ephesians, who have converted a large church built entirely of marble into a mosque, and I don't know that the edifice looks

6. *Journey,* II, 64.
7. *Travels in Spain and the East,* pp. 106–07. In his account Darwin remarks that
"we anchored in the harbour of Piraeus, and found Lord Byron and Mr. Hobhouse
here visiting the remains of Grecian splendour."
8. *Journey,* II, 70.   9. *Journey,* II, 70–3.   1. *Journey,* II, 94 ff.

the worse for it."[2] Among the ruins the melancholy wail of hundreds of jackals was to be heard.[3]

The journey from Smyrna to Ephesus furnished Byron with the setting and much of the material for a fragment of a novel which he wrote in Switzerland during June, 1816. At that time Byron, Shelley, Mary Shelley, and Dr. Polidori had been reading German ghost stories together to help pass away a rainy period when, according to Mrs. Shelley, Byron suggested that each of the group write an original ghost story. This they set about doing; Shelley's and Polidori's contributions came to nought but Mary Shelley's was the first draft of her famous novel, *Frankenstein*. And Byron's own incomplete story is extremely interesting both as a reminiscence of his travels in Asia Minor and as a striking example of the self-absorption of his imaginative faculties, particularly in times of emotional stress.[4]

The surviving fragment purports to be a story told by a young Englishman who "In the year 17—" traveled through the southern part of Europe to the East in the company of one Augustus Darvell, a college friend of considerable fortune and ancient family. When they were journeying from Smyrna to Ephesus, the friend's health, which had steadily been declining, failed him completely and he died in mysterious fashion in a Turkish cemetery, after gaining from his horrified companion a promise that he would never tell of the death. Here, probably at the point where it was just getting under way, the story very unsatisfactorily breaks off.[5]

What is first remarkable about this fragmentary tale is the very accurate description it gives of the journey which Byron himself had taken to Ephesus six years before. The following passage is surprisingly close in its details to Hobhouse's description of the first half of the trip to Ephesus:

We had passed halfway towards the remains of Ephesus, leaving behind us the more fertile environs of Smyrna, and were entering upon that wild and tenantless tract through the marshes and defiles which lead to the few huts yet lingering over the broken columns of Diana—the roofless walls of expelled Christianity, and the still more recent but complete desolation of abandoned mosques—when the sudden and rapid illness of my companion obliged us to halt at a Turkish cemetery, the turbaned tomb-

2. *LJ*, I, 268. The previous summer, however, Darwin had noted the foundations of a building that seemed to fit the specifications of the ancient temple. *Op. cit.*, p. 46.

3. *P*, III, 495, n.

4. Byron's fragment is printed and the circumstances that led to its writing are described in Appendix IX to *LJ*, III, 446–53.

5. *LJ*, III, 449–53. Polidori later developed Byron's hints into a story, *The Vampyre* (London, 1819), which was published under mysterious circumstances as Byron's. According to Polidori, Byron had originally intended to have the surviving traveler, upon returning to England, startled to see his supposedly deceased friend moving in society and making love to his former companion's sister. See *LJ*, IV, 286–7, n.

stones of which were the sole indication that human life had ever been a sojourner in this wilderness. The only caravansera we had seen was left some hours behind us, not a vestige of a town or even cottage was within sight of hope, and this "city of the dead" appeared to be the sole refuge of my unfortunate friend, who seemed on the verge of becoming the last of its inhabitants.[6]

In Hobhouse's account of the journey he mentions the imperturbability of Suliman, the Janizary: "But Suliman was not to be persuaded to participate in our impatience; he would not quit his smoking pace (for he had a pipe in his mouth during nearly the whole journey)."[7] One is not surprised to find in Byron's story "Suleiman, our janizary, who stood by us smoking with great tranquillity."[8]

It is worth noting that Byron also included in the markedly autobiographical poem, "The Dream," which he wrote at about this same time,[9] a passage reminiscent of the East and especially of Asia Minor:

> . . . in the wilds
> Of fiery climes he made himself a home,
> And his Soul drank their sunbeams; he was girt
> With strange and dusky aspects; he was not
> Himself like what he had been; on the sea
> And on the shore he was a wanderer;
> There was a mass of many images
> Crowded like waves upon me, but he was
> A part of all; and in the last he lay
> Reposing from the noontide sultriness,
> Couched among fallen columns, in the shade
> Of ruined walls that had survived the names
> Of those who reared them; by his sleeping side
> Stood camels grazing, and some goodly steeds
> Were fastened near a fountain; and a man
> Clad in a flowing garb did watch the while,
> While many of his tribe slumbered around:
> And they were canopied by the blue sky,
> So cloudless, clear, and purely beautiful,
> That God alone was to be seen in Heaven.[1]

Byron's Augustus Darvell is not a particularly absorbing or attractive character. What makes him interesting is his close resemblance to Byron himself. Not only was he a man of family and fortune; he was also reserved and prey to a "shadowy restlessness" that made travel attractive to him. His feelings were acute but unpredictable; he

---

6. *LJ*, III, 451.   7. *Journey*, II, 110.   8. *LJ*, III, 451.
9. The poem is dated July, 1816.
1. Sir Walter Scott highly praised this descriptive scene for its perspective and "true keeping" in the *Quarterly Review*, XVI (1816), 181–3.

showed "an inquietude at times nearly approaching to alienation of mind."[2]

Byron's own state of mind at Smyrna was far from settled. John Galt, coming there toward the end of Byron's stay, observed in him more brusqueness and assertiveness than he had noticed previously. This was especially noticeable one evening during a dinner party at the consul's, where Byron appeared "inclined to exact a deference to his dogmas, that was more lordly than philosophical,"[3] and withdrew petulantly within himself when one of the naval officers ventured to disagree with him on a point of politics. Underneath such displays of temperament Galt detected for the first time in Byron a seeming dissatisfaction and purposelessness; he was forcibly struck by the "undetermined state of his mind."[4]

One might say with some truth that this was "simply Byron" but Galt had seen a good deal of Byron previously and it seems reasonable to believe that he was observing him now in one of his recurrent and frequently prolonged moods of depression. Galt was ready to attribute Byron's unrest to his anxiety about remittances from his lawyer Hanson[5] but it is probably true also that by this time the novelty and excitement of travel had begun to wear off somewhat and Byron was impatient to get on to Constantinople.

At Smyrna Byron completed his first draft of *Childe Harold* on March 28.[6] Two weeks later he and Hobhouse embarked on the *Salsette* frigate, under command of Captain Bathurst, for Constantinople.[7] The *Salsette* had been ordered there to convey the British Ambassador, Mr. Robert Adair, from the Porte. As Byron departed from Smyrna, Mrs. Werry, the wife of the English Consul, clipped a lock from his hair and shed many tears— "Pretty well for fifty-six years at least," Hobhouse drily observed.[8]

The *Salsette* sailed past Lesbos, the modern Mytilene, and came to anchor at Tenedos on April 12.[9] From this island a *Salsette* party, including Byron and Hobhouse, went ashore the following day to visit the ruins of Alexandria Troas.[1] The following morning the passengers found themselves at anchor about a mile and a half below Cape Sigeum; and there, since an imperial order was necessary before they could enter the Dardanelles, they were compelled to linger for over two weeks.[1a] This enforced delay, and a further halt of ten days at the entrance to the straits, offered the travelers ample opportunity to

2. *LJ*, III, 449.   3. Galt, p. 130.   4. Galt, p. 131.
5. *Ibid.* Hanson's recalcitrancy was nothing new, for Byron had been writing letters of complaint to him ever since he arrived at Malta. See *LJ*, VI, 443–8. In October, 1810, Byron was still protesting. *LJ*, VI, 453.
6. *P*, II, xvi.   7. *Journey*, II, 112.   8. *Recollections*, I, 28.
9. *Journey*, II, 114.   1. *Journey*, II, 117–27.   1a. *Journey*, II, 128.

become acquainted with the famous region known as the Troad, which occupies the northwestern promontory of Asia Minor.

The Troad extends from the Dardanelles, or Hellespont, about forty miles south to the Gulf of Adramyttium, and from the Ægean roughly the same distance east to the range of Ida. Not until the late nineteenth century, when the archaeological researches of Schliemann bore such rich fruit, was the exact location of Homer's city of Troy established beyond reasonable doubt as the modern Hissarlik.[3] In Byron's time disputes were still raging not only about the site of the city but also about the very existence of Homer's ancient land. The controversy had received renewed impetus through the early years of the century by the publication in 1796 of Jacob Bryant's *Dissertation Concerning the War of Troy, and the Expedition of the Grecians, as Described by Homer; Showing That No Such Expedition Was Ever Undertaken, and That No Such City of Phrygia Existed.*

Hobhouse, in his *Journey*, devoted many pages to treating with scholarly care and caution the various problems, chiefly geographical, relating to the existence of Troy.[4] Byron, however, in characteristic fashion, exclaimed that

I have stood upon that plain *daily*, for more than a month in 1810; and if any thing diminished my pleasure, it was that the blackguard Bryant had impugned its veracity. It is true I read *Homer Travestied* (the first twelve books), because Hobhouse and others bored me with their learned localities, and I love quizzing. But I still venerated the grand original as the truth of *history* (in the material *facts*) and of *place*. Otherwise it would have given me no delight. Who will persuade me, when I reclined upon a mighty tomb, that it did not contain a hero?—its very magnitude proved this. Men do not labour over the ignoble and petty dead—and why should not the *dead* be *Homer's* dead?[5]

From his cabin window Byron could see the so-called Tomb of Antilochus, one of the huge barrows that rose from the plain of the Troad.[6] And each day the travelers went ashore to explore. Although they could see no traces of the ancient Ilium itself, the mysterious barrows, the river Scamander, and Mount Ida in the distance were enough to excite both wonder and curiosity. Yet the days were not entirely devoted to antiquarianism; as Byron put it, "The Troad is a fine field for conjecture and snipe-shooting, and a good sportsman and an ingenious scholar may exercise their feet and faculties to great advantage upon the spot;—or, if they prefer riding, lose the way

3. See Heinrich Schliemann, *Troja, Results of the Latest Researches and Discoveries on the Site of Homer's Troy and in the Heroic Tumuli and Other Sites, Made in the Year 1882* (New York, 1884).
4. *Journey*, II, 128–211.   5. *LJ*, v, 165–6.   6. *LJ*, I, 262.

(as I did) in a cursed quagmire of the Scamander, who wriggles about as if the Dardan virgins still offered their wonted tribute."[7]

Byron had Pope's *Iliad* with him and took pleasure in reading it "on the spot." He later protested against Wordsworth's and Leigh Hunt's criticism of the inaccuracy of Pope's translation of the well-known moonlight scene at the end of the eighth book. Byron defended Pope's version not on the grounds of its fidelity to the original Greek poem but for its descriptive accuracy and correspondence to the actual scene as he himself saw it:

I have read it on the spot; there is a burst, and a brightness, and a glow about the night in the Troad, which makes the "planets vivid," and the "pole glowing." The moon is—at least the sky is, clearness itself; and I know no more appropriate expression for the expansion of such a heaven —o'er the scene—the plain—the sky—Ida—the Hellespont—Simois— Scamander—and the Isles—than that of a "flood of glory."[8]

Though Childe Harold never reached the Troad, Byron later took Don Juan there, under most distressing circumstances, en route to the slave market at Constantinople. In lighthearted stanzas that contrast with the very heavy heart of poor Don Juan, Byron in 1819 once more admired the high barrows, Ida, and "old Scamander." As for Juan:

> Another time he might have liked to see 'em,
> But now was not much pleased with Cape Sigeum.[9]

A vivid prose passage also shows the lasting impressions made upon Byron during the period the *Salsette* was anchored off the Troad:

I recollect, when anchored off Cape Sigeum in 1810, in an English frigate, a violent squall coming on at sunset, so violent as to make us imagine that the ship would part cable, or drive from her anchorage. Mr. H[obhouse] and myself, and some officers, had been up the Dardanelles to Abydos, and were just returned in time. The aspect of a storm in the Archipelago is as poetical as need be, the sea being particularly short, dashing, and danger-ous, and the navigation intricate and broken by the isles and currents.

---

7. *LJ*, I, 265.

8. *LJ*, III, 241. In the same passage Byron upbraided Wordsworth, for whom he rarely had a good word, for the inaccuracy of his description of Greece in the *Excursion*, which had just appeared. With reference to the lines "Rivers, fertile plains, and sounding shores, Under a cope of variegated sky" (Bk. IV, ll. 719–20) Byron pointed out emphatically that "The rivers are dry half the year, the plains are barren, and the shores *still* and *tideless* as the Mediterranean can make them; the sky is anything but variegated, being for months and months but 'darkly, deeply, beautifully blue.' " *LJ*, III, 240. Byron was always scornful of the ignorance and provinciality of his less-traveled fellow poets, even remarking once of his idol Sir Walter Scott, "Ah! I wish these home-keeping bards could taste a Mediterranean white squall, or the Gut in a gale of wind, or even the Bay of Biscay with no wind at all." *LJ*, III, 117.

9. *Don Juan*, IV, 75.

Cape Sigeum, the tumuli of the Troad, Lemnos, Tenedos, all added to the associations of the time. But what seemed the most *"poetical"* of all at the moment, were the numbers (about two hundred) of Greek and Turkish craft, which were obliged to "cut and run" before the wind, from their unsafe anchorage, some for Tenedos, some for other isles, some for the Main, and some it might be for Eternity. The sight of these little scudding vessels, darting over the foam in the twilight, now appearing and now disappearing between the waves in the cloud of night, with their peculiarly *white* sails, . . . skimming along as quickly, but less safely than the sea-mew which hovered over them; their evident distress, their reduction to fluttering specks in the distance, their crowded succession, their *littleness*, as contending with the giant element, which made our stout 44's *teak* timbers . . . creak again; their aspect and their motion, all struck me as something far more "poetical" than the mere, broad, brawling, shipless sea, and the sullen winds, could possibly have been without them.[1]

This may be a remembrance of the day, April 16, when Byron made his first and unsuccessful attempt to swim across the Hellespont, for he mentioned riding all the way from the Troad on that morning.[2]

On the first day of May the *Salsette* was finally permitted to proceed but the ship had no sooner entered the Dardanelles than breezes failed and it became necessary to anchor off the town of Chanak-Kalessi on the Asiatic shore.[3] There the travelers were delayed for ten more days, first by the lack, then by the violence, of the wind. Those days they mainly spent visiting the shores of the Hellespont and making further excursions back over the Troad;[4] in a small bay they frequently amused themselves by tossing land tortoises into the water and diving for them.[5]

The chief event of the period was, however, Byron's celebrated crossing of the Hellespont, which in partial imitation of Leander he accomplished on May 3.[6] This performance was not merely a great lark but an achievement of which Byron was extremely proud for

1. *LJ*, v, 544–5. This passage is a part of Byron's reply to W. L. Bowles's *Invariable Principles of Poetry, in a Letter Addressed to Thomas Moore, Esq., Occasioned by His "Specimens of British Poetry,"* Particularly Relating to the Poetical Character of Pope (London, 1819): thus Byron's special use of the term "poetical" since he is answering Bowles's contention that the works of nature are more fitting subjects for poetry than the works of art.

2. *P*, III, 13, n.   3. *Journey*, II, 212–5.
4. *Journey*, II, 215–21.   5. *LJ*, V, 250.
6. *LJ*, I, 263–4. Byron first mentioned the exploit in this letter, written to Drury on the very day. There are also references to it in every letter he wrote during the next two months! Byron's fullest account (*LJ*, v, 246–51) was inspired in 1821 by William Turner's depreciatory remarks ·in his *Journal of a Tour in the Levant*. Turner insisted that Byron had performed only the easier part of Leander's feat and that therefore his accomplishment was inconclusive. Byron defends himself with characteristic energy and eloquence. For Turner's reply see Appendix VII to *LJ*, v, 601–03.

the remainder of his life.[7] It was one of those grand gestures of which he was so fond and, despite the skepticism of others, he also considered it substantial proof that Leander could have accomplished his legendary exploit. Byron performed, to be sure, only half of Leander's task but it was enough to give him enormous satisfaction. He can surely be pardoned for the many half-serious, half-humorous references to the feat in the letters he wrote during the weeks to follow.[8] And the lines "Written after Swimming from Sestos to Abydos" rank among Byron's most lively jeux d'esprit.

The crossing of the Hellespont was, indeed, a difficult task and one but rarely performed. Byron and Lieutenant Ekenhead of the *Salsette* swam from a cape on the European shore to a point about a mile and a half below the anchorage of the frigate. The direct distance from shore to shore would have been about a mile but the swimmers were carried so forcibly by the current that they were obliged to swim nearly four miles before they reached the opposite bank. Byron was in the chilly waters for an hour and ten minutes, Ekenhead five minutes less.

Along the Hellespont Byron also got around to writing a long letter, his first, to Henry Drury, and another, the first since Gibraltar, to Hodgson. In these he described his experiences and impressions, telling Drury he found the Turks sensible people, who differed from the English chiefly in their taciturnity and the length of their dresses. His present mood he summed up with the pronouncement that "All countries are much the same in my eyes. I smoke, and stare at mountains, and twirl my mustachios very independently."[9] A few days later he told Hodgson, with how much seriousness it is hard to say, of his vow to reform his way of life, "for I begin to find out that nothing but virtue will do in this damned world."[1]

The shores of the Hellespont were, of course, the setting for *The Bride of Abydos,* which Byron wrote when he could not empty his head of the East[2] in 1813. Not fully content with the nostalgic opening lines, beginning

> Know ye the land where the cypress and myrtle
> Are emblems of deeds that are done in their clime?

7. In *Don Juan,* II, 105, appear the lines:
> A better swimmer you could scarce see ever,
> He could, perhaps, have passed the Hellespont,
> As once (a feat on which ourselves we prided)
> Leander, Mr. Ekenhead, and I did.

8. Miss Mayne loses all sense of perspective and humor (*op. cit.,* p. 115) in devoting a long paragraph to belittling the episode.

9. *LJ,* I, 268.   1. *LJ,* I, 272.

2. *LJ,* III, 407. Byron says, "The scene is in the Hellespont—a favorite *séjour* of mine." In another place he wrote that the composition of this poem wrung his thoughts

and the poignant reminiscences of "Helle's wave" and the Troad at the beginning of the second canto, Byron could not restrain himself from the forthright assertion:

> Oh! yet—for there my steps have been;
> These feet have pressed the sacred shore,
> These limbs that buoyant wave hath borne—[3]

Galt is the authority for the statement that while the *Salsette* lay off the Dardanelles Byron one day "saw the body of a man who had been executed by being cast into the sea, floating on the stream, moving to and fro with the tumbling of the water, which gave to his arms the effect of scaring away several sea-fowl that were hovering to devour."[4] Just so did the body of Selim float "round Sigaeum's steep" at the end of *The Bride of Abydos*.[5]

At least one of the characters in *The Bride of Abydos* derives from Byron's recollections of Asia Minor. The Bey Oglou's kinsman, whom Giaffir intended as the husband of Zuleika, was, to be sure, an imaginary figure but Carasman Oglou, the Bey himself, was a very real person indeed, the powerful governor of the neighboring district of Magnesia and the principal landholder in Turkey.[6] Byron surely heard a great deal about the Bey Oglou during the time the *Salsette* lay off the Troad and the Hellespont. Of him in *The Bride* the unfortunate Selim exclaims:

> . . . a braver man
> Was never seen in battle's van.
>
> .   .   .   .
>
> Enough that he who comes to woo
> Is kinsman of the Bey Oglou.[7]

On the eleventh of May, when the travelers had all but abandoned hope of reaching Constantinople, the winds at last blew gently from the south and the *Salsette* was able to sail up the straits to the Sea of Marmora and the Turkish capital on its farthest shore.[8] In approaching Constantinople Byron was nearing the capital of a nation with which until very recently his own country had been technically at war. When the French influence had succeeded in stirring up war between Russia and Turkey in 1806, the British agreed to send a fleet against Turkey in support of their ally Russia.[9] British prestige suf-

"from selfish regrets to vivid recollections—and recalled me to a country replete with the *brightest* and *darkest*, but always most *lively* colours of my memory." *LJ*, II, 361–2.

3. *The Bride of Abydos*, II, 510–12.   4. Galt, p. 144.
5. Lines 1081–1102 give the very effective picture of Selim's fate.
6. *P*, III, 166, n. See also *Journey*, II, 361.
7. *The Bride of Abydos*, I, 198–9, 205–06.   8. *Journey*, II, 221–9.
9. Fremantle, *England in the Nineteenth Century*, II, 190 ff.

fered when Admiral Duckworth's fleet, after forcing the Dardanelles and threatening Constantinople, was compelled to withdraw down the straits with heavy losses. When, however, after the Treaty of Tilsit Russia broke with England, it was to England's interest to restore peace with Turkey. With this end in view and at the same time to keep Turkey from the toils of France, a mission headed by Sir Robert Adair arrived in Constantinople in July, 1808. Adair succeeded in his task but only with great difficulty and in January, 1809, negotiated the Treaty of the Dardanelles.[1] Thereafter he stayed on a few months as British Ambassador to consolidate the peace and then ill-health kept him there until 1810. Relations between the Porte and England were, then, on a friendly basis when Byron came to Constantinople.[2] Turkey's war with Russia was, however, to continue until 1812.

On the afternoon of May 13 Byron and Hobhouse had their first glimpse of Constantinople as the minarets of Santa Sophia and the mosque of Sultan Ahmet rose dimly before them in the distance.[3] The wind was blowing hard from the north and it was only after considerable tacking that the *Salsette* was able to cast anchor just below Seraglio Point. Soon the stillness and darkness were so complete that it was hard for the Englishmen to believe that they had arrived at one of the great cities of the world.

The following noon, as the wind still blew violently down the Bosphorus upon them, the captain's boat took the passengers a mile along the sea walls of the Seraglio and finally with some difficulty landed them on the farther shore of the famous harbor known as the Golden Horn. From there they rode nearly a mile up the steep hill to a comfortable inn, where they enjoyed the most satisfying meal they had eaten since leaving Falmouth.[4]

As they made their way along the walls of the Seraglio, Byron had viewed a grisly sight that he used later in his poetry. It is certain that the ghastly description of dogs devouring the dead in *The Siege of Corinth*[5] was suggested to Byron by firsthand experience; in a note to the passage he wrote, "This spectacle I have seen, such as described, beneath the wall of the Seraglio in Constantinople, in the little cavities worn by the Bosphorus in the rock, a narrow terrace of which projects between the wall and the water. . . . The bodies were probably those of some refractory Janizaries."[6]

1. The two volumes of Adair's *The Negotiations for the Peace of the Dardanelles* give in detail the steps that led to the eventual success of the mission.

2. Cockerell, who was in Constantinople at the same time as Byron, wrote, "The English have the best reputation of any Franks in this country." *Travels in Southern Europe and the Levant, 1810–1817*, p. 20.

3. *Journey*, II, 229.   4. *Journey*, II, 237–9.

5. The description is found in ll. 454–78.

6. *P*, III, 468, n.: Hobhouse (*Journey*, II, 238) mentions seeing "two dogs gnawing a dead body along the Seraglio walls."

The following day Byron and Hobhouse called on the Ambassador, Mr. Adair, and found young Stratford Canning, the secretary of the British Embassy, performing Adair's functions during his illness.[7] Throughout their first two weeks in Constantinople they were privileged to dine at the Ambassador's palace. Canning had played against Byron in a Harrow-Eton cricket match but had never met him. In his memoirs some years later he recalled that in Constantinople they "took several rides together, and I still retain a most agreeable recollection of his good nature and varied conversation."[8]

Then as now Constantinople was divided by the Golden Horn into two distinct sections: on the western shore Stamboul, the ancient Turkish city, bounded by the walls of Theodosius; and on the east shore the relatively modern suburbs of Galata and Pera. In the latter, which has long been known as the "Frank" quarter, Byron and Hobhouse as a matter of course stayed. This ordinarily pleasant cosmopolitan district was, however, as the European section of Smyrna had been, now divided into hostile national camps, with the result that there was very little sociability or entertainment.[9]

The travelers had not been many days at Pera before they crossed to visit the older part of the city, where almost everything that was of interest and antiquity was to be seen. One day they managed to procure horses and ride along the mouldering and magnificent walls of Theodosius from the Golden Horn.[1] This was one of Byron's most thrilling experiences:

Imagine four miles of immense triple battlements, covered with ivy, surmounted with 218 towers, and, on the other side of the road, Turkish burying-grounds (the loveliest spots on earth), full of enormous cypresses . . . I have traversed great part of Turkey, and many other parts of Europe, and some of Asia; but I never beheld a work of nature or art which yielded an impression like the prospect on each side from the Seven Towers to the end of the Golden Horn.[2]

In the course of their walks about the city the travelers saw also the various antiquities of the Hippodrome, the ancient cisterns and aqueducts, and the extensive, crowded bazaars.[3] On several occasions they watched the astonishing performances of the whirling and howling dervishes.[4] The Seraglio they found surrounded on land as well as sea by high and gloomy walls. Peering through a grating they could see, crowned with red-and-yellow turbans, the sepulchers of the unfortunate Sultans Selim III and Mustapha IV, who had met

7. *LJ*, I, 273; *Recollections*, I, 29.
8. Stanley Lane-Poole, *The Life of the Right Honourable Stratford Canning, Viscount Stratford de Redcliffe . . . from His Memoirs and Private and Official Papers* (London, 1888), I, 84.
9. Cockerell, *op. cit.*, pp. 36–7. 1. *Journey*, II, 319–21.
2. *LJ*, I, 282. 3. *Journey*, II, 331–42. 4. *Journey*, II, 310–18.

violent ends a few years before.[5] In niches on each side of the Seraglio gate it was the custom to expose the heads of state criminals and victims of the Sultan's wrath. Several were on display at the time of Byron's visit; he mentions "among others, the head of the Pasha of Bagdat, a brave young man, cut off by treachery, after a desperate resistance."[6]

During their first week in Constantinople Byron and Hobhouse also went with the officers of the *Salsette* to see the arsenal and to inspect the Turkish fleet.[7] As a preliminary gesture they paid a call upon the Capitan Pasha, or High Admiral. This Turk was a man of great power, with control over all the islands and seaports of the Turkish empire; he was also an important member of the council of state and was surrounded by attendants when the Englishmen visited him. The High Admiral was not, however, very well versed in nautical matters and it soon developed that, though he was fond of the water, he had never actually been to sea.[8] The Pasha's appearance seemed to bear out the reputation for ferocious cruelty which he enjoyed; when Byron came to write *The Giaour* he recalled that "the Capitan Pacha's whiskers at a diplomatic audience were no less lively with indignation than a tiger cat's, to the horror of all the dragomans; the portentous mustachios twisted, they stood erect of their own accord, and were expected every moment to change their colour, but at last condescended to subside, which, probably, saved more heads than they contained hairs."[9]

As the Englishmen examined the port of Constantinople, the sight of several hundred Russian prisoners was a reminder that Turkey was at war.[1] With Turkish officers the visitors later went on board the *Sultan Selim*, the fine ship of the Capitan Pasha, and they were also received with great cordiality aboard a Turkish seventy-four. Troops, picturesquely and brightly arrayed, were departing daily. In every street there were bustle and the sound of arms. Yet mingled with the quickened military activity was a note of despondency, for the Turks were aware of a prophecy that the empire would expire with the line of Mahmoud; and the present sultan remained childless.

Among the chief glories of Constantinople were, of course, the

5. *Recollections*, I, 30. During the rebellion of the Janizaries in 1807, Selim, who had reigned for eighteen years, was first deposed and later killed. His nephew Mustapha, who succeeded him, was put to death the following year.

6. *P*, III, 167, n.   7. *LJ*, I, 273–5; *Journey*, II, 292–300.

8. Hobhouse may be overstating here (*Journey*, II, 294) but an article in *The New Monthly Magazine*, XVII (1826), emphasizes the inefficiency and half-heartedness of the Turkish Navy under the Capitan Pasha, Haffiz-Ali. See especially p. 309.

9. *P*, III, 114, n. On July 4 Byron told Hodgson, "The Russians and Turks are at it, and the Sultan in person is soon to head the army; the Captain Pasha cuts off heads every day, and a Frenchman's ears; the last is a serious affair." *LJ*, I, 286–7.

1. *Journey*, II, 296–7.

spacious mosques whose minarets rose at almost every hand. These the travelers did not visit until they had been in the city for over a month; and they were fortunate in being able to see the mosques at all for, with the exception of Santa Sophia, the sacred buildings could be visited by foreigners only by special permission, rarely granted, of the Sultan himself. Fortunately, however, as a compliment to the departing Ambassador, the English in Constantinople were allowed to view the mosques on June 15 and Byron and Hobhouse, along with other foreigners, had the opportunity to inspect Santa Sophia, Little Santa Sophia, and the royal mosques of Ahmed, Osman, and Suleiman.[2] Both were disappointed in the famous Santa Sophia; Byron wrote that it was "inferior in beauty and size to some of the mosques, particularly 'Soleyman,' etc., and not to be mentioned in the same page with St. Paul's."[3]

Byron and Hobhouse also made excursions to the environs of Constantinople; the most rewarding of these were the trips they took up the Bosphorus.[4] The Ambassador's barge carried them one day to the edge of the Black Sea, where Byron took great delight in scrambling up the sides of the famous rocks, the Symplegades, with the appropriate lines from the *Medea* in his head. Reaching the summit, he composed his own brief but exuberant translation of Euripides' passage and sent it in a letter to Drury.[5] They also visited on the European side the village and vast forest of Belgrade and the resort town Buyukdere; on the Asiatic shore the chief point of interest was a mountain known as the "Giant's Grave." All along the Bosphorus were the brightly painted villas of the leading families of Constantinople.[6] Byron spoke from memory when in *Don Juan* he wrote:

> The wind swept down the Euxine, and the wave
> Broke foaming o'er the blue Symplegades;

2. *Journey*, II, 345–56.
3. *LJ*, I, 282. The comparison with St. Paul's was suggested by Byron's mistaken recollection that Lady Mary Wortley Montagu had preferred Santa Sophia to it. See *LJ*, I, 281–2 and n. The architect Cockerell was a member of the party with Byron and Hobhouse; feeling himself fortunate in an opportunity to view the mosques, he found them, however, "ill-built and barbarous." *Op. cit.*, p. 15.
4. *Journey*, II, 258–77. There is evidence that while at Constantinople Byron also engaged in some boating on a *smaller* scale. An unpublished note, dated June 20 and addressed simply to "Dear Doctor," reads: "They tell me the wind is too high for an expedition to Serajlio Point, and I cannot think of putting your precious life in peril but I hope to have the pleasure another day." *Catalogue of the Renowned Collection of Autograph Letters and Historical Manuscripts Formed by the Late Alfred Morrison* (London, 1917), p. 341.
5. *LJ*, I, 276–7.
6. *Don Juan*, V, 46:
> Each villa on the Bosphorus looks a screen
> New painted, or a pretty opera-scene.

One of Byron's translations from the Armenian in 1816 was "The Pleasure Houses of the Summer of Byzantium." *LJ*, IV, 434–6.

> 'Tis a grand sight from off "The Giant's Grave"
> To watch the progress of those rolling seas
> Between the Bosphorus, as they lash and lave
> Europe and Asia, you being quite at ease:
> There's not a sea the passenger e'er pukes in
> Turns up more dangerous breakers than the Euxine.[7]

Early on the morning of May 28 the Englishmen in Constantinople assembled to accompany their Ambassador to his audience with the Camaicam,[8] who represented the Grand Vizier during the latter's absence in the Russian wars. Byron, arriving at the Ambassador's palace in scarlet regimentals and a profusely feathered cocked hat, inquired first of Canning and then of Adair what place he was to occupy in the procession. When it developed that, according to Turkish etiquette, he would have to follow the members of the Embassy Byron stalked away "with that look of scornful indignation which so well became his fine imperious features"[9] and took no part in the ceremony. In a few days, to be sure, he realized his foolishness and wrote to the Ambassador that another time he would cheerfully follow "not only your Excellency, 'but your servant or your maid, your ox, or your ass, or anything that is yours.' "[1]

An Englishman who lived for some years in Constantinople has described the appearance one day of a young countryman of his, accompanied by a Janizary and guide, in a shop where each had come to purchase some pipes. The Englishman had heard of Byron's recent arrival on the *Salsette* and when he noticed this young man's very visible lameness he was convinced that the purchaser must be Byron. He described him thus:

He wore a scarlet coat, richly embroidered with gold, in the style of an English aide-de-camp's dress-uniform, with two heavy epaulettes. His countenance announced him to be about the age of two-and-twenty. His features were remarkably delicate, and would have given him a feminine appearance but for the manly expression of his fine blue eyes. On entering the inner shop, he took off his feathered cocked-hat, and showed a head of curly auburn hair, which improved in no small degree the uncommon beauty of his face. The impression which his whole appearance made on my mind was such, that it has ever since remained deeply engraven on it.[2]

When Byron experienced difficulty in making his desires known to the shopkeeper, his fellow purchaser addressed him in English and offered to interpret for him. The result was gratifying:

When his Lordship thus discovered me to be an Englishman, he shook me cordially by the hand, and assured me, with some warmth in his manner,

7. *Don Juan*, v, 5.   8. *Journey*, II, 357–9.   9. Lane-Poole, *op. cit.*, I, 86.
1. *LBC*, I, 9.   2. *The New Monthly Magazine*, XVII (1826), 310–1.

that he always felt great pleasure when he met with a countryman abroad. His purchase and my bargain being completed, we walked out together and rambled about the streets, in several of which I had the pleasure of directing his attention to some of the most remarkable curiosities in Constantinople. The peculiar circumstances under which our acquaintance took place, established between us in one day a certain degree of intimacy, which two or three years frequenting each other's company in England would most likely not have accomplished.[3]

When, however, this same Englishman saw Byron later in the week at the Ambassador's and requested that he be regularly introduced, to his surprise and chagrin Byron spoke coldly and immediately turned his back on him.[4]

The more agreeable third scene in this very characteristic little drama of the Byronic temperament is also best described in the words of the original teller:

It was not, therefore, without some surprise, that, some days after, I saw him in the street coming up to me with a smile of good nature in his countenance. He accosted me in a familiar manner; and, offering me his hand, said—"I am an enemy to English etiquette, especially out of England; and I always make my own acquaintances without waiting for the formality of an introduction. If you have nothing to do, and are disposed for another ramble, I shall be glad of your company." There was that irresistible attraction in his manner, of which those who have had the good luck to be admitted into his intimacy, can alone have felt the power in his moments of good humor; and I readily accepted his proposal. We visited again more of the most remarkable curiosities of the capital, . . . but his Lordship expressed much disappointment at their want of interest. He praised the picturesque beauty of the town itself, and its surrounding scenery; and seemed of the opinion, that nothing else was worth looking at. He spoke of the Turks in a manner which might have given reason to suppose he had made a long residence among them, and closed his observations with these words:—"The Greeks will sooner or later rise against them; but, if they do not make haste, I hope Bonaparte will come and drive the useless rascals away."[5]

On July 10 the long-awaited audience with the Sultan took place. Byron, though attired in his brilliant English staff uniform, now went along as a simple individual, "delighting those who were nearest him," in the words of Canning, "by his well-bred cheerfulness and good-humoured wit."[6] Rather surprisingly, Byron gives no details of the episode in his letters, merely referring to the fact that at Adair's audience of leave he "saw Sultan Mahmout."[7] Hobhouse, however, describes the occasion at great length.[8]

3. *Idem*, p. 311.   4. *Idem*, pp. 311–2.   5. *Idem*, p. 312.
6. Lane-Poole, *op. cit.*, I, 86.   7. *LJ*, I, 287.   8. *Journey*, II, 363–72.

In accordance with Turkish custom, the elaborate ceremony commenced at 4.30 A.M. with a processional on horseback from the Ambassador's palace to the shore. As the party, consisting of the Ambassador and his suite and English friends, was rowed across the harbor to the Seraglio, the guns of the *Salsette* saluted them. On the grounds of the imperial residence, after passing through two courts, they reached the council chamber, where in the presence of the Englishmen the Caimacam, or Vice-Vizier, rather ostentatiously distributed moneybags to the Janizaries. It was part of the ritual of the Sublime Porte that foreigners should be fed and clothed before they could be presented to the imperial presence. At the hour of ten, therefore, under the auspices of the Caimacam, dinner was served in the council chamber. Byron and Hobhouse were among the few who were permitted to sit as they "tasted" a banquet consisting of twenty-two dishes.

After the visitors had been fed they were duly clothed; the fifteen or twenty who had been selected to witness the audience of the Sultan were now provided with fur robes and, thus attired, were conducted into the presence chamber. In that small dark room, which was almost completely filled by the resplendent throne on which the Sultan reclined, the English Ambassador took his leave. Adair delivered a short address to his Imperial Majesty, expressing his hope for enduring friendship between England and Turkey and his confidence that the present war against Russia would reach a favorable conclusion under the Sultan's leadership.[9] To these sentiments the Sultan replied briefly but politely and delivered into the Ambassador's hands a letter for his sovereign George III. Through this ceremony, for the sake of effect "the dead silence was broken only by the speeches, a lighted lamp glimmered, a small fountain trickled, in their respective corners, and two spare turbans of imperial shape surmounted with plumes from the bird of paradise, appeared in a recess near the throne."[1]

Apparently Sultan Mahmoud made no lasting impression upon Byron. No further references to him exist in Byron's very abundant writings and the Gilbertian Sultan in the fifth canto of *Don Juan* shows only a very general resemblance to the flesh-and-blood monarch whom Byron saw in Constantinople. Hobhouse describes Mahmoud as a gorgeously attired young man of less than thirty years whose glossy, jet-black eyes, brows, and beard gave him an unmistakable air of majesty.[2] Yet the fact seems to be that the Sultan was more impressed with Byron than was Byron with the Sultan, for it has been recorded that "His youthful and striking appearance and the splendour of his dress, visible as it was by the looseness of the

9. *Op. cit.*, II, 87.   1. Lane-Poole, *op. cit.*, I, 85.   2. *Journey*, II, 369–70.

pelisse over it, attracted greatly the Sultan's attention, and seemed to have excited his curiosity."[3]

Byron intended to go on with *Childe Harold* when he was in the Troad and Constantinople but failed to do so.[4] There is some reference to the Turkish capital in the stanzas added to the second canto in 1814[5] but in them Byron does not so much introduce Constantinople in an explicit manner as he uses it for contrast with Greece, which is his first concern. Constantinople, "the city won for Allah from the Giaour," may be freed some day, Byron writes, but Freedom will never seek the fated soil of Greece. Speaking of the pre-Lenten carnival in Athens, he alludes again to Constantinople and in three stanzas (79–81) describes the spirited song and merriment he observed along the Bosphorus.

Byron, in fact, disdained at the time to write any extended description of Constantinople, feeling that task had been adequately performed by Gibbon, Lady Mary Wortley Montagu, and other travelers.[6] He later spoke of the port of Constantinople as "the most beautiful of harbours," especially at night when the Turkish vessels of war were illuminated in very picturesque manner.[7] And in *Don Juan* he summed up the beauties of Constantinople in one stanza:

> The European with the Asian shore
>   Sprinkled with palaces—the Ocean stream
> Here and there studded with a seventy-four,
>   Sophia's Cupola with golden gleam,
> The cypress groves, Olympus high and hoar,
>   The twelve isles, and the more than I could dream,
> Far less describe, present the view
> Which charmed the charming Mary Montagu.[8]

For the more particularized descriptions in *Don Juan* Byron does not seem to have drawn in any precise way upon memories of 1810. Galt is right in saying of the vague descriptions of the slave market and the harem that "they have not that air of truth and fact about them which render the pictures of Byron so generally valuable, independ-

3. *The New Monthly Magazine*, xix (1827), 147. Here the same anonymous writer who had seen Byron previously mentions also that in 1824 the Sultan insisted that the English lord whom he saw in 1810 was not Byron but a woman dressed in man's clothes.

4. *LJ*, ii, 28. Byron writes, "I feel honoured by the wish . . . that the poem should be continued, but to do that I must return to Greece and Asia; I must have a warm sun, a blue sky; I cannot describe scenes so dear to me by a sea-coal fire. I had projected an additional canto when I was in the Troad and Constantinople, and if I saw them again, it would go on; but under existing circumstances I have neither 'heart nor voice' to proceed."

5. *Childe Harold*, ii, 77–83.

6. *History of the Decline and Fall of the Roman Empire* (London, 1789), ii, 1–15; *Letters of Lady Mary Wortley Montagu Written During Her Travels in Europe, Asia, and Africa* (London, 1793), i, 146–52, and ii, 1–53.

7. *LJ*, v, 545.   8. *Don Juan*, v, 3.

ent of their poetical excellence."[9] The harem, one can be certain, Byron never saw and if he did see the slave market it was an unimpressive and pitiful sight at that time.[1] But of what he *did* see in 1810, it is indeed surprising that ten years later Byron remembered as much as he did. Also, it was probably significant for the development of *Don Juan* that "On the borders of the Black Sea, we heard only of the Russians."[2]

There was, all this time, little opportunity really to know the Turkish people at first hand.[3] Natives and foreigners were divided geographically by the Golden Horn and since none but Turks were allowed to live in the old city it was impossible to establish any intimacy with the natives. In addition there were the formidable barriers of language, religion, and custom, and the natural reticence of the Turks. On the basis of what he was able to observe, however, Byron was inclined to rate the men of Turkey above the Greeks, Spaniards, and Portuguese.[4] He was quick to defend them from charges of ignorance and intolerance and, pointing out that schools were established (and regularly attended) in all the mosques, he insisted that the Turks were not deficient in education or in the common arts of life. Byron declared:

The Ottomans with all their defects, are not a people to be despised . . . If it be difficult to pronounce what they are, we can at least say what they are *not;* they are *not* treacherous, they are *not* cowardly, they do *not* burn heretics, they are *not* assassins, nor has an enemy advanced to *their* capital. They are faithful to their sultan till he becomes unfit to govern, and devout to their God without an inquisition. Were they driven from St. Sophia tomorrow, and the French or Russians enthroned in their stead, it would become a question whether Europe would gain by the exchange. England would certainly be the loser.[5]

Byron had nothing but praise for the Turks' high sense of honor in all business transactions. Nowhere, he felt, was there "a more honourable, friendly, and high-spirited character than the true Turkish provincial Aga, or Moslem country gentleman."[6] Of the Turkish women, however, he could say nothing, for the Turks "take too much care of their women to permit them to be scrutinized."[7]

Galt mentions that the self-abstraction he had noticed about Byron at Smyrna was also observed by others at Constantinople.[8] The re-

---

9. Galt, p. 151.   1. *Journey,* II, 254.   2. *LJ,* II, 11.

3. *Journey,* II, 231–3. Cockerell, too, makes the point that "it is not easy to get into any intimacy with Turks." *Op. cit.,* p. 32.

4. *LJ,* I, 281. Byron seems here, however, to be using the term "Turk" in its broadest sense, to include all the Mohammedans of the Near East. He apparently has the "Albanian Turks" in mind as well as those he saw in Asia Minor and Constantinople.

5. *P,* II, 206.   6. *P,* II, 205.   7. *LJ,* I, 271.

8. Galt, p. 153. See also Moore, I, 235.

marks of that same Englishman who had met Byron in the pipe shop and seen a good deal of him thereafter, tend to bear this out:

The eccentricities of his manners and mode of living already distinguished him from other men. The kind of unconcern with which he seemed to view mankind in general, and the little intercourse he held even with his most intimate acquaintances, were calculated to impede his knowledge of men, or at least confine it within a very narrow space. His principal studies were of an abstract kind, or such as to divert the attention from the common occurrences of life. The profound knowledge of the human heart which he has exhibited in all his writings, . . . appears, therefore, to have been the result of a remarkable quickness of perception, assisted by much theoretical information.[9]

Indeed, at times Byron's manner was so difficult to understand that some foreign residents in Pera went to the extreme of pronouncing him insane.[1] It is impossible to judge how much of the impression Byron created at this time was conscious and how much was the natural expression of his temperament. He wrote rather mysteriously to Adair that "The fact is, I am never very well adapted for, or very happy in, society, and I happen at this time, from some particular circumstances, to be even less so than usual."[2]

Byron was uncertain about the future. By the time he reached Constantinople it was becoming evident that he would have neither the energy nor the funds to proceed on into Persia and India as he had originally intended. By now, too, a certain travel-weariness had no doubt set in. And there was no *Childe Harold* to occupy his thoughts. The writing of that poem, subjective as much of it was, had been both an emotional strain and release. Now he was somehow not ready to go on with the poem. And, fond though he was of Hobhouse, it was hard for Byron to be so close to any human being for so long a time.[3] But soon it developed that Hobhouse would have to return to England; for a while Byron thought he would have to do the same but he finally decided, without any great conviction, to return to Greece. "But I am quicksilver," he told Drury, "and say nothing positively."[4]

From the easternmost bounds of his pilgrimage a new and more serious note appeared in the letters to his mother. In late June he wrote:

All I am afraid of is that I shall contract a gipsylike wandering disposition, which will make home tiresome to me . . . I have not been disappointed

9. *The New Monthly Magazine*, xix (1827), 147–8.
1. *Ibid.*   2. *LBC*, i, 9.
3. *LJ*, i, 286. On June 7 Byron had written the gay "Farewell Petition to J. C. H. Esqre," in which he poked fun at that unheroic servant Fletcher and at Hobhouse's projected book of travels.
4. *LJ*, i, 278.

or disgusted. I have lived with the highest and the lowest. I have been for days in a Pacha's palace, and have passed many a night in a cowhouse, and I find the people inoffensive and kind . . . God knows, I have been guilty of many excesses, but . . . I have laid down a resolution of reform, and lately kept it.[5]

To Dallas he conveyed his convictions that

all climates and nations are equally interesting to me; that mankind are everywhere despicable in their different absurdities; that the farther I proceed from your country the less I regret leaving it, and the only advantage you have over the rest of mankind is the sea, which divides you from your foes; your other superiorities are merely imaginary. I would be a citizen of the world, but I fear some indispensable affairs will soon call me back; and as I left the land without regret, I shall return without pleasure.[6]

The echo of Byron's sentiments as he left Falmouth a year before is unmistakable.[7] On July 14 he departed from Constantinople on the *Salsette*, which was England-bound. Three days later he bade Hobhouse farewell at the port of Zea and proceeded to Athens.[8]

5. *LJ*, I, 280–3.   6. *LJ*, VI, 452.   7. Cf. *LJ*, I, 225.
8. *Journey*, II, 407; *LJ*, I, 287. In his *Recollections* (I, 32) Hobhouse rather melodramatically described the farewell: "Took leave, *non sine lacrymis*, of this singular young person, on a little stone terrace at the end of the bay, dividing with him a little nosegay of flowers; the last thing perhaps I shall ever divide with him."

IV

Second Year: Greece and Return to England

WHEN Byron returned to Greece on July 18, 1811, he was, according to his own words, "woefully sick of travelling companions."[1] Yet no sooner had he reached Athens than he was greeted by the Marquess of Sligo,[2] who, when he heard that Byron intended to visit the Morea, expressed the desire to go with him as far as Corinth. It was with some reluctance that Byron consented. Sligo, the unhappy possessor of "a brig with 50 men who won't work, 12 guns that refuse to go off, and sails that cut every wind except a contrary one,"[3] was now temporarily forced to give up the sea and travel by land. So on July 21 twenty-nine horses carried the joint Byron-Sligo party "over the hills and far away" toward Corinth; Byron, who had mentioned in a letter to his mother the day before that "Your northern gentry can have no conception of a Greek summer,"[4] observed that the temperature was 125 degrees![5]

Byron informed Hobhouse that en route Sligo told him "some things that ought to set you and me by the ears"[6] but what those things were he refused to divulge. It is evident that Byron did some confiding himself. Along the way he spoke often and unfavorably to Sligo of his mother and when they stopped to bathe in the Gulf of Corinth Byron pointed to his own leg and foot, exclaiming, "Look there!—it is to her false delicacy at my birth that I owe my deformity; and yet, as long as I can remember, she has never ceased to taunt and reproach me with it. Even a few days before we parted for the last time, on my leaving England, she, in one of her fits of passion, uttered an imprecation upon me, praying that I might prove as ill-formed in mind as I am in body!"[7] Sligo offered to take his friend for a long cruise but Byron did not find the prospect very attractive. At Corinth, after a rather trying trip, their lordships separated, Byron and his five attendants bound for Patras, Sligo and his for Tripolitza.

At Patras Byron had some business with the Consul, Mr. Strané; otherwise, as he remarked, he spent his time "alone very much to my

1. *LJ*, I, 290–1. For the chronology of Byron's second year in Greece see Appendix A, sec. II.
2. Howe Peter Browne, Lord Altamont (1788–1845), who became the second Marquess of Sligo in 1809, had been a Cambridge friend of Byron's.
3. *LBC*, I, 10.   4. *LJ*, I, 289.   5. *LBC*, I, 10.
6. *LBC*, I, 11.   7. Moore, I, 242.

satisfaction, riding, bathing, sweating, hearing Mr. Paul's musical clock, looking at his red breeches."[8] To his mother he wrote:

I am very well, and neither more nor less happy than I usually am; except that I am very glad to be once more alone, for I was sick of my companion, —not that he was a bad one, but because my nature leads me to solitude, and that every day adds to this disposition . . . The greater part of Greece is already my own, so that I shall only go over my old ground, and look upon my old seas and mountains, the only acquaintances I ever found improve upon me.[9]

From Patras Byron journeyed southward to Tripolitza, the capital of the Morea. There, as Veli Pasha prepared to march with his troops to join the Sultan against the Russians, Byron found more of the atmosphere of warfare than he had experienced since he left Spain.[1] Ali Pasha's son, the Vizier of the Morea, received Byron with even greater pomp and attention than his father had done, presenting him with a handsome stallion, conducting him to the door with his arm around his waist, and urging that he meet him with his army later at Larissa.[2] "He honoured me," wrote Byron, "with the appellations of his *friend* and *brother,* and hoped that we should be on good terms, not for a few days but for life."[3] After such a gratifying reception it is not surprising that Byron for a time seriously considered the possibility of traveling to Larissa to see the Pasha again.

Returning by way of Argos, Byron met Sligo once more[4] and continued on his way to Athens. There he "auspiciously settled" himself for the remainder of his stay in ample quarters at the Capuchin monastery. The famous monument of Lysicrates had been converted into a study which was an ideal retreat for reading and writing.[5] In one of his gayest letters Byron described the manner of existence he led during the weeks that followed. One wonders whether his craving for solitude was satisfied, for the monastery housed not merely the friar, the six boys who were his scholars, and Byron but also Byron's "suite," which now numbered five men of assorted nationalities.[6] "These gentlemen," Byron wrote of the schoolboys, were "almost (saving Fauvel and Lusieri) my only associates."[7] The tempo of life at the monastery was far from ecclesiastical: "We have nothing but riot from noon to night."[7a] The boys romped, Byron's servants divided their time between drink and intrigue, and several Albanian women devoted their leisure hours to "running pins into Fletcher's backside."[7b]

8. *LBC*, I, 11.   9. *LJ*, I, 295.   1. *LBC*, I, 12.
2. *LJ*, I, 303.   3. *LBC*, I, 12.   4. *LBC*, I, 14.
5. William Miller, *Essays in the Latin Orient* (Cambridge, England, 1921), p. 386.
6. These were Fletcher, the Albanians Dervish and Vasilly, the Greek Andreas Zantachi, and "Sullee, my new Tartar." *LBC*, I, 16.
7. *LBC*, I, 14.   7a. *LBC*, I, 14.   7b. *LBC*, I, 15.

And far from objecting to such invasions upon his privacy, Byron declared himself to be "vastly happy and childish."

His special favorite was the Greek boy, Nicolo Giraud. Byron wrote to Hobhouse, "I am his 'Padrone' and his 'amico,' and the Lord knows what besides. It is about two hours since, that, after informing me he was most desirous to follow *him* (that is me) over the world, he concluded by telling me it was proper for us not only to live, but 'morire insieme.'" Nicolo was instructing him in Italian, Byron revealed, "but my lessons, though very long, are sadly interrupted by scamperings, and eating fruit, and peltings and playings; and I am in fact at school again, and make as little improvement now as I did there, my time being wasted in the same way."[1] Perhaps his friendship with Nicolo had something to do with Byron's changed attitude at this time toward Elgin's agent Lusieri; Nicolo was the son of Lusieri's "should-be wife."[2] Byron now spoke of Lusieri as "a new ally of mine."[3]

At about this time in Athens Byron became involved in an incident which, he said, first suggested to him the story of *The Giaour*.[4] Several versions of the episode have survived and Byron, far from attempting to clarify the details, seems to have taken pleasure in confusing the curious and leaving the whole matter shrouded in mystery. That something *did* happen is almost certain. But, on the basis of Byron's own hints, of a letter written to him about the affair by Sligo, and of the not always consistent reports of others, one can feel sure only that Byron somehow concerned himself in an incident involving the imminent death of a Greek girl who, like her counterpart in *The Giaour*, was to be tossed into the sea in the customary Turkish manner.

According to Sligo's account,[5] Byron, returning from the Piraeus one day, met the procession which was conducting the unfortunate victim to the waterside. When he became aware of their purpose and of the identity of the girl, he was said to have drawn a pistol and forced the leader of the group to return with him to Athens to the Governor's house. There, by threats, bribery, and entreaty, Byron reputedly succeeded in gaining the girl's pardon but only with the understanding that she leave Athens; he had her conveyed to safety in Thebes.

Byron wrote later that Sligo's account was not far from the truth. But he hinted that there was more to the story. One phase of the incident, he insisted, was more singular than any of the Giaour's adventures[6] but "to describe the *feelings* of *that situation* were impossible—it is *icy* even to recollect them."[7] Medwin recounted the adventure with Byron himself as the lover of a female slave,[8] while

---

1. *LBC*, I, 16.   2. *LBC*, I, 23.   3. *LBC*, I, 16.
4. *LJ*, II, 311.   5. *LJ*, II, 257-8, n.   6. *LJ*, II, 311.
7. *LJ*, II, 361.   8. *Conversations of Lord Byron*, pp. 121-4.

Hobhouse thought Byron's Turkish servant was the girl's love.[9] The true facts remain obscure.

Byron rode to the Piraeus each day and swam for an hour or so in the harbor.[1] On one occasion as he was diving from the molehead there he was observed by Lady Hester Stanhope, who, with her friend Michael Bruce and her physician Dr. Meryon, was crossing from Corinth under the guidance of Lord Sligo.[2] The fame of Byron's swim across the Hellespont had already reached these travelers and they could hardly have had a more appropriate first glimpse of Byron. Byron saw a good deal of Lady Hester and her companions at the beginning of their stay in Athens but a few days after their arrival he surprised them by pleading urgent business at Patras and disappearing from Athens for several weeks.[3]

One cannot say for certain whether Lady Hester's presence in Athens caused Byron to hurry away so unexpectedly but in the light of the opinion he expressed of her to Hobhouse it seems highly probable that she was at least an important factor:

I saw the Lady Hester Stanhope at Athens, and do not admire "that dangerous thing a female wit." . . . She evinced a . . . disposition to *argufy* with me, which I avoided by either laughing or yielding. I despise the sex too much to squabble with them. . . . I have seen too little of the Lady to form any decisive opinion, but I have discovered nothing different from other she-things, except a great disregard of received notions in her conversation as well as conduct. I don't know whether this will recommend her to our sex, but I am sure it won't to her own.[4]

And Lady Hester, herself a headstrong person, was no more complimentary in her opinion of Byron. She afterward amused her friends by mimicking his little affectations, especially his habit of solemnly giving orders to his Greek servant in Romaic.[5] Years after, she recollected him as a temperamental, self-interested, quixotic individual and, with very little knowledge of it, deprecated his poetry.[6] Lady Hester's strongest indictment was the statement, "He had a great deal of vice in his looks—his eyes set close together, and a contracted brow."

Byron took Nicolo Giraud with him to the Morea. On the way they were blown ashore on the island of Salamis[7] but apparently traveled

9. *Westminster Review*, III (1825), 27. Kampouroglou has availed himself of this incident in his *Attikoi Erotes*, where the victim is none other than the melancholy Turkish girl who had mysteriously appeared and vanished from Byron's sight in the opening scene at the Acropolis.

1. *LBC*, I, 16.

2. C. L. Meryon, *Travels of Lady Hester Stanhope* (London, 1846), I, 36.

3. *Idem*, p. 42.   4. *LJ*, I, 302–03.

5. A. W. Kinglake, *Eothen* (London, 1879), p. 123.

6. Meryon, *Memoirs of Lady Hester Stanhope* (London, 1848), III, 193–4. Moore, however (I, 243) speaks of them as becoming "most cordial friends."

7. *LJ*, I, 307.

on undeterred. Their goal seemed to be Olympia but at Patras Byron contracted a violent fever and we next find him recovering there. It would be hard to find better examples of that "relish for the ridiculous which makes my life supportable"[8] than the three gay poems Byron composed during his illness and sent to his friends.[9] One, an epitaph, fortunately did not have to be used; his picture of himself on his bed of pain is diverting to the reader and seems to have been so to Byron:

> Poor B-r-n sweats, alas! how changed from him,
> So plump in feature, and so round in limb.[1]

The fever was a violent one and Byron enjoyed attributing his recovery not to the "assassins"[2] in the shape of physicians who attended him but to his loyal Albanians who "nursed me with an attention which would have done honour to civilization."[3]

To Hodgson Byron wrote from Patras in what seems a mood of mock self-pity:

I have really no friends in the world; though all my old school companions are gone forth into that world, and walk about there in monstrous disguises, in the garb of guardsmen, lawyers, parsons, fine gentlemen, and such other masquerade dresses. So, I have shaken hands and cut with all these busy people, none of whom write to me. Indeed, I asked it not;—and here I am, a poor traveller and heathenish philosopher, who hath perambulated the greatest part of the Levant, and seen a great quantity of very improvable land and sea, and, after all, am no better than when I set out—Lord help me![4]

The next day, on the other hand, he had exciting news for Hobhouse: all Albania was in an uproar since Ibrahim Pasha and an ally had retaken Berat from Ali and were threatening Tepelini. The very mountains Byron and Hobhouse crossed the year before were now the scene of warfare; Veli Pasha was, to the Sultan's consternation, hurrying to his father's assistance.[5]

Nicolo caught the fever also but as soon as both were sufficiently recovered they set out for Athens again.[6] At Corinth for the second time an unpleasant episode took place when both the Bey and Codja-

8. *LBC*, I, 17.   9. *LBC*, I, 17–18; *LJ*, I, 298.
1. *LBC*, I, 18.   2. *LJ*, I, 298.
3. *P*, II, 175. Byron later enjoyed telling how his Harrow friend Robert Peel (later Sir Robert) insisted he had passed him on St. James Street twice within a few days in the fall of 1810. Moreover, it was reported to Byron that he had been seen writing down his name among those inquiring after the health of the King, then attacked by insanity, at this same period. "Now," Byron told Murray, "at this period, as nearly as I could make out, I was ill of a *strong fever* at Patras, caught in the marshes near Olympia, from the *Malaria*. If I had died there, this would have been a new Ghost Story for you." *LJ*, v, 87.
4. *LJ*, I, 298–9.   5. *LJ*, I, 303.   6. *LBC*, I, 18.

bashee refused Byron a lodging despite the inclemency of the weather; eventually he was able to acquire a "miserable cottage."[7] Also it was probably during this "tolerable tour of the Morea"[8] that Byron was the guest of a retired Arnout robber near Gastouni. His picturesque buskins, "plated in scales one over the other, like the back of an armadillo [and] . . . sheathed behind with silver,"[9] suggested to Byron details for the description of Selim in *The Bride of Abydos:*

> The greaves below his knee that wound
> With silvery scales were sheathed and bound.[1]

Back at Athens, Byron now found his appetite for travel pretty well satisfied.[2] For the most part he was content to settle back into the life of Athens, spending the greater part of his time at the monastery, with "Hymettus before me, the Acropolis behind, the Temple of Jove to my right, the Stadium in front, the town to the left."[3] Byron rode regularly to the Piraeus and its environs, to be sure, and made occasional excursions to Marathon, Sunium, Hymettus, and across the Isthmus of Corinth.[4] In February he thought for a while of a trip to Egypt and Syria.[5] But most of his days during the next six months he passed contentedly in Athens and came to know the city and its people much more intimately than he had been able to do previously.

During this second winter in Athens Byron involved himself in a curious controversy over the placing in the Theseum of an epitaph in memory of the English traveler and antiquary John Tweddell. Ever since Tweddell had died in Athens in 1799, unavailing efforts had been made to erect an appropriate memorial.[6] In 1803 Lord Elgin had gone to the trouble of composing a long Latin inscription but it was not put to use; two years later the Reverend Robert Walpole composed an epitaph of his own in Greek. At this point the loyal Lusieri

---

7. See in Appendix B Byron's letter of complaint, dated October 13, 1810, to Stratford Canning, who had succeeded Adair as Ambassador to the Porte.

8. *LBC*, I, 18.   9. *P*, III, 184, n.   1. *The Bride of Abydos*, ll. 627–8.

2. *LJ*, I, 306.   3. *LBC*, I, 29–30.

4. *Ibid.* In speaking of *The Siege of Corinth* Byron wrote in 1815, "The Ground is quite familiar to me, for I have passed the Isthmus *six*, I think—*eight*, times in my way to and fro." *LJ*, III, 229. Byron also mentions (*LJ*, V, 574) several statues he saw on the island of Ægina.

5. *LJ*, VI, 455–6. Byron had received a firman from the Porte and told Hanson he would not return to England "before I have seen Jerusalem and Grand Cairo." In *Englische Studien*, XXV (1898), 152, there appears a letter from Hobhouse to Hanson, dated April 23, 1811, in which Hobhouse quotes from a letter written to him by Fletcher: "me Lord thinks of meaking a tower to Yerusalim." Hobhouse goes on to say, "I do not think that his Lordship will make the said tower; and, indeed, I very much wonder that he should like staying so long amongst such uninformed uninforming barbarians as the Turks. I was sick of them long before I came to the resolution of leaving their country."

6. William B. Dinsmoor, "Observations on the Hephaisteion," *Hesperia*, Suppl. v (1941), pp. 17–18.

rose in support of Elgin's contribution and a competition ensued between Lusieri, the champion of the Elgin inscription, and some of
the English in Athens, who backed Walpole's.[7]

In the winter of 1811 Byron and his friend John Fiott joined the
Walpole faction. A correspondent of Walpole's, perhaps Fiott, gives
a lively account of the civil war that followed. When Lusieri pro-
posed first that the Walpole inscription be engraved on a marble slab
below the Elgin epitaph and then that it be engraved on the wall of
the temple, Byron, according to Walpole's correspondent, "entered
most heartily into the cause, and supported your [Walpole's] inscription." Two other Englishmen, Cockerell and Foster, also gave their
support and nothing remained "but to act in defiance of Lusieri; and
to act a l'Italienne, in secret, lest he should place his stone in the
temple before we could get another ready."[8]

While Lusieri was preparing his own tablet, the English conspira-
tors set about procuring a marble slab of their own. There were many
difficulties: "The Disdar offered to sell any marble in the Acropolis;
but Athens could not furnish means to remove one thence on account
of the size; and no person possessed a cart but Lusieri. A beautiful
marble next fell in our way, and it required sawing through the
middle; but no one in Athens had a saw but Lusieri." Finally, however, a slab of convenient size was found in a private home and was
dragged to the temple. There, on February 15, it was placed in the
exact center, where Fauvel had been careful to have Tweddell's grave
dug a dozen years before in the hope of finding some remains of
Theseus! So Byron and his confederates had the satisfaction of tri-
umphing over Lusieri and Elgin. The engraving on the tablet was
completed a week later with the assistance of Lusieri's rival Fauvel.
Apparently the Latin epitaph of the vanquished Lusieri was placed
somewhere in the Theseum but neither survives today.[9]

Byron's memorializing activities in Athens did not stop there. The
summer before, a Mr. George Watson had died in the Greek capital
and was also buried in the Theseum.[1] Ten days after the Tweddell
victory the Englishmen succeeded in getting hold of yet another
marble and on it was engraved a Latin epitaph of Byron's own composition. Byron's epitaph commemorates not a close friend but a
countryman who died in a land far from home. The epitaph, which

---

7. *Remains of John Tweddell*, Reverend Robert Tweddell, ed., (London, 1816), pp.
13–14.

8. *Idem*, p. 16.   9. Dinsmoor, *op. cit.*, pp. 20–4.

1. Byron wrote to Hobhouse on August 23: "Here hath been an Englishman ycleped
Watson, who died and is buried in the Tempio of Theseus. I knew him not, but I am
told that the surgeon of Lord Sligo's brig slew him with an improper potion, and a cold
bath." *LBC*, I, 16.

can still be seen in the Theseum although it is footworn and partially obliterated, reads:[2]

HIC OSSA QUIESCUNT

GEORGII WATSON ARM: BRITANNI

QUEM

NEC ANIMI VIRTUTES CORPORIS VIRES

JUVENTUTIS VER NEC HAEC SALUBERRIMA REGIO

CONSERVARENT

OBIIT XVII KAL. SEP. MDCCCX

SI MISERANDUS IN MORTE

SALTEM IN SEPULCHRO FELIX

Early in December Byron rode one day with several of his friends to Sunium. Although they did not realize it until several days afterward, the party had a narrow escape from some Mainote pirates who were concealed in the caves below with some Greek boatmen as their prisoners. Only the sight of Byron's Albanian attendants, it developed, deterred the pirates from attacking the "Franks" on the cliff above. Byron's Dervish had had a presentiment of danger as they approached the cape but his alarm was ridiculed by the others. A few days later, however, Dervish was redeemed when one of the Greek victims, who had been released, described the appearance and behavior of the travelers on the cliff so accurately that there could be no doubt that they had seen them from the cave below.[3]

There were many more English in Athens than there had been during the preceding winter. The day after he first returned from Constantinople Byron noted that "Messrs. North,[4] Knight,[5] and Fazak-

2. William Miller, *The English in Athens before 1821*, p. 17.

3. The episode is described in *P*, II, 169; *P*, III, 134–5; and *LBC*, I, 24–5.

4. The Honorable Frederick North (1776–1827), the youngest son of George IV's Prime Minister, had been an ardent lover of Greece since his Oxford days. In 1810 he had already traveled widely and had been Governor of Ceylon. North became the first president of the Society for Promotion of Culture at Athens in 1814 and ten years later he was one of the founders of the Ionian University. As chancellor of that institution he aroused ridicule in England by wearing the ancient classical costume. He became the fifth Earl of Guilford in 1817. Though other travelers, notably Holland, Hughes, and Williams, paid high tribute to North's accomplishments as a scholar and a philhellene, Byron always spoke scornfully of him. His designation of North as "the most illustrious humbug of his age and country" (*LJ*, IV, 182) is but one of Byron's milder judgments.

5. Henry Gally Knight (1786–1846) had been known to Byron at Cambridge. In August, 1809, he joined Byron and Hobhouse at Cadiz. He had since been traveling in the company of North and Fazakerly. Knight rivaled North in the disesteem of Byron, who in 1820 exclaimed, "I would rather be a Galley Slave than a Galley Knight—so utterly do I despise the middling mountebank's mediocrity in everything but his income." *LJ*, V, 68. Knight dedicated his *Eastern Sketches* (London, 1819) to his former Mediterranean companions, North and Fazakerly. Knight later became noted for his writings on architecture.

erly[6] paid me visits."[7] Now Byron mentioned other fellow countrymen who had come to Athens, most of them to engage in antiquarian
or architectural pursuits. Among them were Charles R. Cockerell[8]
and John Foster,[9] whom he had seen in Constantinople, and Sandford
Graham,[1] an old Trinity friend. Later the names of John Fiott[2] and
William Haygarth[3] appear in Byron's letters. With the exception of

6. John Nicholas Fazakerly (1787–1852), who became known as a scholar and antiquary, was educated at Eton and Oxford. He spent the years 1810–11 traveling in Spain
and the Near East with his friends North and Knight. Fazakerly later became a member of Parliament. There is a reference to his interview with Napoleon in the *Memoirs
of John Murray*, I, 350–1. Fazakerly was a witness at the Select Committee inquiry into
the Elgin marbles in February, 1816, and he expressed at that time his impression that
the marbles at Athens had been exposed to very considerable danger of deterioration.

7. *LBC*, I, 10. The editor makes no effort to identify Byron's Athens acquaintances
beyond giving their last names.

8. *LBC*, I, 23. Charles Robert Cockerell (1788–1863) was commencing his profes-
sional studies by exploring Greece, Turkey, and Asia Minor in 1810. At about the time
of Byron's departure from Greece in the spring of 1811, Cockerell and his companions
discovered the famous Ægina Marbles. Cockerell became one of England's most distinguished architects. He was professor of architecture at the Royal Academy and president of the Royal Institute of Architecture. The book, *Travels in Southern Europe and
the Levant, 1810–1817*, edited by his son S. P. Cockerell, consists largely of extracts
from the journal Cockerell kept in the Near East.

9. John Foster (1787?–1846) was a Liverpool architect, later the designer of some
of his city's chief buildings. Foster and Cockerell met at Constantinople in 1810 and
continued their travels and researches together in Greece. A letter written by Byron to
Foster shortly after the latter's arrival at Athens in December, 1810, reveals a slight con-
tretemps resulting from the disputed possession of that prime essential to travelers in
the Near East—a horse. The quarrel, which arose when Byron met Foster riding a horse
he claimed was his own, was speedily terminated when Byron wrote to Foster as follows: "No written agreement exists between the owner of the horse in question and
myself, but I assure you upon my *honour* the horse was to be mine at a certain sum a
day during my stay in Athens, and so far from its being in Giorgi's option to let him to
another, he obtained him under the pretext of his fatigue after a journey, to rest for a
few days only. As for the man, he is a liar and a rascal, and has contradicted himself
today twenty times before the Waywode and also before me, pretending 'that the horse
was taken by force,' 'that he wanted to sell him,' &c., &c. His object at present appears
to be that of causing a quarrel between the parties, in which, if he succeeds, it will not
be the. . . ." Here the letter, preserved only in part, breaks off. The text appears in
*The Collection of Autograph Letters and Historical Documents Formed by Alfred Mor-
rison*, Ser. 2, Vol. 1 (1893), 448.

1. Sandford Graham (1788–1852) was educated at Eton and Trinity College, Cambridge. In later life he was a member of Parliament and Fellow of the Society of Antiquaries. Graham became a baronet in 1824. Byron probably referred to Graham when,
in a note to a note to *Childe Harold* (*P*, II, 197, n.) he mentioned an excellent lexicon
he "received in exchange from S. G—, Esq., for a small gem: my antiquarian friends
have never forgotten it or forgiven me."

2. John Fiott (1783–1866), a graduate of St. John's College, Cambridge, was touring
the Near East from 1807–10 as a "travelling bachelor" of his college; he was primarily
engaged in collecting objects of antiquity, including manuscripts, coins, and medals. In
1815 Fiott assumed the name of Lee by royal license. He became eminent as a collector
and man of science. A Fellow of the Society of Antiquaries, Fiott-Lee was an original
member and later president of the Royal Astronomical Society.

3. William Haygarth (1784–1825), a graduate of Rugby, must have been known to
Byron at Trinity College, Cambridge, from which he received the B.A. in 1805 and
M.A. in 1808. During his visit to Greece in 1810–11 Haygarth began a poem in blank

North, all of these were young men, contemporaries of Byron's; few of them, however, had such unspecified ends in view as Byron. None, on the other hand, showed interest equal to Byron's in the Greeks as living people.

Also in Athens was a group of distinguished Continental men of the arts; Byron wrote in mid-November that he was "on good terms with five Teutones and Cimbri, Danes and Germans, who are travelling for an Academy."[4] Though Byron mentions only three of these by name, from other sources it is possible to identify the two companions of Baron Haller, Dr. Brönsted of Copenhagen and "a Bavarian Baron named 'Lynch' (pronounce it *Lynk*),"[5] as well as to provide further information about those three travelers themselves.[6] Two young Danish archaeologists, Peter Oluf Brønsted and George H. C. Koës, had shared since early youth the desire to visit Greece and to study the language and antiquities of classical lands.[7] When, after preparatory studies in France, they reached Rome in 1809, Brønsted

verse, which was published in London in 1814 as *Greece; a Poem, in Three Parts.* A panoramic view of Athens drawn by Haygarth appears facing p. 541 of the second volume of Walpole's *Travels in Various Countries of the East.*

4. *LJ*, I, 307.   5. *LBC*, I, 29.

6. Haller is mentioned by name in a letter to Hobhouse. *LBC*, I, 23. There are references to this interesting group in contemporary travel books but the fullest source of information regarding the men and their activities is an article by Peter Goessler, "Nordische Gäste in Athen um 1810," *Ephemeris Archiaolog.* (1937), 69–72. There is also useful material regarding the five travelers in Goessler's *Jakob Linckh, ein württembergischer Italienfahrer, Philhellene, Kunstsammler und Maler* (Stuttgart, 1930).

7. Peter Oluf Brönsted (1780–1842) and George H. C. Koës (1783–1811) were fellow archaeologists at the University of Copenhagen. In his *Voyages et recherches dans la Grèce* (Paris, 1826, 1830. 2 vols.) Brönsted wrote with respect to the Greek journey that "le désir de visiter le pays où avaient vécu, agi et écrit ces génies supérieurs, se transforma insensiblement en une ferme résolution." I, x. At Rome in 1810 Brönsted and Koës won over their new friends, Haller and Linckh, to the idea of an expedition to Greece, while Linckh in turn persuaded the less impulsive Stackelberg. So it turned out that Brönsted and Koës arrived with Linckh at the Piraeus in mid-September, a bare two weeks before the arrival of Haller and Stackelberg. Byron, who had been in the Peloponnesus in late summer and early fall, first mentions the travelers in a letter to Hodgson dated November 14. *LJ*, I, 307. Once arrived in Athens, Brönsted and Koës enthusiastically devoted the fall and early winter to explorations in and about the city, often in company with Stackelberg and their German companions, sometimes also with the Englishmen Cockerell and Foster. Later in the winter the two Danes set off with Stackelberg through Boeotia and Thessaly and across the Ægean to Asia Minor and Constantinople. At Ephesus they examined the remains of the Temple of Diana. The tragic death of Koës, who succumbed to a fever at Zante in September, 1811, cut short the close friendship of the two countrymen. Brönsted remained on in Greece, however, until 1813. His investigations with Linckh of the antiquities of the island of Zea and his archaeological and historical study of the Acropolis in the winter of 1812 provided the basis for his valuable two-volume work, *Voyages et recherches dans la Grèce.* Forty-four lectures, chiefly archaeological and topographical, delivered at the University of Copenhagen from 1815 to 1817, constitute Brönsted's *Reise i Graekenland i Varene 1810–13*, R. B. Dorph, ed. (Copenhagen, 1844). The volume also contains a biographical sketch by J. P. Mynster. In his later career Brönsted became a Chevalier of the Order of Denmark and was sent by his Government as Minister to Rome.

and Koës happened to meet three men whose enthusiasm for Greece matched their own. These were Karl Freiherr Haller von Hallerstein, an architect from Nuremberg;[8] Jacob Linckh, a Württemberg painter;[9] and Otto Magnus Freiherr von Stackelberg, an Esthonian archaeologist.[1] It was all but inevitable that the five kindred spirits

8. Karl Freiherr Haller von Hallerstein (1774–1817) was architect to Prince Louis of Bavaria and was traveling on a small allowance from his patron. He had been a student at Stuttgart, then studied architecture in Naples and Rome before joining the expedition to Greece. There he joined in the archaeological researches of his companions and also produced many noteworthy drawings and landscapes. Haller accompanied Linckh, Cockerell, and Foster to Ægina in the spring of 1811, assisted Cockerell and Stackelberg in the excavations of the Temple of Apollo at Bassae, and with Stackelberg engaged in investigations of ancient Athenian graves. Haller died suddenly in Thessaly in November, 1817. Brönsted, Cockerell, and others paid tribute to Haller's sterling abilities and generous nature; H. W. Williams (*Travels in Italy, Greece and the Ionian Islands,* I, 330–5) praised at some length the taste and expressiveness of his art. A portrait of Haller appears as an illustration in Cockerell's *The Temples of Jupiter Panhellenius at Ægina, and of Apollo Epicurius at Bassae near Phigaleia in Arcadia* (London, 1860).

9. Jacob Linckh (1787–1841), a native of Cannstatt, first sensed the appeal of an artistic career when he visited Rome as a boy of seventeen in 1804–05. Meeting at that time Thorwaldsen, Koch, and other important figures in the world of art, he returned to Rome in 1808 with the firm resolve to follow in their footsteps. When in 1810 a tour to Greece was projected, Linckh was quick to join his new-found friends Brönsted, Koës, and Haller in this venture and to win over his companion Stackelberg to the plan. The fall and winter of 1810–11 were devoted chiefly to excavations in Attica; Linckh did, however, visit Corinth in November and sketched the palace of Nari Bey there. In April, 1811, just as Byron was leaving for Malta, Linckh went with Cockerell, Foster, and Haller to Ægina, where the excavations on the site of the Temple of Jupiter proved so rewarding. Linckh's copious Ægina journal, edited by Paul Wolters, was published in the *Münchner Jahrbuch der Bildenden Kunst,* XII (1937–38), 151 ff. This journal and another kept at Bassae in July and August, together with many sketches of scenes, monuments, and ruins in Greece and Turkey, are in the possession of descendants at Schloss Rauhenzell near Immenstadt, Germany. Goessler, in his biography of Linckh (*op. cit.,* p. 21) points to Linckh's special talent for water colors, ink and sepia drawings, and miniatures. In 1812 Linckh engaged in excavations with Brönsted in the island of Zea, investigated Salamis with Stackelberg, and accompanied several of his friends to the Ionian Islands. In the summer of 1813 he visited Constantinople with the Austrian Vice-Consul at Athens, Gropius. Linckh left Greece for good in the spring of 1814. His close friendship with Stackelberg was renewed in Italy in later years; both were members of a society which later became the German Archaeological Institute. Linckh devoted the remaining years of his life to a creditable career as an artist and collector of vases, bronzes, and other art objects. A portrait of him by Vogel von Vogelstein is reproduced on p. 3 of Goessler's biography.

1. Otto Magnus Freiherr von Stackelberg (1787–1837) studied for a diplomatic career at the University of Göttingen but a growing interest in ancient art took him to Rome in 1808. There he became a close friend of the young Cannstatt painter Jacob Linckh; Linckh's influence and Stackelberg's own interest in the classical world prompted him to undertake the journey to Greece in 1810. The extent of Stackelberg's artistic pursuits in Greece and his interest in the people and country are shown by the paintings in his *Costumes et usages des peuples de la Grèce* (Rome, 1825) and *La Grèce; vues pittoresques et topographiques* (Paris, 1834). His chief contributions to archaeology are contained in *Der Apollotempel zu Bassæ in Arcadien* (Rome, 1826) and *Gräber der Hellenen* (Berlin, 1837). Stackelberg was, according to Thomas S. Hughes, "an accomplished young nobleman, who has rendered himself an universal favorite by his talents and engaging manners." *Travels in Sicily, Greece, and Albania,*

should shortly determine to visit Greece together. With the exception of Haller, all were under thirty and by good fortune they arrived in Greece at the beginning of a new epoch in the appreciation of Greek art, a period of new archaeological discoveries in which they were to play a leading part.

These were, then, the five "Teutones and Cimbri" with whom Byron had considerable contact during his second stay in Athens. Haller and Stackelberg accompanied him on several expeditions;[2] Linckh, the most talented and experienced painter of the group, Byron persuaded to do landscapes for him;[3] while Brönsted earned from him the tribute of being "a pretty philosopher as you'd wish to see." All were men of unusual talent and learning and other travelers who met them in Greece attested to their agreeable personal qualities. Byron's companionship with men of such strong enthusiasm and extensive knowledge of Greece past and present must indeed have quickened his own appreciation of Athens and its surroundings. And, great as were their contributions to knowledge of the classical glories of Greece, it is clear that their curiosity and interest extended also to contemporary conditions. Brönsted defended the modern Greeks against their detractors in much the same manner that Byron was himself to do.[4] In 1813 Haller, Stackelberg and Linckh were among the members of a society aiming to establish a library, museum, and schools in Athens and to assist needy Greek students. A year later Stackelberg became identified with another organization designed not only to protect Athenian antiquities but also to send young Greeks abroad for artistic training.[5] Here are early manifestations of that zeal for intellectual and artistic awakening that nourished the Greek revolutionary movement.

These distinguished foreigners, with Fauvel and Lusieri and some of the principal Greeks and Turks, made up a strongly cosmopolitan society. Byron's intercourse with such people led him to conclude:

I, 278. I have been unable to gain access to a memoir of Stackelberg by his niece Natalie von Stackelberg based on her uncle's diaries and letters; this work, which was available to Goessler, is entitled *O. M. von Stackelberg, Schilderung seines Lebens und seiner Reisen in Italien und Griechenland* (Heidelberg, 1882).

2. *LBC*, I, 23–4. Goessler (*Ephemeris Archiaolog.*, p. 75) gives from Natalie von Stackelberg's biography of her uncle the information that Stackelberg was with Byron at Sunium on November 18, 1810.

3. *LBC*, I, 29.

4. "On prétend que les Grecs sont dégénérés, et, chose assez singulière, des écrivains qui sont redevables aux Grecs de ce qu'ils ont appris at fait de mieux dans ce pays même, prennent à tache d'accréditer cette opinion. . . . Je demanderai seulement si un peuple européen, quel qu'il soit, après quatres siècles d'un honteux esclavage, ne serait pas encore plus dégénéré?" *Voyages et recherches dans la Grèce*, I, XVI.

5. Goessler, *Ephemeris Archiaolog.*, pp. 79–80. Also listed as members of the first society are Cockerell, Foster, and, interestingly enough, the three Macri sisters.

I am so convinced of the advantages of looking at mankind instead of reading about them, and the bitter effects of staying at home with all the narrow prejudices of an islander, that I think there should be a law amongst us, to set our young men abroad, for a term, among the few allies our wars have left us. Here I see and have conversed with French, Italians, Germans, Danes, Greeks, Turks, Americans, etc., etc., etc.; and without losing sight of my own, I can judge of the countries and manners of others.[6]

Byron had far more extensive and immediate intercourse with the Greeks than he had with the people of any of the other countries he visited. Not only were there the Greeks among whom he lived and those officials with whom he inevitably came into contact but it seems clear that during his second stay he became better acquainted also with some of the Greek families in the capital. In January he wrote, "We have had balls and a variety of fooleries with the females of Athens,"[7] and in March, "I am living here very amicably with English, French, Turks and Greeks."[8] Byron now had opportunity for a fuller and more considered judgment of the Greeks.

Byron did not find it easy to make up his mind. He could not overlook the cunning of the Greeks[9] nor could he deny that in their subjugated state they suffered from "all the moral and physical ills that can afflict humanity."[1] Yet now on closer acquaintance he did not find the Greeks without hope. He no longer looked upon them as

The helpless warriors of a willing doom.[2]

Byron now protested vigorously against those judgments he had been inclined to take for granted a year before—that the national degradation of the Greeks was complete and that there were no grounds for hoping for an improvement in their condition. Such views were universally maintained by the Franks in Athens: Fauvel insisted that by reason of their depravity the Greeks did not *deserve* to be emancipated; and the French merchant Roque exclaimed, "Sir, they are the same *canaille* that existed in the days of Themistocles."[3] But this wholesale condemnation of the Greeks now struck Byron as being both petty and unfair; he could not help feeling that it was "rather hard to declare so positively and pertinaciously, as almost everybody has declared, that the Greeks, because they are bad, will never be better."[4]

Byron still felt that the Greeks would never be independent, nor did he feel it was practicable or desirable that they should be completely so. But they could be "subjects, without being slaves."[5] They

6. *LJ*, I, 309. 7. *LBC*, I, 25. 8. *LBC*, I, 31. 9. *P*, II, 190.
1. *P*, II, 191. 2. *Childe Harold*, II, 73.
3. *P*, II, 190. 4. *P*, II, 190–1. 5. *P*, II, 191.

could be free and industrious in much the same way that England's colonies were free and industrious. And it was hardly fair to accuse them of ingratitude in their present state; indeed, the Greeks had little to be thankful for:

Where is the human being that conferred a benefit on Greek or Greeks? They are to be grateful to the Turks for their fetters, and to the Franks for their broken promises and lying counsels. They are to be grateful to the artist who engraves their ruins, and to the antiquary who carries them away; to the traveller whose janissary flogs them, and to the scribbler whose journal abuses them. This is the amount of their obligations to foreigners.[6]

Yet only the intervention of foreigners, Byron felt, could emancipate the Greeks.[7] This point of view is in strong contrast to his earlier cry:

> Hereditary Bondsmen! know ye not
> *Who* would be free *themselves* must strike the blow?[8]

Byron now blames the indifference of foreigners rather than that of the Greeks. A slight effort, he insists, is required for the Greeks to strike off their chains and only the apathy of the Franks prevents this from happening. The Greeks look now to the Russians, now to the French, now to the English for deliverance: "But whoever appear with arms in their hands will be welcome; and when that day arrives, Heaven have mercy on the Ottomans; they cannot expect it from the Giaours."[9]

It is worth noting also that Byron links the problem of the Greeks with that of other oppressed races and creeds, with the plight of the Negroes and Catholics in England, and of the Jews the world over. He prefaces one of his extended notes on the Greeks with the general statement that "Amongst the remnants of the barbarous policy of the earlier ages, are the traces of bondage which yet exist in different countries; whose inhabitants, however divided in religion and manners, almost all agree in oppression."[1]

The extremes to which most observers had gone in their opinions of the Greeks aroused Byron's special wrath. While some debased them unduly, others praised them far beyond what was reasonable.[2] Above all Byron insisted that one must look upon the Greeks as they *are*, without allowing himself to be blinded by what they once *were*. There was, unfortunately, a deplorable lack of correct and accurate information concerning these suffering people.[3] Byron stated his conclusion judiciously, that "there is a reasonable hope of the redemption of a race of men, who, whatever may be the errors of their religion and

6. *Ibid.*   7. *P*, II, 192.   8. *Childe Harold*, II, 76.   9. *P*, II, 193.
1. *P*, II, 192.   2. *P*, II, 191, 193–6.   3. *P*, II, 194–5.

policy, have been amply punished by three centuries and a half of captivity."[4]

There were already some stirrings of nationalism in Greece in 1811 but these were to be found in the sullen resentment of the people and in the strong convictions of such individuals as Andreas Londos[5] rather than in any organized movement. The patriotic songs of Rhigas were circulated among the people but there was more real activity for Greek regeneration in Vienna and Paris than there was in Athens itself.[6] In those foreign capitals, high-minded Greeks, most prominent among them Adamantios Korais,[7] were endeavoring by emphasis upon an intellectual revival to lift the local patriotism of the Greeks above its present impotence. Korais laid special stress upon the importance of a standardization and purification of the spoken language, the Romaic, as a means toward promoting national unity and strength. Byron was aware of the activities of Korais. In his notes he remarks of him that "to his exertions, literary and patriotic, great praise is undoubtedly due."[8] But Byron does not seem to have been aware that the process of purifying the Romaic was already under way and becoming a factor toward Greek regeneration.[9]

Byron's considerable efforts to gain further information about the Greeks are commendable. He frequently emphasized the fact that he was more interested in the modern language and the inhabitants than he was in antiquities. And in Greece Byron did more than merely master a few colloquial phrases of the language; during his second stay he settled down to studying the language under the direction of a tutor.[1] It has been pointed out that this tutor, Marmaratouri, was a leader among the Greek patriots and doubtless had something to do with Byron's change of opinion with regard to the future of the Greek people.[2] Marmaratouri was attempting at the time to publish his translation of Barthelemy's *Voyage du jeune Anacharsis* as a means to awakening national feeling; Byron included a prospectus of the translation in the Appendix to *Childe Harold*.[3]

Byron had a natural facility for languages. Moreover, his translations of Rhigas' Greek war song and of two Romaic love songs make it clear that he had attained considerable mastery of the native language by the time he left Athens. Though he mistook the meter of the Greek

4. *P*, II, 196.   5. See above, pp. 86–7.
6. Finlay, *History of the Greek Revolution*, I, 118 ff.
7. Korais, who was born in Smyrna in 1748, was one of the most distinguished classical scholars of his time as well as a powerful force in the promotion of modern Hellenism. See Stephen George Chaconas, *Adamantios Korais: A Study in Greek Nationalism* (New York, 1942).
8. *P*, II, 197.   9. *P*, II, 200.   1. *LJ*, I, 308.
2. Panos Morphopoulos, "Byron's Translation and Use of Modern Greek Writings," *Modern Language Notes*, LIV (1939), 318, n.
3. *P*, II, 208.

original of the war song, Byron did in several places enrich the expression of that work.[4] And comparison of the "Romaic Song," beginning "I enter thy garden of roses, Beloved and fair Haidee," with the words of the Greek text has revealed both Byron's excellent knowledge of Greek and his skill in creating an integrated poem.[5] This last song was a great favorite among the young girls of Athens; Byron heard it sung frequently during the winter of 1810–11 and described the air as "plaintive and pretty."[6] So much, indeed, did the song impress him that he had it copied for him just before leaving Greece in the spring of 1811.[7] To the second of the love songs, beginning "Ah! Love was never yet without / The pang, the agony, the doubt," Byron gave in translation a more impetuous tone than was evident in the more subdued Greek text.[8]

A further if less ambitious experiment in translation was Byron's English version of the opening passage of a long dramatic satire in modern Greek. In this work a Russian, Englishman, and Frenchman in turn interrogate a Greek patriot, an archbishop, a prince, a merchant, and a cogia bachi or primate concerning the miserable state of Greece. Although Byron did not make any great claims either for the poem or for his translation, it is interesting that the lines he rendered into English begin with an accusation very similar in tone to his own *Childe Harold* stanzas:

> Thou friend of thy country! to strangers record
> Why bear ye the yoke of the Ottoman lord?
> Why bear ye these fetters thus tamely display'd,
> The wrongs of the matron, the stripling, and maid?[9]

Once he had gained fair mastery of the Romaic, Byron had the opportunity to realize that the Greeks were not intellectually dormant but that, despite the necessity for having their work printed abroad, they were writing a surprising number of books. These had to be limited for the most part to religious works but Byron found it encouraging that books were being published at all.[1] His interest in making correct information about the Greeks more widely available

---

4. Morphopoulos, *op. cit.*, p. 322.

5. C. M. Dawson and A. E. Raubitschek, "A Greek Folksong Copied for Lord Byron," in *Hesperia*, XIV, No. 1 (1945), 33–57. With this valuable article are reproduced the MSS. of the poem as it was copied for Byron and of Byron's translation. The Greek version is in the possession of the Yale University Library; Professor Chauncey Brewster Tinker is the owner of Byron's manuscript.

6. *P*, III, 22, n.

7. The copyist was Dudu Roque. See Dawson and Raubitschek, *op. cit.*, p. 33.

8. Morphopoulos, *op. cit.*, p. 324. The poem appears in *P*, III, 62–3.

9. *Childe Harold's Pilgrimage, a Romaunt: and Other Poems* (London, 1812), p. 277.

1. *P*, II, 208.

is evident from his remarks in the third long note to *Childe Harold;*[2] in the further remarks, the Romaic extracts and translations, and the list of Romaic authors he included in the Appendix to that poem.

In mid-January Byron told his mother he was done with authorship and would not jeopardize what reputation *English Bards* had gained him by any further poetic efforts. He did not deny, to be sure, that he had some verses in manuscript but they would not be published in his lifetime; and he would write no more.[3] By the middle of March Byron had completed over seven hundred lines of *Hints from Horace*[4] and shortly afterward he appears to have written nearly two hundred lines of *The Curse of Minerva.*[5]

It is significant that Byron intended the *Hints from Horace* as a sequel to *English Bards.* His numerous references at this time to his first satire show how sensitive he was to that poem's reception.[6] Not forever would "the Mediterranean and the Atlantic roll between me and criticism"[7] and it is typical of Byron that, as he began to face the prospect of returning to England, he should want to have another arrow ready in his quiver. The mere accident that there was a copy of Horace in the Capuchin monastery must have had something to do with Byron's choice of subject matter.[8] But it was also inevitable that sooner or later so devoted an admirer of Pope should try what Pope had tried—an imitation of Horace. Nor could there be a more effective way of strengthening the attack upon the poets of the day than by indicting them through the words of so authoritative a spokesman of neoclassical orthodoxy as Horace.

Unfortunately *Hints from Horace* has impressed almost everyone except Byron himself as a mediocre poem and a far from worthy

---

2. *P*, II, 196–204.   3. *LJ*, I, 309.

4. *P*, I, 450. There are three known manuscripts of *Hints from Horace*. The last page of the earliest of these is dated March 11–12, 1811; the final date on the others is March 14. Of these last, one was probably completed in Greece and the other, the Murray MS., copied from it at Malta. See also *P*, I, 387.

5. It is impossible to say with certainty at just what time in 1811 *The Curse of Minerva* was written. The Stanhope MS., to which Coleridge referred in preparing his edition, is dated March 17 (*P*, I, 453) but *Hints from Horace* had been completed only on March 14; Byron could hardly have written and copied *The Curse of Minerva* in three days. There are two reasonable possibilities: Byron may have written *The Curse* in a rough form earlier in the winter and revised or copied it on March 17; or he may have begun the poem on March 17. On the following day in a letter to Hobhouse he remarked, "You see my scribbling propensities, though 'expelled with a fork,' are coming on again." *LBC*, I, 31. For a discussion of the manuscripts of *The Curse of Minerva* see Appendix C.

6. A typical passage is the following from *LBC*, I, 20: "If anybody is savage and wants satisfaction for my satire, write, that I may return and give it."

7. *LJ*, I, 267.

8. Claude M. Fuess, *Lord Byron as a Satirist in Verse* (New York, 1912), p. 77. On August 23, 1810, Byron had translated into Italian the famous thirtieth ode of the third book, beginning "Exegi monumentum." *LBC*, I, 16.

sequel to *English Bards*. Byron's diligence and ingenuity are undeniable; particularly in the first three hundred lines the poem is a surprisingly faithful and at times adroit rendition of its Latin original. But this is precisely the trouble—the ideas, and usually the very images, are Horace's, not Byron's. Only occasionally does a personal note enter in, as when Byron continues his attack upon Jeffrey[9] and when he presents an English nobleman's version of the "ages of man" theme.[1] For a moment, too, there is some freshness as Byron addresses his former companion:

> Hobhouse, since we have roved through Eastern climes,
> While all the Aegean echoed to our rhymes,
> And bound to Momus by some pagan spell
> Laughed, sang and quaffed at "Vive la Bagatelle!"[2]

But even this passage Byron Latinized when he came to think of publication and "Hobhouse" became "Moschus." There are no new and interesting literary judgments; Byron is sometimes dexterous in replacing classical references with English parallels but oftener these substitutions are forced and uninspired. *Hints from Horace* is, in fact, chiefly memorable as an indication of Byron's instinctive allegiance to the neoclassical creed at the very time when he was acquiring the materials and mood for a very different style of poetry.

Hints from Horace was always a favorite with Byron. *Childe Harold* crowded it out in 1812 but in 1820, after the appropriate nine years, Byron again made efforts to publish the poem.[3] Looking back upon his earlier work, he was astonished to see how little he had improved since 1811: "I wrote better then than now; but that comes from my having fallen into the atrocious bad taste of the times—partly."[4] Byron's high opinion of the *Hints* was probably to a large extent attributable to his conviction of the eternal rightness of most of its literary judgments and to his experience of the strict discipline that the task of adaptation required. In 1821 he was still insisting that "The *Hints* must be printed with the *Latin*, otherwise there is no sense."[5]

The Curse of Minerva is really three poems—the first, a beautiful, serene descriptive tableau, in the best eighteenth-century manner, of

---

9. *Hints from Horace*, ll. 589–626.   1. *Idem*, ll. 220–62.

2. *P*, 1, 413, n. To Hobhouse Byron wrote on March 18, "I have just finished an imitation in English verse (rhyme of course) of Horace's 'Art of Poetry,' . . . This poem I have addressed, and shall dedicate to you. In it you will fill the same part that the 'Pisones' do in Horace." *LBC*, 1, 31.

3. The poem was not published until 1830.

4. *LJ*, v, 77.

5. *LJ*, v, 245. Albert S. Cook, in his edition of *The Art of Poetry; the Poetical Treatises of Horace, Vida, and Boileau* . . . (New York, 1926), includes in his notes to the *Ars Poetica* many parallel passages from *Hints from Horace*.

Athens and its surroundings;[6] the second, a violent and ill-tempered attack upon Lord Elgin;[7] and the third, a vigorous denunciation of the foreign and domestic policies of the British Government.[8] When in 1815 it became apparent to Byron that he would not publish *The Curse of Minerva*,[9] he included the opening lines, which rank among the best he ever wrote, as an introductory passage to the third canto of *The Corsair*.[1] And there they are much more appropriate to their context in mood and spirit. One wonders, indeed, if Byron did not perhaps originally write the passage as an isolated descriptive piece without particular reference to *The Curse of Minerva*. No lines he ever wrote show more vividly his delight in the changing moods of the Greek landscape and the warm devotion to Greece that was growing within him.

The central section of the poem affords ample proof that, though Byron altered his earlier views on some matters during his second stay in Athens, he did not soften in the slightest degree his scorn for the activities of Lord Elgin. Indeed, Byron's wrath appears to have increased rather than diminished.[2] The attack on Elgin in *The Curse* is even more unfair than the stanzas in *Childe Harold* had been. As satire the couplets fail, despite occasional felicity and sharpness of phrase, because they utterly lack restraint and the saving grace of humor.

The transition from Byron's abuse of Elgin to his indictment of the policies of the British Government comes in the couplet:

> Hers were the deeds that taught her lawless son
> To do what oft Britannia's self had done.[3]

The remaining hundred lines of the poem are of genuine interest for the indications they give of the stimulus Byron's political and social consciousness received during the course of his travels. This quickening had begun in Spain and it continued as Byron gained further grounds for comparing his country with others. In January he wrote to his mother, "Where I see the superiority of England (which, by the by, we are a good deal mistaken about in many things), I am pleased, and where I find her inferior, I am at least enlightened."[4] In *The Curse of Minerva* Byron's emphasis is decidedly on the latter.

6. *The Curse of Minerva*, ll. 1–54.   7. *Idem*, ll. 55–210.
8. *Idem*, ll. 211–312.
9. The poem was privately printed in 1812 and was surreptitiously published, both in part and in its entirety, frequently during Byron's lifetime.
1. *The Corsair*, ll. 1169–1222.
2. As late as 1821 Byron still maintained, "I opposed, and will ever oppose, the robbery of ruins from Athens, to instruct the English in sculpture (who are as capable of sculpture as the Egyptians are of skating)." *LJ*, v, 5.
3. *The Curse of Minerva*, ll. 211–2.   4. *LJ*, I, 309.

Byron's criticism, expressed through the accusations of Minerva, is first directed back to Britain's highhanded behavior in seizing the Danish fleet at Copenhagen in September, 1807. Next he turns attention to India, where rebellions in 1809 and 1810 threatened British supremacy:

> Look to the East, where Ganges' swarthy race
> Shall shake your tyrant empire to its base.[5]

And then inevitably Byron points to Spain and what he considers the failure of British arms in the Peninsular operations; as evidence that the Spanish do not trust their British allies, he cites their lack of cooperation in the recent battle of Barossa.[6]

It may seem surprising that Byron should at this time have had even more to say about the state of affairs at home than of the situation abroad. It is clear, however, that he was in reasonably close touch with what was going on in England; in late July he had protested against his mother's habit of filling her letters with "things from the papers, as if English papers were not found all over the world. I have at this moment a dozen before me."[7] At home, he now wrote, there were poverty and despair. Goods were rotting on the wharves while

> The starved mechanic breaks his rusting loom,
> And desperate mans him 'gainst the coming doom.[8]

War was solving none of England's pressing problems and even if that war were to be turned upon her own shores England could not complain:

> Nay, frown not, Albion! for the torch was thine
> That lit such pyres from Tagus to the Rhine.[9]

These are harsh views and by no means the reactions of one who knew little and cared less about political matters.[1] The period of Byron's comparative indifference to politics was over.

Byron's letters show that his thoughts were turning more and more toward England through the winter of 1811, partly from curiosity about his friends and affairs but more from the realization that practical considerations must soon require his return. He had sent Fletcher back in November[2] and despite his uncertain financial status Byron kept reasserting through the winter his refusal to sell Newstead.[3] If such an expedient were to prove necessary, he insisted, he would pass his life abroad. He wrote his mother to that effect in late

---

5. *The Curse of Minerva*, ll. 221–2.   6. The battle took place on March 5, 1811.
7. *LJ*, I, 295.   8. *The Curse of Minerva*, ll. 271–2.   9. *Idem*, ll. 307–08.
1. See above, p. 4.   2. *LJ*, I, 306; *LJ*, VI, 453.   3. *LBC*, I, 19–20, 24, 26.

February: "I feel myself so much a citizen of the world, that the spot where I can enjoy a delicious climate, and every luxury, at a less expense than a common college life in England, will always be a country to me; and such are in fact the shores of the Archipelago."[4]

But by April Byron could postpone his departure from Greece no longer. As he prepared to leave Athens, he was deeply touched by the grief of his Albanian, Dervish, who wept bitterly and refused to be consoled up to the very hour of Byron's embarkation. This was Byron's last and most moving experience of the intense loyalty of the rough Albanian: "That Dervish would leave me with some regret was to be expected; when master and man have been scrambling over the mountains of a dozen provinces together, they are unwilling to separate; but his present feelings, contrasted with his native ferocity, improved my opinion of the human heart."[5]

On April 19 Byron gave a farewell dinner. Two days later he left Athens and Cockerell, Foster, and Linckh saw him aboard the transport ship *Hydra*. When on their way to Ægina his friends came to the Piraeus again the next evening, they saw to their surprise that Byron's ship was still in the harbor.[6] Our last glimpse of Byron before he set foot again on British soil is Cockerell's description of the second farewell visit he, Foster, Haller, and Linckh paid him in the Piraeus that evening:

As we were sailing out of the port in our open boat we overtook the ship with Lord Byron on board. Passing under the stern we sang a favourite song of his, on which he looked out of the windows and invited us in. There we drank a glass of port with him, Colonel Travers, and two of the English officers, and talked of the three English frigates that had attacked five Turkish ones and a sloop off Corfu, and had taken and burnt three of them.[7]

Linckh supplements Cockerell's account with the detail that after an hour's time the pilot interrupted the sociability to inform them that their boat was under sail and so he and his companions departed for Ægina. From the site of the Temple of Jupiter the following day the *Hydra* remained visible to them, still held up by contrary winds and it was not until late the next afternoon, April 24, that Byron's friends finally watched his ship, passing Cape Colonna, slowly move toward Zea and disappear beyond that small island.

Along with Byron the *Hydra* carried a load of Elgin marbles, the last large shipment to be dispatched for England. Moreover, Lusieri,

4. *LJ*, I, 310–1.   5. *P*, II, 176–7.
6. *Münchner Jahrbuch der Bildenden Kunst*, XII, 151. These early entries in Linckh's Ægina journal deal with Byron's departure.
7. *Travels in Southern Europe and the Levant*, p. 50.

Elgin's chief agent, took the trip with the marbles.[8] Thus we have the incongruous situation of a ship carrying, on the one hand, Byron and *The Curse of Minerva*, on the the other, Lusieri and the last considerable collection of the Elgin "plunder." Byron's young friend Nicolo Giraud was also aboard and Byron took with him two Greek servants, Demetrius and Andreas.

The *Hydra* reached Malta on the last day of April. Over a year and a half had passed since Byron left the island and his "fair Florence" for Albania; now, his passion less intense, he returned to find Constance Spencer Smith there awaiting him. Their interview is best described in Byron's own words:

But she *was* there, and we met at the Palace. The Governor (the most accommodating of all possible chief magistrates) was kind enough to leave us to come to the most diabolical of explanations. It was in the dog-days, during a sirocco (I almost perspire now with the thoughts of it), during the intervals of an intermittent fever (my love had also intermitted with my malady), and I certainly feared the ague and my passion would both return in full force. I however got the better of both, and she sailed up the Adriatic and I down to the Straits.[9]

Byron has exercised dramatic compression in the final details of his account, for he actually lingered on for over a month at Malta. This last period at Malta was anticlimactic. The excitement of travel was over, there was nothing new to discover or explore. And to add to his discomfiture, Byron was stricken again with a violent tertian fever; "it killed Falstaff and may me," he told Hobhouse.[1] One is not surprised that this illness and the heat of Malta combined with Byron's listlessness and lack of enthusiasm in returning to England to reduce him to very low spirits—to one of those morbid moods of melancholy to which he was always susceptible. Byron's depressed state of mind at this time is dramatically displayed in some notes, entitled "Four or Five reasons in favour of a Change," which he wrote down on May 22. Before he finished his self-analysis, however, Byron found *seven* reasons. Through the kindness of Professor Chauncey Brewster Tinker, the owner of the manuscript, I am permitted to present these melancholy reflections here:

8. Smith, *Lord Elgin and His Collection*, p. 281. A Hydriote polacca had taken forty-eight cases to Malta a year before, representing the accumulation of five years' work in Athens, but had been forced to leave the largest and heaviest objects behind, including a capital and drum of the Parthenon, a Doric capital of the Propylaea, an Ionic column of the monastery of Daphne, and a colossal sepulchral cippus. These, in addition to the fifteen cases of additional material (including vases, etc.) which had accumulated during the year between March, 1810, and April, 1811, were transported to Malta on the *Hydra*.

9. *LBC*, I, 78. The passage occurs in a letter to Lady Melbourne, dated September 15, 1812.

1. *LBC*, I, 32.

1st At twenty three the best of life is over and its bitters double.

2ndly I have seen mankind in various Countries and find them equally despicable, if anything the Balance is rather in favour of the Turks.

3dly I am sick at heart.

> "Me jam nec *faemina* . . .
> Nec *Spes animi credula mutui*
> Nec *certare* juvat *Mero.*[2]

4thly A man who is lame of one leg is in a state of bodily inferiority which increases with years and must render his old age more peevish & intolerable. Besides in another existence I expect to have *two* if not *four* legs by way of compensation.

5thly I grow selfish & misanthropical, something like the "jolly Miller" "I care for nobody no not I and Nobody cares for me."

6thly My affairs at home and abroad are gloomy enough.

7thly I have outlived all my appetites and most of my vanities aye even the vanity of authorship.[3]

One must not assume from the morbidity of these lines that Byron's travels had affected him adversely or that his depression, though no doubt genuine enough, was as profound as he suggests. Here again we are confronted not with the whole Byron but with one side of his exceedingly complicated and variable nature. Four days later the same man was writing one of his gayest poems, "Farewell to Malta:"[4]

> Adieu, ye joys of La Valette!
> Adieu, Sirocco, sun, and sweat!
>
> .　　.　　.　　.　　.　　.　　.
>
> Adieu, thou damned'st quarantine,
> That gave me fever, and the spleen!
> Adieu that stage which makes us yawn, Sirs,
> Adieu his Excellency's dancers!
>
> .　　.　　.　　.　　.　　.　　.
>
> Adieu, ye females fraught with graces!
> Adieu red coats, and redder faces!

The chief source of interest at Malta during the months of April and May of 1811 was the presence of the British naval heroes of the recent action off Lissa, on the Dalmatian coast. In that battle on

2. Byron was quoting, somewhat inaccurately, Horace's first ode of the fourth book. The correct text of the passage, ll. 29–32, is:

> me nec faemina nec puer
> iam nec spes animi creduli mutui
> nec certare juvat mero
> nec vincire novis tempora floribus.

3. A poem on suicide in another hand but signed "B., 1814," appears on the same sheet. The manuscript in Professor Tinker's possession of the "Epitaph for Mr. Joseph Blackett late poet & shoemaker," written in Byron's hand at Malta on May 16, refutes Coleridge's statement (*P*, VII, 11, n.) that the poem is "of doubtful authenticity."

4. "Farewell to Malta," ll. 1–2, 11–14, 17–18.

March 13 four English frigates, under the command of Captain William Hoste, had decisively defeated a combined French and Italian squadron and brought their prizes triumphantly into Malta. Since then, while their ships were receiving necessary repairs, the officers and crews had been constantly entertained and acclaimed at Malta. In one of the victorious frigates, the *Volage,* Byron planned to return to England in early June.[5]

The *Volage* sailed for England, with its sister ship the *Amphion* and two enemy prize ships, on June 2.[6] Again there is irony in the fact that Byron carried personally to England a note from Lusieri to his master Lord Elgin.[7] The marbles, however, did not leave Malta until the following year. Byron parted reluctantly with his young friend Nicolo and as a farewell gesture presented to him a considerable sum of money.[8] The voyage home was long and tedious. Byron had recovered from the fever but still kept to a restricted vegetable diet. His spirits, as he told Hobhouse, were not "as rampant as usual."[9] Literary matters occupied his mind somewhat; Byron expressed regret that he had published *English Bards* but looked forward with some anticipation to the publication of *Hints from Horace.*[1] He suggested in a letter to Hobhouse that with Matthews they might soon set about founding a new literary periodical.[2] But such thoughts were hardly sufficient to keep Byron diverted over a period of six weeks—there was all too much time for introspection and the inevitable mood of melancholy resulted. Byron's words to Hodgson as he approached England were as theatrical as those with which he had departed two years before: "Embarrassed in my private affairs, indifferent to public, solitary without the wish to be social, with a body a little enfeebled by a succession of fevers, but a spirit I trust, yet unbroken, I am returning *home* without a hope, and almost without a desire."[3] Byron set foot on his native soil at Portsmouth on July 11.[4]

5. *P,* III, 25–6, n.   6. *LBC,* I, 35.   7. Smith, *op. cit.,* pp. 282–3.
8. Moore, I, 244. In the will he drew up in August (*LJ,* I, 328–30) Byron assigned seven thousand pounds to Nicolo upon his coming of age. The clause was later excluded, however.
9. *LBC,* I, 35.   1. *LJ,* I, 314–5.   2. *LBC,* I, 39.   3. *LJ,* I, 316.
4. The *Morning Chronicle* for July 13, 1811, reports: "Portsmouth, July 11—Arrived from Malta and sailed again for Chatham, the Amphion, 36, Captain Hoste, and Volage, 24, Captain Hornby, with their prizes, La Corona and La Bellone, French frigates, which they so gallantly took, in a most gallant action, in the Adriatic."

CONCLUSION

DURING Byron's first weeks back in England it seemed that the gloom he felt in approaching his native land had been a premonition. Hardly had he returned when he was stunned by the sudden deaths of his mother and his close friend Matthews and by learning shortly afterward that both Wingfield and Edleston had died the previous spring.[1] The shock of these events was such as to drive most other considerations from his mind during the fall of 1811.

Byron did, however, busy himself in preparing his poems for the press. *Childe Harold,* about which he showed noticeable hesitancy, impressed his friends much more favorably than did the luke-warm *Hints from Horace;* the first was put in the hands of John Murray, the latter committed to James Cawthorn, who had published *English Bards.* But as plans for *Childe Harold* progressed apace, it became increasingly apparent that the publication of the *Hints* must be postponed indefinitely. In the late months of 1811 Byron wrote additional notes for *Childe Harold* at Newstead and gathered together the materials for his Appendix. More important, he revised his original stanzas, as has been pointed out earlier, and added substantially to both cantos. Several of the new stanzas reflect his anguish and perplexity at this time of bereavement.[2] It is rather pleasantly ironic that to the very last Byron was uncertain about the reception of *Childe Harold;* there is something disarming about his admission to Hobhouse in December that, "I begin to be rather alarmed as the moment of publication approaches, but must man myself."[3] Byron had not yet awakened to find himself famous.

The enormous success of *Childe Harold* when it appeared in March is, of course, one of the most famous episodes in literary history. The energy, freshness, and immediacy of the poem rendered it irresistible to most readers; and the hints of personal mystery only enhanced its interest. Already a self-conscious person, Byron was to be immeasurably more so when a curious and eager audience began to watch his every movement and take a morbid delight in comparing him with

---

1. *LJ,* I, 320–7; *LJ,* II, 52–3. Mrs. Byron died on August 1; Matthews was drowned in the Cam a few days later. Byron's friend John Wingfield had died of a fever at Coimbra, Portugal, in May. Edleston, the Cambridge chorister, died of consumption in the same month.

2. Stanzas 91–2 of Canto I are addressed to Wingfield, Stanzas 9, 95–6 of Canto II probably to Edleston. The last two stanzas of Canto II are Byron's reflections in this difficult period.

3. *LBC,* I, 68.

the misanthropical creature of his imagination. The Byronic legend now began to take real and lasting shape.

The effects upon Byron of his two years in foreign lands were not immediately discernible. Superficially the mood of his letters might even lend credence to his offhand remark that, "I don't know that I have acquired anything by my travels, but a smattering of two languages and a habit of chewing Tobacco."[4] But the very considerable impact of his experiences was not long in manifesting itself and in many different ways.

It is difficult to conceive what Byron's literary career would have been like if he had not traveled at this early and impressionable age. Moore suggests that he might have turned into a "querulous satirist."[5] Perhaps so. The point may not be worth pursuing too far, since in the light of Byron's nature it seems that he *must* have traveled sooner or later. But one cannot escape the fact that both in material and point of view Byron's poetry is much more dependent upon the exact data of experience than is that of most of his contemporaries. "Material" in its baldest sense was of more importance to him than to many poets. He was dealing always with a more readily perceptible and tangible world than a Shelley or a Wordsworth, to whom travel was thus less important. It is a sign both of the vitality and of the limitations of Byron's talent that he should insist there must "always be some foundation of fact for the most airy fabric, and pure invention is but the talent of a liar,"[6] and should exclaim, "A Pilgrimage to Jerusalem! How the devil should I write about *Jerusalem,* never having yet been there."[7]

But it was something more than the mere surface appeal of the subject matter that led Byron to write *The Giaour* and *The Bride of Abydos, The Corsair* and *The Siege of Corinth* in the years immediately following his return from the East. The sharp contrasts, the violence, and the melodrama in those tales were in a sense akin to his own nature. He found an emotional outlet in turning his mind to "the land of the cedar and vine."[8] The long passage at the beginning of *The Giaour* shows that his concern with the deplorable state of Greece was genuine and lasting. And in these poems the element of nostalgia was also strong; this is perhaps most directly discernible in the long opening passage to *The Siege of Corinth,* where in defiance of strict chronological accuracy Byron begins:

> In the year since Jesus died for men,
> Eighteen hundred years and ten,

4. *LJ,* II, 31.   5. Moore, I, 257.   6. *LJ,* IV, 93.
7. *LJ,* IV, 22.   8. *The Bride of Abydos,* I, 5.

> We were a gallant company,
> Riding o'er land and sailing o'er sea . . .

There is significance, too, in the fact that Byron's last major poem, and his greatest poem, is rich in reminiscences of his early travels; it is no accident that Don Juan sailed from Spain through the Mediterranean and eventually arrived at Constantinople.

Byron's observations abroad made him less ready than ever to accept what he considered the narrow prejudices and dogmas of his native island. His distrust of religious orthodoxy increased as he observed adherents to other creeds than the Christian: "I will bring you ten Mussulmans shall shame you in all goodwill towards men, prayer to God, and duty to their neighbors."[9] To some extent, to be sure, Byron's stress upon the superiority of things non-English was affectation. He did not expect to be taken too seriously when he wrote, "Oh! in the East women are in their proper sphere, and one has—no conversation at all."[1] Yet it is possible that his experience of the debasement of women in Turkish society influenced Byron somewhat in the rather callous attitude toward the opposite sex that he himself too frequently adopted.

Byron, stirred by his experiences in Spain and the East, returned with an enlivened interest in political and social matters and a breadth of outlook that could never have been his without the advantages of travel. Despite the brevity of his Parliamentary career, political questions continued to engage his active attention for the remainder of his life. Byron now affiliated himself more formally with the Whig party and in his maiden speech on February 27, 1812, speaking against the Framework Bill, declared, "I have traversed the seat of war in the Peninsula, I have been in some of the most oppressed provinces of Turkey; but never under the most despotic of infidel governments did I behold such squalid wretchedness as I have seen since my return in the very heart of a Christian country."[2] Less than two months later Byron bitterly condemned Britain's policy in granting aid willingly to her Catholic allies while maintaining restrictions upon Catholics at home.[3] His hatred for oppressions that stood in the way of human liberty, whether in England or in Spain or in Greece, had now become a living thing. Medwin quotes Byron as saying:

Perhaps, if I had never travelled,—never left my own country young,—my views would have been more limited. They extend to the good of mankind in general—of the world at large. Perhaps the prostrate situation of Portugal and Spain—the tyranny of the Turks in Greece—the oppression of the Austrian Government at Venice—the mental debasement of the Papal

9. *LJ*, ii, 22.   1. *LJ*, ii, 33.   2. *LJ*, ii, 429.   3. *LJ*, ii, 431–43.

states, (not to mention Ireland,)—tended to inspire me with a love of liberty. No Italian could have rejoiced more than I, to have seen a Constitution established on this side of the Alps. I felt for Romagna as if she had been my own country, and would have risked my life and fortune for her, as I may yet for the Greeks. I am become a citizen of the world.[4]

Already in these early years Byron had begun to acquire something of that cosmopolitan and worldly-wise outlook that was to inform his finest poetry. He had, as he later wrote, "seen a little of all sorts of society, from the Christian prince and the Mussulman sultan and pacha, and the higher ranks of their countries, down to the London boxer, the '*flash and the swell*,' the Spanish muleteer, the wandering Turkish dervise, the Scotch highlander, and the Albanian robber."[5]

Byron ever after felt himself more a "citizen of the world" than an Englishman. Indeed, his sense of detachment and immunity from the responsibilities of his native land goes a long way toward explaining his behavior during the last four years he spend in England. For Byron the boat was always on the shore; he was constantly on the point of returning to the warm shores and blue skies of the Mediterranean world. The East was a refuge toward which he could turn whenever the complications of life at home became too overwhelming; it became truly "the greenest island of my imagination."[6]

When circumstances finally forced the issue and Byron left England forever in 1816, he soon found Italy almost equally congenial to his tastes and temperament. Yet his loyalty and instinctive inclination toward regions farther east persisted. He told of the occasion when "we were divided in choice between Switzerland and Tuscany, and I gave my vote for Pisa, as nearer the Mediterranean, which I love for the sake of the shores which it washes, and for my young recollections of 1809."[7]

Finally in 1823 Byron's affections and convictions combined to take him on his last pilgrimage to Greece, on sterner business than he had ever before undertaken. Even then, under such different circumstances, he found his pen quickened by the grateful atmosphere of the land he had known a dozen years before. Taking up his journal at Cephalonia in October, 1823, Byron wrote:

"I know not why I resume it even now, except that, standing at the window of my apartment in this beautiful village, the calm though cool serenity of

4. Medwin, *Conversations of Lord Byron*, pp. 351–2.   5. *LJ*, v, 591.

6. *LJ*, IV, 7. Through the years 1812 and 1813, and into 1814, Byron kept planning and then putting off his departure for the Mediterranean. A typical passage, one among dozens, is the following written in December, 1813: "I trust your third will be out before I sail next month; can I say or do anything for you in the Levant? I am now in all the agonies of equipment, and full of schemes, some impracticable, and most of them improbable." *LJ*, II, 310.

7. *LJ*, v, 365.

a beautiful and transparent Moonlight, showing the Islands, the Mountains, the Sea, with a distant outline of the Morea traced between the double Azure of the waves and skies, has quieted me enough to be able to write, which (however difficult it may seem for one who has written so much publicly to refrain) is, and always has been, to me a task and a painful one. I could summon testimonies, were it necessary; but my hand-writing is sufficient. It is that of one who thinks much, rapidly, perhaps deeply, but rarely with pleasure."[8]

8. *LJ*, VI, 249.

APPENDIX A

I. Byron in Portugal and Spain:
A Revised Itinerary

THE Itinerary prefixed to Coleridge's edition of *Childe Harold* (*P*, II, xxi) is based entirely upon indications in Byron's letters. But, as we have already shown with regard to the date of sailing from Falmouth, Byron's expectations of departure were not always fulfilled. Nor is this surprising in a journey the course of which was often determined by accident or sudden whim. The present Itinerary, which agrees with Coleridge's only in the first date, is based largely upon Hobhouse's (Broughton's) *Recollections*. Not only is there an immediacy about many of Hobhouse's entries that lends credibility to their dates but they also fit into a more reasonable chronology.

1809:

July 2	Sailed from Falmouth in *Princess Elizabeth* packet for Lisbon
July 7	Arrived at Lisbon
July 12	Visited Cintra and Mafra
July 21	Left Lisbon to ride post to Seville
July 22	Passed through Elvas and crossed Caia into Spain
July 24	Passed through Monastereo in crossing the Sierra Morena
July 25	Reached Seville
July 28	Left Seville for Cadiz
July 29	Arrived at Xeres
July 30	Reached Puerta Santa Maria. Witnessed bullfight. Arrived at Cadiz
August 3	Left Cadiz in *Hyperion* frigate for Gibraltar
August 4	Arrived at Gibraltar
August 19	Sailed from Gibraltar in *Townshend* packet for Malta

II. Chronology of the Second Year

The details of Byron's activities from July, 1810 to July, 1811 have always been obscure but it is possible to arrange a more precise chronology of his movements than has existed to date. The publication of the two volumes of *Lord Byron's Correspondence* in 1922 made available much new and valuable material, and uncollected data from several other sources now help to fill in the picture. On the basis of Byron's statement that he returned to Athens the day after he had disembarked from the *Salsette* at the island of Zea,[1] it is clear that he reached Athens on July 18. My examination of

1. *LBC*, I, 10.

the manuscript of the first letter Byron wrote to his mother from Athens has revealed it to be dated July 20 rather than July 25, as Prothero gives it;[2] Byron mentions in that letter his intention to proceed into the Morea the next day.[3] Since his first letter to Hobhouse from Patras makes it evident that he had already been there several days on July 29,[4] it seems reasonable to believe that Byron *did* leave Athens on July 21 and, considering the length and necessary slowness of the journey, probably arrived at Patras four or five days later.

In a letter to his mother from Patras dated July 30, Byron announced his intention to visit Veli Pasha at Tripolitza "in a few days."[5] This intention he must have fulfilled, for on August 16 he had been for some time at Tripolitza, half way down the Peloponnesus, and was about to return to Athens by way of Argos.[6] On August 23 he was writing to Hobhouse from Athens and his remarks give the impression that he had been settled there for several days.[7] At this point Byron must have spent three or four weeks in Athens before setting off again for Patras, where his next letter was written on September 25.[8] Lady Hester Stanhope arrived in Athens on September 12 and on the third or fourth day after her arrival Byron left again for the Morea.[9] Thus it must have been mid-September when Byron departed once more for Patras. The last extant letter from Patras is dated October 4.[1] Byron returned to Athens shortly after that date, for an unpublished letter written from Athens is dated October 13.[1a] From that time on, as far as we can determine, Byron's time was spent in and around Athens until the spring of 1811.

2. *LJ*, I, 287. I have been allowed to inspect this letter through the courtesy of the Pierpont Morgan Library. It is worth noting also that in the original letter the passage which Prothero prints on p. 289 as ll. 2–8 follows the first sentence of the letter.

3. *LJ*, I, 289.

4. *LBC*, I, 11. Speaking of the Imperial Consul, Mr. Paul, Byron says "we visit him every evening." The fact that Byron must have been in Patras on July 27 is a good reason for doubting further the already suspect letter, deriving from Schultess-Young, that appears in *LJ*, I, 292–3, dated "Athens, July 27, 1810."

5. *LJ*, I, 294.   6. *LBC*, I, 12.   7. *LBC*, I, 13–17.

8. *LBC*, I, 11.   9. *Travels of Lady Hester Stanhope*, I, 42.

1. *LJ*, I, 301.   1a. This letter appears in Appendix B below.

APPENDIX B

Supplementary Letters (1809–11)

THE following six letters, all written during Byron's first journey, have not appeared in the collected editions of his correspondence and three still remain unpublished. Letters 1 and 2 are reprinted from an article, "Zehn Byroniana," by E. Kölbing, in *Englische Studien*, XXV, 1898, p. 141. For permission to present letters 3, 4, and 5 for the first time I am indebted to Miss Belle dacosta Greene, of the Pierpont Morgan Library. Letter 6 is reprinted from *Poems and Letters of Lord Byron*, edited from the original manuscripts in the possession of W. K. Bixby of St. Louis, by W. N. C. Carlton, Chicago, 1912, pp. 23–4.

1. *To John Hanson*

Constantinople, June 15th 1810

Sir,

This letter will be delivered by Mr. Hobhouse. I find by Hammersley that it was the sum of £1000 & not £500 as I supposed which was added to my credit last December, but half of this being lodged at Malta & half at Constantinople, I conceive it better in future either to place the entire sum (whatever it may be) with one Banker, or to send me a general credit for the same on both as was the case in my letters of credit when I left England. I should also have deemed it as well for you to have written at the same time in reply to my repeated requests to that effect.—Perhaps you have done so, but your letters have never reached me, which they would if addressed to Malta. Mr. H. will inform you as to my progress, and present my respects to the family.

I remain, Sir,
your very obed^t Servt.
Byron

2. *To John Hanson*

Constantinople, June 30th 1810

Sir,

In case of any accident befalling the letter which Mr. Hobhouse has in charge for you, I send a second merely to state that my own return will not take place for some time, and to request you will continue to remit regularly, according to circumstances, but I think it better instead of dividing the sum between two bankers, either to lodge it entire with one, or to send me a general letter of credit for the amount, as when I left England. You will present my best regards to your family & believe me

yours very sincerely
Byron

P.S. I shall not return to England for two years at least (from this date) except in case of war.

3. *To James Cawthorn*

Constantinople, July 1st 1810

Mr. Cawthorne,

You have paid much *attention* to my desire that you would send a copy of the second Edition of my Satire to Malta for me; I presume if the sale is successful it is nothing to you hot-press gentry what becomes of the author. I again request however that you will attend to my order, though you have not written to give the smallest intimation of its progress. I have heard through other channels that the work goes on tolerably. I suppose that my directions have been obeyed with regard to the additions &c before I left London, and it is said to be in a third Edition. Wishing you success and a little more politeness I remain

&c &c

Byron

4. *To Stratford Canning*

Athens, October 13th 1810

Sir,

I cannot address you without an apology the more especially as I write in the character of a complainant. In travelling from the Morea to Athens, the Bey of Corinth for some time refused me a lodging, and this at a time when the inclemency of the weather made it an act not only of impoliteness, but of inhumanity. It was indeed one of those days when "an enemy's dog" would have been sheltered. The Greek Cogia Bachi was equally unwilling to order a house, and I at last with difficulty procured a miserable cottage. As the last circumstance has happened twice to myself in the same place, and once to others, I have nothing left but to request your interference. I know no circumstance of explanation, as a word from the Bey or the Cogia Bachi would have admitted me into any house in the village, where I had before (in the time of Vely Pacha) found much better accommodation. I therefore do hope and venture to request that the "circumcised dog" may not pass (I cannot say unpunished) but unreprimanded. I believe it to be the inclination, as I know it to be the power of the British minister to protect the subjects of his Sovereign from Insult. I conceive that brutality will not be countenanced even by the Turks, as we are taught hospitality is a barbarian's virtue. Your interference may be esteemed a favour not only to me but to all future travellers. By land or sea we must pass the Isthmus in our excursions from Athens to the Morea, and you will be informed of the accuracy of my statement of the Bey's conduct by the Marquis of Sligo, who does me the honour to deliver this letter.—I again solicit your interposition, and have the honour to be, Sir,

Your most obedient
humble Servant
Byron

5. *To James Cawthorn*

Malta, May 9th, 1811

Mr. Cawthorn,

I have seen here your third Edition of "E.B.&S.R." and observe that it is printed on the very type you rejected for the *second edition.*—Now why is the 3d to be published in a worse form than the 2d? which was more creditable to you & me.—I hope if the poem reaches a 4th you will attend to what I have observed, and, if we *must* change, don't let it be for the worse.

I shall soon probably be in England, if my health (which is very precarious) permit me, & I have a poem finished, which I designed for you to publish, but if you make these retrograde movements I must look elsewhere. If you see Mr Dallas present my compts.

I am
yr. obed't serv't
Byron

6. *To James Cawthorn*

Volage Frigate, off Ushant
July 7th 1811

Mr. Cawthorn:

I have been scolding you (like almost all Scolders) without a reason, for I found your two parcels, one at Athens, & the other at Malta on my way down. In a few days on our arrival at Portsmouth, which we expect to make about the 10th, I shall send this off, however the date on the outside will apprize you of the day. I shall thence proceed to town where I expect you to pay me a visit either at Dorant's or Reddish's Hotels in Albemarle or St. James's Street. I hope the Satire has answered your purpose, & of course it has answered mine. I have a poem in the same style, & much about the same length which I intend as a kind of Sequel to the former; it is ready for publication, but as my scrawl is impenetrable to Printers, & the Manuscript is a good deal blotted with Alterations etc, you must have an Amanuensis ready to copy it out fair on my arrival. I suppose you have not lost by the last, but my only motive for asking is a wish that you *may not;* the present shall be yours for the risk of printing, as the last was. But neither you nor I must suppose because the first has succeeded tolerably, a second will have the same fate, though its style is similar. However, it will serve to make a tolerable volume with the other, with which it is in some degree connected. The Nature of it I will explain more fully when I see you. If you see Mr. Dallas or any other of my acquaintance, you will present my Compts. I remain

Yr obed^t Servt,
Byron

P.S. Accept my excuse for blaming you for what you did not deserve. I am sorry for it; the fault lay with my Maltese Correspondents.

APPENDIX C

A Note Concerning the Manuscripts and Early State of The Curse of Minerva

THE acquisition by the Yale University Library of what purports to be a "Fair Copy" of *The Curse of Minerva* has invited comparison with the manuscript of the poem, which is now in the Berg Collection of the New York Public Library. Comparison of the Berg MS. with the Fair Copy[1] has revealed:

1. This "Fair Copy" was, I feel sure, copied directly from the Berg MS. There are only three variations: the word "maid" appears instead of "nymph" in line 193 of the FC.; and in the lines added in another hand (lines 157–62) "counsels" and "will tell" appear in place of "councils" and "shall tell." The original omission of those six lines is explained by the fact that in the MS. the lines preceding (lines 149–56) were added to the MS. by Byron and pasted over the six lines in question. Thus the copyist must have passed over those lines. All the changes made in the MS. are embodied in the FC. Moreover, in many cases the arrangement (number of lines to a page, etc.) is identical.

2. Comparison with the MS. shows that those six lines in another hand were clearly *not* written by Byron. They have great similarity, however, to the handwriting of Dallas, who has written and signed (initials) a brief statement on the outside of the MS. Comparison of the lines in the FC. with this statement convinces me that the six lines were added to the FC. by Dallas. Also, the title on the outside of the FC. coincides almost perfectly with that in Dallas' handwriting on the MS.

3. Although I am practically certain that nothing else in the FC. is in Byron's hand, the word "Socrates" on page 2 seems to differ from both the other hands and resembles Byron's own handwriting very closely. There is no "Socrates" note in the MS.; the FC. follows the MS. in all others. The FC. embodies several corrections (lines crossed out and amended) made in the MS.

4. There is no doubt that the handwriting throughout the Berg MS. is Byron's. Dallas has written on the outside, "I prize this MS. as a great curiosity, pray take great care of it for me." He calls it "The original, written at Athens." At the head of the first page of the MS. Byron himself has written "Nov. 17, 1811 (Athens, March, 1811)." The watermark is "Cray Mill 1808."

5. There remains some doubt in my mind about the date or dates of the writing of the Berg MS. Dallas calls it "The original, written at Athens" but without further proof I am not ready to assume that this is so. The problem

1. Hereafter referred to as FC.

is complicated by the fact that Coleridge, in preparing his text of the poem, consulted another, probably an earlier MS., which he calls "the MS. in the possession of Lord Stanhope." *P*, 1, 452. The nature of the variations Coleridge gives from this document and its incompleteness (lines 149–56 and lines 202–65 do not appear at all) would seem to indicate that it preceded the Berg MS. I have been unable to discover the whereabouts of this "Stanhope MS." A note, in a hand unknown to me, at the beginning of the Berg MS. says, "Lord Stanhope possesses the rough notes of this poem." These "rough notes" may be the Stanhope MS. referred to by Coleridge. Interestingly enough, the lines in which Byron satirizes his contemporary Lord Stanhope do not appear in the Stanhope MS. The name "Stanhope" appears in line 251 of the Berg MS.

6. Coleridge also mentions (but never saw) a "second MS., formerly in the possession of the Duke of Newcastle," which he says "is believed to have perished in a fire which broke out at Clumber in 1879." This "second MS." may well be the present Berg MS.

7. The next question is the relation of the FC. to the privately printed 1812 quarto. It cannot be the *direct* and *complete* basis of that volume, because there are several discrepancies, but Byron may well have sent these minor alterations by letter, as was his custom, while the volume was being set up in print.

LIST OF WORKS CITED

"A. H." "Upon Reading Lord Byron's Reflections on the Battle of Talavera in Childe Harold," *Gentleman's Magazine*, LXXXII, I, (1812), 566. (Poem.)

Abrantes, Duchess of. See Junot, Laure.

Adair, Sir Robert. *The Negotiations for the Peace of the Dardanelles*. London, 1845. 2 vols.

Albania: Handbooks prepared under the direction of the Historical Section of the Foreign Office, No. 17. London, 1920.

Art of Poetry, The; Poetical Treatises of Horace, Vida, and Boileau. Albert S. Cook, ed. New York, 1926.

Atchley, Shirley C. *Bios kai drasis tou Byronos en Helladi*. Athens, 1918.

Baggally, John W. *Ali Pasha and Great Britain*. Oxford, 1938.

Beckford, William. *Italy; With Sketches of Spain and Portugal*. London, 1834. 2 vols.

Bessborough, Earl of. See Ponsonby, Vere Brabazon.

Best, Capt. James J. *Excursions in Albania*. London, 1842.

Blessington, Countess of. See Gardiner, Margaret Farmer.

Boppe, Auguste. *L'Albanie et Napoleon, 1797–1814*. Paris, 1914.

Borrow, George. *The Bible in Spain*. London, 1843.

Brönsted, Peter O. *Voyages et recherches dans la Grèce*. Paris, 1826, 1830. 2 vols.

— *Reise i Graekenland i Varene* 1810–13. R. B. Dorph, ed. Copenhagen, 1844.

Broughton, Lord. See Hobhouse, John Cam.

Brouzas, C. G. "Teresa Macri, the Maid of Athens," *West Virginia University Bulletin, Philological Papers*, v (1947), 1–31.

Brown, Wallace Cable. "Byron and English Interest in the Near East," *Studies in Philology*, xxxiv (1937), 55–64.

— "The Popularity of English Travel Books about the Near East, 1775–1825," *Philological Quarterly*, xv (1936), 70–80.

Bryant, Arthur. *Years of Victory*. London, 1945.

Bryant, Jacob. *Dissertation Concerning the War of Troy, and the Expedition of the Grecians as Described by Homer; Showing That No Such Expedition Was Ever Undertaken, and That No Such City of Phrygia Existed*. London, 1796.

Byron, George Gordon, Lord. *Catalogue of the Renowned Collection of Autograph Letters and Historical Manuscripts Formed by the Late Alfred Morrison*. London, 1917–19.

— *Childe Harold's Pilgrimage, A Romaunt: and Other Poems*. London, 1812.

— *Childe Harold's Pilgrimage and Other Romantic Poems*. Samuel C. Chew, ed. New York, 1936.

— (Translation of Canto I into Portuguese) *Peregrinaçoes de Childe*

Harold, Canto Primero, traducção do inglez por Alberto Telles. Portugal e Hespanha, 1881.

— *The Collection of Autograph Letters and Historical Documents Formed by Alfred Morrison.* Ser. 2, 1 (1882–93).

— *Le Messager d'Athènes,* No. 220, Special Supplement in English and French. Athens, April 19, 1924. Articles, addresses, and poem by John Drinkwater in honor of Byron centenary.

— *Lord Byron's Correspondence.* John Murray, ed. London, 1922. 2 vols.

— *Poems and Letters of Lord Byron,* edited from the original manuscripts in the possession of W. K. Bixby of St. Louis, by W. N. C. Carlton. Chicago, 1912.

— *Poetry of Byron,* chosen and arranged by Matthew Arnold. London, 1881.

— *The Unpublished Letters of Lord Byron.* Edited with a critical essay on the poet's philosophy and character by H. S. Schultess-Young. London, 1872.

— *The Works of Lord Bryon; in Verse and Prose.* FitzGreene Halleck, ed. New York, 1833.

— *The Works of Lord Byron, Letters, 1804–1813.* William Ernest Henley, ed. New York, 1897.

— *The Works of Lord Byron, Letters and Journals.* Rowland E. Prothero, ed. London, 1898–1901. 6 vols.

— *The Works of Lord Byron, Poetry.* Ernest Hartley Coleridge, ed. London, 1898–1905. 7 vols.

— "Zehn Byroniana," E. Kolbing, ed., *Englische Studien,* xxv (1898), 130–62.

Carr, Sir John. *Descriptive Travels in the Southern and Eastern Parts of Spain and the Balearic Isles in the Year 1809.* London, 1811.

Castelar, Emilio. *Vida de Lord Byron.* Habana, 1873. Translated by Mrs. Arthur Arnold as *Life of Lord Byron and Other Sketches.* New York, 1876.

Chaconas, Stephen George. *Adamantios Korais: A Study in Greek Nationalism.* New York, 1942.

Chapman, Guy. *Beckford.* London, 1937.

Choiseul-Gouffier, Marie Gabriel, Count of. *Voyage pittoresque de la Grèce.* Paris, 1787, 1809. 2 vols.

Churchman, Philip H. "Lord Byron's Experiences in the Spanish Peninsula," *Bulletin Hispanique,* xi (1909), 55–95, 125–71.

Cockerell, Charles R. *The Temples of Jupiter Panhellenius at Aegina, and of Apollo Epicurius at Bassae Near Phigaleia in Arcadia.* London, 1860.

— *Travels in Southern Europe and the Levant, 1810–1817.* S. P. Cockerell, ed. London, 1903.

Cotton, Walter. *Ship and Shore: or Leaves from the Journal of a Cruise to the Levant.* New York, 1835.

Cristowe, Stefan. *The Lion of Janina.* New York, 1941.

Cust, Lionel. *History of the Society of Dilettanti.* London, 1898.

Dalgado, D. G. *Lord Byron's Childe Harold's Pilgrimage to Portugal.* Lisbon, Imprensa Nacional, 1919.

Dallas, Robert. *Recollections of the Life of Lord Byron.* London, 1824.

Darwin, Francis S. *Travels in Spain and the East, 1808–1810.* London, 1927.

Davenport, Richard A. *The Life of Ali Pasha, of Tepelini.* London, 1837.

Davis, H. W. C. *The Age of Grey and Peel.* Oxford, 1929.

Dawson, Christopher M., and Raubitschek, Anthony E. "A Greek Folksong Copied for Lord Byron," *Hesperia,* xiv, No. I (1945), 33–57.

Dinsmoor, William B. "Observations on the Hephaisteion," *Hesperia,* Suppl. v. (1941).

Disraeli, Isaac. *The Literary Character.* London, 1822.

Drinkwater, John. *The Pilgrim of Eternity: Byron—A Conflict.* London, 1925.

Dudley, Earl of. See Ward, John W.

Dumas, Alexandre Père. *Le Comte de Monte Cristo.* Paris, 1846.

Eggert, Gerhard. *Lord Byron und Napoleon.* Weimar, Leipzig, 1933.

Fielding, Henry. *Journal of a Voyage to Lisbon.* Leslie Stephen, ed. London, 1882.

Finlay, George. *History of the Greek Revolution.* London, 1861. 2 vols.

Fox, Elizabeth Vassall, Lady Holland. *The Spanish Journal of Elizabeth Lady Holland.* London, 1910.

Fremantle, Alan F. *England in the Nineteenth Century,* Vol. i. London, 1930.

Fuess, Claude M. *Lord Byron as a Satirist in Verse.* New York, 1912.

Galt, John. *Letters from the Levant.* London, 1813.

— *The Life of Lord Byron.* London, 1830.

Gamba, Count Pietro. *Narrative of Lord Byron's Last Journey to Greece.* London, 1825.

Gardiner, Margaret Farmer, Countess of Blessington. *A Journal of the Conversations of Lord Byron with the Countess of Blessington.* New York, 1893.

Gell, Sir William. *Geography and Antiquities of Ithaca.* London, 1807.

— *Itinerary of Greece.* London, 1808.

— *Topography of Troy.* London, 1804.

Gentleman's Magazine, LXXVIII, 1 (1808), 560. Obituary of Capt. George Bettesworth.

Gibbon, Edward. *History of the Decline and Fall of the Roman Empire.* London, 1789.

Goessler, Peter. *Jakob Linckh, ein württembergischer Italienfahrer, Philhellene, Kunstsammler und Maler.* Stuttgart, 1930.

— "Nordische Gäste in Athen um 1810," *Ephemeris Archiaologikē* (1937), pp. 69–82.

Gordon, Sir Arthur. *The Earl of Aberdeen.* London, 1893.

Gronow, Rees Howell. *The Reminiscences and Recollections of Captain Gronow.* London, 1892. 2 vols.

Haygarth, William. *Greece; a Poem in Three Parts.* London, 1814.

Herculano, Alexandre. "O Parocho" (*Estudos Morais,* vol. II), *O Panorama,* Lisbon, 1844.

Hobhouse, John Cam, Lord Broughton. *A Journey through Albania and Other Provinces of Turkey in Europe and Asia to Constantinople during the Years 1809 and 1810.* London, 1813. 2 vols.

— *Imitations and Translations from the Ancient and Modern Classics.* London, 1809.

— "Letter to John Hanson," April 23, 1811, *Englische Studien,* xxv (1898), 151–2.

— (Lord Broughton). *Recollections of a Long Life.* Lady Dorchester, ed. London, 1909–11. 6 vols.

— (Lord Broughton). *Travels in Albania and Other Provinces of Turkey in 1809 and 1810.* London, 1855. 2 vols.

— Review of Dallas' *Recollections* and Medwin's *Conversations, Westminster Review,* vol. III (1825).

Hodgson, Francis. *Lady Jane Grey; a Tale; and Other Poems.* London, 1809.

— *Translation of Juvenal.* London, 1807.

Hodgson, James T. *Memoir of the Rev. Francis Hodgson.* London, 1878. 2 vols.

Holland, Lady. See Fox, Elizabeth Vassall.

Holland, Dr. Henry. *Travels in the Ionian Isles, Albania, Thessaly, and Greece.* London, 1815.

Holzhausen, Paul. *Bonaparte, Byron, und die Briten.* Frankfurt, 1904.

Hughes, Thomas S. *Travels in Sicily, Greece and Albania.* London, 1820.

Jacob, William. *Travels in the South of Spain, in Letters Written A. D. 1809 and 1810.* London, 1811.

Jókai, Mór. *The Lion of Janina.* London, 1898.

Junot, Laure, Duchess of Abrantes. *Mémoires,* Paris, 1834. Vol. xv.

Kampouroglou, D. G. *Attikoi Erotes.* Athens, 1921.

Kinglake, Alexander W. *Eothen.* London, 1879.

Knight, Henry Gally. *Eastern Sketches.* London, 1819.

— *Phrosyne, a Grecian Tale.* London, 1817.

Knighton, Lady Dorothea Hawker. *Memoirs of Sir William Knighton.* London, 1838.

Lane-Poole, Stanley. *The Life of the Right Honourable Stratford Canning, Viscount Stratford de Redcliffe.* London, 1888.

Larrabee, Stephen A. *English Bards and Grecian Marbles.* New York, 1943.

Leake, William Martin. *Travels in Northern Greece.* London, 1835.

— *Researches in Greece.* London, 1814.

Lear, Edward. *Journal of a Landscape Painter in Albania, Illyria, etc.* London, 1851.

Legrand, Phillipe Ernest. "Biographie de Louis-François-Sébastien Fauvel, Antiquaire et Consul," *Revue Archaeologique,* Ser. 3, xxx (1897), 41–66, 185–201, 385–404; xxxi (1897), 94–103, 185–223.

Lemos, João De. *Cancioneiro,* vol. II. Lisbon, 1859.

Linckh, Jacob. "Aegina Journal," *Münchner Jahrbuch der Bildenden Kunst,* xII (1937–38), 151 ff.

Link, Henry F. *Travels in Portugal and through France and Spain; With a Dissertation on the Literature of Portugal, and the Spanish and Portuguese Languages.* John Hinckley, ed. London, 1801.

Maier, Hans. *Entstehungsgeschichte von Byrons "Childe Harold's Pilgrimage," Gesang I und II.* Berlin, 1911.

Malakis, Emile. *French Travellers in Greece, 1770–1820: An Early Phase of French Philhellenism.* Philadelphia, 1925.

Marsden, John H. *A Brief Memoir of the Life and Writings of the Late Lieutenant-Colonel William Martin Leake.* London, 1864.

Matthews, Henry. *The Diary of an Invalid.* London, 1820.

Maurois, André, *Byron.* Hamish Miles, tr. London, 1930.

Mayne, Ethel C. *Byron.* Revised ed. London, 1924.

Medwin, Thomas. *Conversations of Lord Byron: Noted during a Residence with His Lordship at Pisa, in the Years 1821 and 1822.* London, 1824.

Meletius of Janina. *Ancient and Modern Geography.* Venice, 1728.

Meryon, Charles Lewis. See Stanhope, Lady Hester Lucy.

Meyer, Gustav. "Die Albanischen Tanzlieder in Byrons Childe Harold," *Anglia,* xv (1893), 1–8.

Michaelis, Adolf. *Ancient Marbles in Great Britain.* Cambridge, 1882.

Miller, William. *Essays in the Latin Orient.* Cambridge, England, 1921.

— *The English in Athens before 1821.* London, Anglo-Hellenic League, 1926.

Moore, Thomas. *Letters and Journals of Lord Byron: with Notices of His Life.* London, 1830. 2 vols.

Morphopoulos, Panos. "Byron's Translation and Use of Modern Greek Writings," *Modern Language Notes,* LIV (1939), 317–26.

Mountnorris, George Annesley, Earl of. *Voyages and Travels to India, Ceylon, Abyssinia, and Egypt.* London, 1809. 3 vols.

Napier, William F. P. *History of the War in the Peninsula and in the South of France, from the Year 1807 to the Year 1814.* London, 1886. Originally published in 1828–40. 2 vols.

Nicolson, Harold. *Byron: The Last Journey.* New ed. London, 1940.

O'Byrne, William R. *A Naval Biographical Dictionary.* London, 1849.

Paston, George, and Quennell, Peter. *"To Lord Byron," Feminine Profiles Based upon Unpublished Letters 1807–1824.* New York, 1939.

Payne, John Howard. *Ali Pacha; or, the Signet-Ring.* London, 1823.

Plomer, William. *Ali, the Lion.* London, 1936.

Polidori, Dr. John W. *The Vampyre.* London, 1819.

Ponsonby, Vere Brabazon, Earl of Bessborough (In collaboration with A. Aspinall). *Lady Bessborough and Her Family Circle.* London, 1940.

Porter, Sir Robert Ker. *Letters from Portugal and Spain.* London, 1809.

Putnam's Monthly, III (1907), 255. Background and text of lines to Antonio Bailly.

Quennell, Peter. See Paston, George.

Raubitschek, Anthony E. See Dawson, Christopher M.

"Recollections of Turkey," *The New Monthly Magazine,* XVII (1826), 305–14; XIX (1827), 137–49.

Richter, Helene. *Lord Byron: Persönlichkeit und Werk.* Halle, 1929.

Roberts, Michael. *The Whig Party 1807–1812.* London, 1939.

Salvo, Carlo, Marquis de. *Travels in the Year 1806 from Italy to England.* London, 1807.

Schliemann, Heinrich. *Troja, Results of the Latest Researches and Discoveries on the Site of Homer's Troy and in the Heroic Tumuli and Other Sites, Made in the Year 1882.* New York, 1884.

Scott, Sir Walter. Review of *Childe Harold, III, and Other Poems, The Quarterly Review,* XVI (1816), 172–208.

Smith, A. H. "Lord Elgin and His Collection," *Journal of Hellenic Studies,* XXVI (1916), 163–372.

Spenser, Edmund. *The Faerie Queene,* "The Works of Edmund Spenser," Variorum ed. Baltimore, Johns Hopkins Press, 1934, Bk. III.

Stackelberg, Natalie von. *O. M. von Stackelberg, Schilderung seines Lebens und seiner Reisen in Italien und Griechenland.* Heidelberg, 1882.

Stackelberg, Otto Magnus, Freiherr von. *Costumes et usages des peuples de la Grèce.* Rome, 1825.

— *Der Apollotempel zu Bassae in Arcadien.* Rome, 1826.

— *Gräber der Hellenen.* Berlin, 1837.

— *La Grèce; vues pittoresque et topographiques.* Paris, 1834.

Stanhope, Lady Hester Lucy. *Memoirs of the Lady Hester Stanhope, as Related by Herself in Conversations with Her Physician* [Charles L. Meryon]. London, 1846. 3 vols.

— *Travels of Lady Hester Stanhope: Forming the Completion of Her Memoirs.* London, 1846. 3 vols.

Steegman, John. *The Rule of Taste from George I to George IV.* London, 1936.

Strachey, Lytton. *Characters and Commentaries.* London, 1936.

Telles, Alberto. *Lord Byron em Portugal.* Lisbon, 1869.

Ticknor, George. *Life, Letters, and Journals of George Ticknor.* Boston, 1876. 2 vols.

Treimer, Karl. "Byron und die Albanologie," *Seminar za arbanasku filologi ju Arkiv za arbanasku starinu,* III, Pts. I–II (Belgrade, 1926), 176–204.

—Hoopes, J. Review of "Byron und die Albanologie," *Englische Studien,* LXI (1926–27), 297.

Turner, William. *Journal of a Tour in the Levant.* London, 1820. 2 vols.

Tweddell, Robert. *Remains of John Tweddell.* London, 1816.

Valentia, Viscount. See Mountnorris, George Annesley, Earl of.

Vaudoncourt, Guillaume De. *Memoirs of the Ionian Islands . . . , Including the Life and Character of Ali Pacha, the Present Ruler of Greece.* London, 1816.

Vaughan, Charles R. *The Narrative of the Siege of Zaragoza.* London, 1809.

— Review of *The Narrative of the Siege of Zaragoza,* in *The Edinburgh Review,* I (1809), 226–31.

Walpole, Robert. *Travels in Various Countries of the East.* London, 1820. 2 vols.

Ward, John W., Earl of Dudley. *Letters to "Ivy" from the First Earl of Dudley.* S. H. Romilly, ed. London, 1905.

Watkins, John. *Memoirs of the Life and Writings of the Right Honorable Lord Byron.* London, 1822.

Wiener, Harold S. L. "Byron and the East: Literary Sources of the 'Turkish Tales,'" *Nineteenth Century Studies,* (Ithaca, Cornell University Press, 1940), pp. 89–129.

— *The Eastern Background of Byron's Turkish Tales.* Unpublished doctoral dissertation, Yale University, 1938.

Williams, Hugh W. *Travels in Italy, Greece and the Ionian Islands.* Edinburgh, 1820. 2 vols.

Wordsworth, William. *Tract on the Convention of Cintra.* A. V. Dicey, ed. London, 1915.

Young, George. *Portugal Old and Young, a Historical Study.* Oxford, 1917.

INDEXES

Names listed in Index I are those of persons either anterior to or contemporary with Byron; later writers and commentators appear in the List of Works Cited. I have also omitted the names of Byron and Hobhouse, since almost every page of the book contains references to the two travelers. In Index II, I have listed only places that Byron actually saw or visited during his 1809–11 journey, with the exception of a few towns in the Peninsula, Albania, and Greece that were closely connected with his thought or experience at the time. These latter appear in italics. I have not, I hope, stretched too far the strict meaning of the term "places" by using it to include mountains, islands, and rivers as well as cities and villages.

I. Index of Persons

II. Index of Places

III.. Index of Poems by Byron